Jack Marx was born in Maitland in 1965. A freelance journalist and author of two books, Jack has been writing for newspapers and magazines both in Australia and abroad since 1992. He is the recipient of the 2006 Walkley Award for Newspaper Feature Writing, which he received for 'I Was Russell Crowe's Stooge', his online account of the unfolding relationship between himself and the Hollywood Oscar winner. He lives in Broken Hill.

Also by Jack Marx

Sorry – the Wretched Tale of Little Stevie Wright
The Damage Done – Twelve Years of Hell in a Bangkok Prison
(with Warren Fellows)

AUSTRALIAN TRAGIC

GRIPPING TALES FROM THE DARK SIDE OF OUR HISTORY

JACK MARX

hachette
AUSTRALIA

hachette
AUSTRALIA

First published in Australia and New Zealand in 2009
by Hachette Australia
(An imprint of Hachette Australia Pty Limited)
Level 17, 207 Kent Street, Sydney NSW 2000
www.hachette.com.au

This edition published in 2015

National Library of Australia
Cataloguing-in-Publication data

Marx, Jack.
Australian tragic: gripping tales from the dark side of our history/Jack Marx.

978 0 7336 2733 0 (paperback)

Tales – Australia.
Tragic, The.
Australia – History.

994

Cover illustration and design by bookdesignbysaso.com.au
Author photo courtesy of Simon Obarzanek and Karen Woodbury Gallery, Melbourne
Text design by bookdesignbysaso.com.au and Bookhouse, Sydney
Typeset in Birka by Bookhouse, Sydney
Printed and bound in Australia by McPherson's Printing Group

MIX
Paper from
responsible sources
FSC
www.fsc.org
FSC® C001695

The paper this book is printed on is certified against the
Forest Stewardship Council® Standards. McPherson's Printing
Group holds FSC® chain of custody certification SA-COC-005379.
FSC® promotes environmentally responsible, socially beneficial
and economically viable management of the world's forests.

This book is dedicated with thanks to Matt Richell

CONTENTS

INTRODUCTION

On a winter's evening in Melbourne in 1880, during the opening night of *Les Huguenots* at the old Opera House in Bourke Street, a man named Greer stormed the dress circle during the climactic third act, a pistol in his hand. What happened next – and how the public reacted to it – is a good illustration of the moral values that shepherded Australian society of old, and it's a shame that the keepers of colonial record regarded such episodes as embarrassments rather than as events of historical interest. No doubt there are thousands of similar tales buried in the same dungeon where I found this one: in the pages of old newspapers, readily accessible through our libraries, but forgotten where the national history is concerned. That's a pity.

Anyone who has ever snored through lessons at an Australian school knows that the official history of our nation is as boring as milk. Where American kids get to thrill to tales from the War of Independence, the Civil War, the various bloody encounters of the Wild West and enough assassinations to keep conspiracy theorists busy for a century yet, our poor little bastards are forced to dream up ingenious ways to stay awake during lectures on the Gold Rush, Federation, and the 'adventures' of Blaxland, Lawson and Wentworth. Gallipoli, the military tragedy trumpeted as being 'the birth of our nation', was undoubtedly one of the most tedious battles in the history of armed conflict, and our most intriguing politician – by a long way – is only interesting for the fact that he went missing while in office (but that more of them would).

This is the history that has been chosen for us to read, cherry-picked by custodians of the 'lucky country' myth, a pantomime in which Australia is forever cast as a kingdom of eternal heroism and good, our coastline corralling a population of humble champions, selfless entertainers and assorted larrikins with hearts of gold. In our history books, even a violent bullshit artist like Ned Kelly is varnished with a gallant sheen, so as to make the mongrel a quaint matching bookend for such inoffensive figurines as Bradman, Darcy and Dame Nellie Melba.

When not concerned with the follies, Australia's history, as packaged by bureaucrats in successions of education departments, is – perhaps unsurprisingly – obsessed with authority and victory; those in charge, those who got there first, and those who obeyed their superiors. Thus we are forced to fossick for something interesting in the lives of such pets of the establishment as James Cook, Arthur Phillip, Lachlan Macquarie, Charles Sturt, John Oxley – politicians and surveyors, basically. Such people are important joists in the historical scaffold, but to fixate upon them alone is like going to the football and cheering for the umpires, the security staff and the club secretaries up in the corporate box. Anyone who is honest with themselves knows that the really interesting stuff is happening not in the realm of officialdom, but in the field of play, or sometimes in the stands where the players don't always come with famous names or precious reputations.

Jim Hall, for example, was a Sydney-born boxer who, in a short but explosive nineteenth century career, knocked out more opponents than Les Darcy ever would, and whose fight with world champion Bob Fitzsimmons in New Orleans in 1893 was billed as 'the Fight of the Century', its purse of $40 000 being the largest the American ring had ever seen. There are no books about Jim Hall, no entry for him in the *Australian Dictionary of Biography*, no mention of his name in our sporting halls of fame. The reason you haven't heard of Jim Hall is because he was a bastard, a shocking drinker who fought whether he was in the ring or not, some of his most noteworthy brawls including drunken rages against friends, trainers and doctors. Unlike Darcy, Jim Hall was not the type of role model our educators like to push on Australian kids.

But history's not just about education. It's about storytelling, wonder, and pointless, amoral voyeurism. With the increasing digitisation of old newspaper pages, once only available on microfilm, a whole new door is being opened to those who are tired of the salt-of-the-earth blokes, passionately politicised murderers and stoic hand-to-breast heroines of Australia's official history. Beyond are thousands of characters like Jim Hall and J. J. Greer, whose faces will never appear on bank notes, but whose value to the history of this country is inestimable.

Though my purpose in writing *Australian Tragic* was to present real stories in the sensational 'dime novel' style of old, I have invented no people or events and I have been careful to invent no dialogue. All action comes from official documents, contemporaneous reports or eyewitness testimony, and any liberties I have taken with presumed thoughts or observations have been based, I believe, upon guesses whose sound educations can be found in the rear of this book.

Some may wonder why many of the events and characters herein deserve to be so remembered. But Australian life is built within the hours of the dead – lives that are summarised in the end with a few words in the obituary column and some verse on a headstone but which were as long and nourishing, charming and boring, hurt and spiteful as our own. Perhaps they, too, thought their lives insignificant, when in fact they instruct us in death. We can, in the words of Alan Feuer, 'hear their whispers drifting down the hallway: Eat well, drink much, love whatever you can on that side of the pavement. These are things we know.'

Jack Marx, Sydney

MOLOCH

Ancient legend speaks of Moloch, a fiery Prince of Hell who takes pleasure in the sorrow of mothers. The pagans sacrificed their young to him, in temples built in his likeness – giant effigies of iron, a creature with the body of a man and the head of a bull. Fires burned in his belly, the tips of flames seen to dance in the darkness of a mouth that was open to receive the loved. Parents were forbidden to cry as their children burned – to do so was an insult to Moloch, who desired his gifts be delivered by disciples willingly, joyfully, and with no regret. And so that mothers might not be moved by the anguished cries of their suffering babes, there was music and drumming, cheering, the piping of flutes and the hammering of tambourines – the sounds of a carnival to lure children to their doom and hide the screams of death.

Those who take their ancient texts literally can see his face in the rise of the modern world. He appeared in Fritz Lang's Metropolis, *his visage revealing itself in the machine of industry as it became a furnace into which the workers were flung for all their lives. And there are those who saw his face appear in the emergence of the amusement parks of the late nineteenth century, in the 'cities of light' that rose from the filth and the vice of New York's Coney Island, on the esplanade of Melbourne's St Kilda, and on the shores of Sydney Harbour . . .*

1

Jenny Poidevin was sixteen years old when she met John Godson, a twenty-year-old apprentice builder from the town of Warren in central New South Wales. She'd been having trouble at home – the type of turmoil that would make a girl run into the arms of a stranger. Strong, quiet and uncomplicated, John was her protector, her liberator. Even his name told of a saviour.

They were married during the summer floods of '71, John rowing his bride in a little boat that ferried them from the church to his parents' property, where the couple would live until they could afford a place of their own. It was here, in their flat at the end of the house, that John and Jenny fell into a weatherboard harmony, the weekly highlight being Friday night at the local bowling club – a game of darts, a scotch on the rocks, a few cigarettes and some laughs with friends. Jenny felt she was as happy as she had ever been.

Within a year Jenny was expecting, but miscarried. She miscarried again. And again. She travelled to Sydney for tests which suggested she may never bear a child. Then, just when she'd begun to accept that she may never know the joys of motherhood, she fell pregnant with Damian, a boy so precious that surgical intervention was required to keep him growing inside. Every day he remained within her was a small miracle. Jenny was careful with every movement, every thing she ate, the very air she breathed. Damian was delivered on 13 August, 1973. The following year, on 15 December, 1974, Jenny gave birth to another boy, Craig. She now had two little lives to nurture and shepherd through life's vast mystery.

One day, only weeks after bringing Craig home from the hospital, Jenny was preparing to bathe him when the family hound came scratching at the door. Jenny went out to investigate, following the animal as it bounded through the briar to the creek that ran at the back of the property. There she found Damian, face down in the water. She dived in and dragged him to the banks of the creek and resuscitated him back to life. The boys lungs were damaged and he lay in hospital for a week, but he survived. Not for the last time, the family Godson made the front page of the local newspaper.

The Godsons bought their own little house in Warren, not far from where John's parents lived. Jenny took great joy in her boys, and marvelled at the otherness of their ripening personalities. Damian was sensitive, fragile, easily intimidated, constantly bullied at school. When another child threw his hand-knitted jumper into the creek, Damian suffered terribly. He thought deeply, quietly, like his father. It was the product of Jenny's attention to him, as her first child, the one who had been so precious from the start. She'd been so frightened of hurting him. To Jenny, he'd been like a holy thing.

Craig was different. He was strong, with a noble little way. He laughed easily, wore his feelings openly. So unique was his character – so distinct from the other people who had conceived him – that Jenny often wondered if young minds didn't grow long before the womb, families chosen by little spirits for reasons we will never know.

Together the two boys clung to their father as an army of three, marching out to collect wood from the fields, returning from adventures with centipedes or other creatures from the bush, which they'd nurture for days or until those lives ceased. John was so proud of being their father it forever showed upon his face.

To make ends meet John began driving tankers for a petroleum company, his travels taking him away from his family for days on end. Jenny began to suffer a recurring dream in which John was trapped, his truck overturned, his body burning in a storm of fire. She would wake not knowing whether to thank the Lord for the life she had, or curse Him for taunting her with a pain she dared not imagine. She began to wonder what life would be like without John, whether her love for him was as strong as it should be. Life would be so long – longer than could ever be furnished by little contentments and the kind words of saviours. Could this be all that life had in store for her? A voice from where she knew not seemed to whisper that she was meant for something greater. Such thoughts worried her deeply.

One day, while taking tea with a neighbour, Jenny began to feel an ache growing inside her head. It grew louder and louder until she felt no longer part of the world. An ambulance was called. Her blood pressure soared beyond the survivable. She was airlifted to a hospital in Sydney. At twenty-five years old, Jenny Godson had suffered a brain hemorrhage. For a time the doctors couldn't say whether she was going to make it.

Jenny remained in hospital for months, in agony – not just physical pain, but emotional, too. The flood in her brain seemed to have released long-suppressed thoughts and buried dreams. She couldn't stop crying. Something had changed within her, and there was nobody on earth to whom she could talk. She confided some of it to John – ugly childhood memories. She tried to talk to her parents, but they wouldn't have it. There are some things parents do not wish to hear from their children.

But for Jenny, the worst realisation of all was that she didn't love her husband like she should. She had no idea why she was feeling such a thing – he'd been so good to her, a wonderful husband and a beautiful father to their boys. But her feeling was strong that this was not the man whom she would love for all of her life.

When Jenny returned to the family home, she was not the same woman who had left months before, close to death. She felt disconnected from John and the boys, who stepped carefully around her, as if she were a ghost in her own house.

John saw the change in Jenny and, in his own way, panicked. He suggested they get away for some time together, just the two of them. They'd both been working so hard at being providers for the family they had forgotten about each other. A week in Sydney together might be just what was needed to make things right, to return their world to the charm of before, when they'd been happy with what little they had. The boys could stay with relatives while John and Jenny went to nightclubs and restaurants, and strolled through the city like lovers do. Before coming home, they could treat Damian and Craig to a day out in Sydney – the zoo, the harbour, the dazzling lights, and the thrills that awaited at Luna Park.

For a week, John and Jenny were as teens on a date, while their real lives waited in some unspoken place. Jenny didn't dwell on the voices in her heart – whether her feelings for John were being changed or renewed – but simply went with the moment. Only when they returned to the normalcy of life back home, the mundane struggle of each day, would she know.

On their last day in Sydney, they met their boys for the adventure that had been promised them. They rode on ferries in the harbour and visited the zoo, but the boys never stopped talking about Luna Park, their hands clutching their loins in childish excitement.

Late in the afternoon, as the family waited at Circular Quay for a ferry to take them to Luna Park on the other side of the harbour, a strange pagan procession of minstrels and dancing girls snaked through the crowd. They seemed to come from nowhere, and nobody was ever to learn who they were or why they were there on that day. Leading the band was a man wearing the head of a bull. As Damian sought refuge behind his mother, the creature seemed to catch sight of him, leaving his post at the head of the procession and approaching the boy, as if with something to say. But the creature said nothing, only stood for a moment before slowly raising his hand and placing it upon the frightened boy's shoulder. Jenny quickly snapped a photograph. It was the last image of the boy ever to be captured.

It was half-past nine on 9 June, 1979, when the Godson family emerged from the madness of Luna Park's Coney Island, from the slides, the mirror mazes, the spinning floors, the unreal world. They had been at Luna Park for hours, and had sampled every amusement on offer: the Big Dipper, which sped them along a crazy track of loops and dives; the River Caves, a romantic journey by boat through tunnels that emerged into scenes from lands far away and others never known; and the Ghost Train, whose tiny carriages careened on a rail that twisted and turned and crashed through doors to reveal ghastly scenes of severed heads and skeletal remains, all to the sound of ghoulish howls from the dying and the dead, which mingled with the screams of the living children who trembled in their seats.

Jenny saw that they had four tickets left – just enough for a ride they could all enjoy together – and so she asked the boys which ride they would like to take as the last for the evening. The boys wanted to ride on the Ghost Train. It was the one that had excited them the most.

As they walked toward the leering ghouls and spooks that howled in the distance, Jenny, for reasons she could never explain, felt a heat inside her that made her thirst. It was a desire that seemed to come from a place that made no sense – her family were headed for the gates of the ride, and she with them – but the feeling was strong enough to drag her away from her family. She told John and the boys to go ahead without her, that she would join them later, once she had purchased an ice cream.

When Jenny returned, her boys were nowhere to be seen. Believing they had headed to the Ghost Train without her, she walked in the direction of the ride. It was as she approached that she saw smoke – just a wisp of it, a slight haze above the skulls and ghouls that adorned the facade. But as she watched she saw the smoke become thicker, and heard people beginning to cry out.

A car appeared from the exit door, its occupants, a teenage boy and girl, frantically crying out to the attendant. There was a fire inside, they screamed, and he had to stop the ride and get help. The man didn't seem to understand. He had his foot on the front of a car that contained two young boys, who heard the screaming and began to cry, saying to the attendant that they wanted to get off. But the man removed his foot from the carriage, which accelerated along the tracks and propelled the two crying boys through the doors, their anxious faces turned to the crowd as they disappeared into the smoky darkness beyond.

Within moments, the ribbons of smoke became lashing flames that rose high above the skeletons and corpses that danced on the roof of the building. Fire burst upwards as if propelled by a hot wind, upon which, every now and then, a scream or a cry seemed to ride into the night, nobody knowing if it were real or pretend. The train continued motoring through the furnace, cars on fire emerging from the exit doors, empty of the passengers who'd entered within them. The crowd began to scream horribly as they realised people were dying inside.

Attendants hastened the throng toward the gates of the park. Jenny protested – she had lost her family, she cried, and feared they might be some of those who were in the belly of the pyre. She was shuffled along with the others, away from what was now an inferno, until she stood at the gates, scanning the crowd for John and Damian and Craig. The sounds of the carnival continued to drone – the calliope song of the merry-go-round, the recorded barking of spruikers, the laughter from beneath the wide open mouth. Jenny could take no more and ran back into the park, over the gates and past the guards. She was finally stopped by men in front of what had moments before been the Ghost Train, and was now but a hot, glowing pile of cinder, charcoaled timber and twisted metal . . . and rising from the ashes, a skeleton, untouched by flame, its mouth open, mocking the living and the dead. The blood ran to her head and everything went black and disappeared.

Many years passed before Jenny could bring herself to read the coroner's report into what happened inside the Ghost Train on that winter night in 1979. It was ruled that the fire was an accident, a discarded cigarette or flaming match setting ablaze a dark and dusty room made from plywood and asbestos, the ceiling coated with bitumen that rained molten tears of flame on those who were trapped in the dark. Seven people died that night. Jenny's saviour and her little boys were found huddled together, an army of three. They had burned alive.

The woman who was the mother and wife died in the fire that night, too. For years Jenny shuffled through psychiatric wards where doctors told her she was getting better, though she knew it could never be true, that one never recovers from the world in which she dwells. Her family's absence defines her, the flames that took them wreaking destruction beyond the mad midnight moments and trembling sorrows. She married again but it couldn't last, her husband doomed to forever compete with a ghost who could do no wrong, and her daughter, now in her teens, has lived with a sibling relationship with the spectres of two perfect boys. The tragedy never ends, but waits each day in a new hiding place.

Jenny remains convinced that there was human evil at work that night. The fire, she believes, was lit by hand. There are too many questions, a silence too loud. Somebody knows something and they'll take it to their grave. Perhaps there lives a man who smoked but does no longer, and why he quit he'll never tell. The fire left more burdens than can be counted by those who need to know.

But no one placed her family there that night, in the ride that burned at Luna Park on Sydney Harbour, so far from home. Jenny has been haunted for decades by the tormenting idea that it was she who had ultimately taken them there. They were all led, like children to the mouth of Moloch, by desire, the architect of all tragic ends. Some sacrifice the things they love for money, others for fame, or power, or lust, or revenge. For Jenny, it was simply a tantalising belief in an existence more fulfilling than that which she had. She imagined a life different to her own, and so it was delivered her, by a hand both generous and cruel. She has lived, she believes, to learn this, to value the stillness of love and life. She has faith that something good will come of it.

Jenny doesn't like to dwell upon the grotesque last moments suffered by those she loved – the terror in the boys as they clung to John for salvation in the dark, or the agony in their proud father's mind as the flames came closer and took their bodies. She tries to remember the sweet things – John's lovely smile, or the way the boys laughed as they fought for the icing mix when she made a cake on summer days. But her mind's eye wanders, always, back to the darkness on Sydney Harbour, through the open mouth and into the lights, to a moment when her boys were so excited, clutching themselves, eyes wide with desire. Jenny can see them still, their young faces aglow with a radiant light, as if they can somehow feel that all the love they will ever know is here, on a night that will make them beautiful for all of time.

CLOSER

The long jetty reaching out from Brighton Beach just south of Adelaide was once a message board that fluttered with notes to those lost to the sea, the war, love's fickle winds and other things that swallow the foolish and the brave. A man called Honey laid the timber deck in 1886, but a storm in 1915 weakened the wharf and shook the faith of those who'd waved goodbye to cherished ones as they departed for the Great War. In 1926 schoolchildren watched in horror as their heroine, Kitty Whyte, who'd famously saved a drowning soul from these very waters seven years before, dived from the jetty and into the jaws of a great white shark. In Kitty's memory, the women of Brighton built a drinking fountain, which survived the storm that wrecked the pier and felled the Arch of Remembrance in '95.

Today the jetty at Brighton is rebuilt, stronger in the broken places, the messages of love and hate, sad tidings and good ones, too, now beamed from a communications tower that rises as a sentinel at the end of the wharf. We must now turn back, walk north along the shore, just a little way past the Norfolk Island pines that hide the houses from the sea, to a lonely place in the sand, no less a monument for being unheralded by artefact. Sit down here in the sand, your eyes to the many sorrows that live beyond the bay, and know that a farewell as desperate and tragic as any other was once said here . . .

He still walks with a limp, the only outward sign of that wartime business from so long ago. He lives in the same house in Tarlton Street, just a short walk from the shores of Brighton Beach on Holdfast Bay. Over the years the old flyboys have sought him out and come to visit, to talk about the old times, the old war, the lucky escape, and the ones they so wish could be here. They are careful with the old man, protective of him, as they feel they should be. He will always be one of them.

Robert William Bungey was born in Adelaide on 4 October, 1915, the first child of Ernest and Ada Bungey, whose love for music and amateur dramatics drew them together. He was educated first at Glenelg Public School and then Adelaide Boys High School, beginning his working life as a clerk for a local life insurance firm. But young Bob Bungey had a fascination with aircraft, his room in Tarlton Street bejewelled with models and sketches of Sopwith Camels and others from the bygone war, and when he heard the RAAF was accepting applications for Flight Training School he was quick to enlist as an Air Cadet, accepted into the flying course at Point Cook, Victoria, in 1936.

A quiet boy, Bob Bungey took to flying like a child to a secret place. Suspended in the sky, looking down upon the once tall buildings and impassible rivers, their tributaries now silver little lightning bolts impressed into the earth, he felt as one having leapt from the frame in which all life remained, the streets and houses, the people going to and fro about their tiny business, all captives of some vast equation only he had solved. All the things that ever mattered were now literally beneath him, falling away from his panorama with the tilting of the wings, all humankind's existence made to wait for his return. It was the greatest thing in life, and risking life was worth it.

Robert knew that England would need young pilots for the storm that was darkening Europe. The newspapers were saying they were German planes that had bombed the Spanish city of Guernica, killing hundreds of women and children in a pyre of burning timber and falling brick from crumbling buildings. This would be a war fought in the air, and Bob was good with the machines that would fight it. Upon graduating from Point Cook in 1937, the young pilot immediately sailed for England, to offer his services to the RAF.

Bob's skills were quickly noted and, as the threat of war grew louder, he was posted to the 226 Squadron at Harwell, Berkshire, where he learned to fly the Fairey Battle bomber, a three-man machine designed for low-altitude ground assaults on infantry and light mechanics. Some feared the slow, lightly-armed bomber would be a suicide machine when pitted against the slick German Messerschmitt or Focke Wulf, but the RAF had failed to keep pace with the output of the Luftwaffe and needed every craft they had to match the German numbers in the air.

When German troops invaded Poland, Bob's squadron was ordered immediately to France as part of the British Expeditionary Force, arriving in Rheims the very next day to be housed in barns and abandoned cottages, or rooms in the houses of kindly French villagers, as they awaited an onslaught that never seemed to come. This was the the 'Phoney War' and Bob and his comrades saw plenty of it. When not bombarding German towns and villages along the French border with anti-Nazi leaflets, the 226 ran reconnaissance sweeps over German territories, the mist that hovered on the ground along the Moselle valley glowing eerily in the moonlight. Occasionally they'd be forced to play a dodging game with a single German searchlight that lurched at them through the dark, but the dangers of war seemed very far away, the daylight hours spent engaged in fake dogfights and affecting speeding passes over fields, inching ever closer to the ground as pilots dared each other to clip the long grass with their wings.

Bob turned twenty-five in October. A South Australian friend from another squadron flew hundreds of miles to celebrate with him, the cold night charmed in brandy balloons, the radio warm with the sounds of Ray Noble, Bing Crosby, Al Bowlly, and the shrill voice of a French chanteuse who nobody understood, but who somehow made them feel at home. Outside the rain made quagmires of the airfields, and from the murk beneath the meadows emerged bullets, bones and broken things buried since the Great War, rising from the ground like ghoulish emblems of the fate that awaited them.

It was April when the Germans at last launched their blitzkrieg in the West, crushing Denmark and Norway within weeks, the Nazi goliath rolling across the borders in Belgium, Holland, Luxembourg, the speed of the combined ground and air assault taking all defences by complete surprise. The Fairey Battle bombers scrambled, if only to escape being burned on the ground by falling incendiaries, the Luftwaffe having found their airfields while the English slept.

Bob's squadron was thrown into desperate flights of twos and threes against the German soldiers in the north. On that first day, a friend Bob had known from his days at Point Cook in Victoria was sent screaming to his death, bullets ripping through the cockpit as he swooped down in a pass that clipped the daisies from the ground. At day's end, shaken crews returned, their aircraft shredded, cockpit glass all over France, their flight suits spattered with their blood, instrument panels covered in the contents of their stomachs.

They'd seen the Fairey Battle despatched to an airborne grave by the Messerschmitt, though no one dared to speak it.

By May Bob had learned to become as one with his machine, to disengage his conscience from the matter, to be a bomber more than a man. To slow the German advance, Bob's squadron was often called upon to collapse buildings over roadways, or scatter blocks of houses over single village streets. They could only pray the dwellings were deserted. The alternative was unthinkable, and so they didn't think it.

On one day at the end of May, Bob, flying alone, bombed a column of German vehicles and strafed troops running for their lives, cutting them to pieces until his ammunition was exhausted. Another day saw him one of few to return from a determined Allied air assault against the Belgian bridges over which the German columns streamed. He'd watched from his rattling, roaring cockpit as friends fell from the sky, their wings ablaze as they spiralled into fields and buildings, the radio broadcasting their final cries from the insides of doomed machines.

Luck and desperation saw him home again when the entire strength of the Allied bomber group in France was hurled against a German column at Sedan, less than half of all the bombers launched returning to their airfields. They called it the most deadly day the RAF had ever lived.

As France began to fall, what was left of Robert's squadron was ordered from the front, limping home to England in the few Fairey Battle bombers still able to be flown.

After the defeat of France, all thoughts turned to the invasion of Great Britain that was surely coming. Operation Sea Lion was already in the planning, 160 000 German soldiers and their machinery of death poised to cross the channel and enslave the island. Every beach along the English coast became entangled with barbed wire, and old men in the villages were trained in sabotage. The Nazis had overrun western Europe in just a few short weeks, and England was expected to be in German hands by Christmas.

But Hitler's generals feared the RAF – an amphibious invasion, assaulted from the air, could see the stronger army nation founder in the Channel. It was thus agreed that Operation Sea Lion be postponed until the Nazis had achieved complete superiority in the skies. Hermann Göring, commander of the Luftwaffe, assured his Fuhrer this could be accomplished in a matter of weeks, the number of German aircraft outnumbering those of the RAF by four to one, the German pilots more experienced than their British counterparts. All the Luftwaffe had to do was bomb the British airfields, factories and radar stations, the Messerschmitts dealing with the fighters forced into a battle in which they were outclassed.

And so, in July of 1940, the Battle of Britain began. The British losses were terrible – in the first two weeks of August, more than 100 fighter pilots lost their lives in twice as many planes – and the RAF was forced to send up untrained pilots to fight against the experienced German airmen. Bob Bungey was a veteran compared to some of the boys being thrown into the skies, so when he volunteered for Fighter Command he was immediately accepted. Attached to the 145 Squadron, he learned to fly the Hurricane and entered the battle without delay.

It was in these machines that Bob Bungey learned the lonely violence of his war: in a field that had no foxholes, where there were no sandbags to hide behind or medics to attend a wound, and where one had not the luxury to surrender. On this battlefield it was hunt or be the prey, and to hesitate meant death. Better not to think about the other man and who he was, of those who might love him, or the worlds that might be darkened by his never coming home. The enemy were machines. It was an illusion that shattered whenever one heard the sound of a bullet in one's airframe. In that dreadful, unjust, silly moment, it seemed the entire war was aimed at you.

One afternoon in November, Bob was one of eleven Hurricanes of the 145 Squadron patrolling near the Isle of Wight when they were suddenly ambushed by a swarm of Messerschmitt 109s, led by the notorious German ace Helmut Wick, who already had fifty RAF fighters to his name. Bob had only just noticed the silvery craft dropping out of the clouds behind them when he heard the appalling sound of shells tearing through the fuselage of his Hurricane, a rapid hammering behind his head that seemed never to stop, a racing of the engine and a shuddering from the wings to the tail. He instinctively cranked his machine over, then into a dive, the ocean racing up to meet him as a map through a looking glass. At the last moment he hauled his stick back and levelled out, sliding his wings left and right to slow his speed before plowing into shallow water near Shanklin on the Isle of Wight. Only slightly injured, Bob managed to escape, and returned to the air with his squadron within days.

By now the German tactics had shifted from assaults upon the fighters to the wholesale bombing of London, to the tortured relief of Fighter Command, which had been close to collapse. More than one out of every six pilots who took part in the Battle of Britain had not survived it. Bob Bungey, once again, was one of the lucky few.

In June of 1941, Bob was made commander of 452 Squadron, the first Australian Spitfire squadron in England. Within a few months of becoming operational, the 452 had become a fearsome presence in the skies over England and the French coast, with the highest tally of enemy aircraft of any squadron in Fighter Command. As with all British squadrons, their success against the enemy owed a lot to the Spitfire, an aircraft destined to become the unicorn of every air veteran's dreams. The young pilots of the 452 owed their lives to the knowledge that Bob had gained in the Battle of Britain and in France before it, the wisdom that belongs to those who've flown in hostile skies and survived: keep the sun behind you; fire only when close; think of nothing else but the target; stay high; always turn and face the attack; hit quickly, hit hard, and get out fast.

But more valuable than any of this was the knowledge – and every pilot in the 452 possessed it – that Bob Bungey was looking out for them. Bob's pilots knew they were safe in an attack because he was always on their rear, protecting them from the enemy against his own instinct for survival. Years later, some would recall how conversations on the ground would abruptly end when Bob heard engines up above, abandoning all earthly talk as his face turned to the sky, like a father looking out for children in his charge.

Some time in 1941, Bob was enjoying leave at a swimming pool in Wallingford when he met Sybil Johnson, a local girl whose father was the stationmaster there. So began a courtship that blossomed in the cauldron of war, and Bob and Sybil were married at the Registry Office at Riegate, in the County of Surrey, on 4 October, 1941.

But now the German blitz was spreading from London to the counties. There was no village or town that was safe from the raining death. More than 50 000 civilians had been killed by Nazi night raids, and there was talk of weird new weapons – flying bombs that would travel from occupied France to England in just a few minutes, obliterating neighbourhoods no enemy would even see. Plymouth, Portsmouth, Liverpool, towns as far north as Newcastle were not spared. To be in England during the Blitz was to be on the front line of the war.

When Sybil became pregnant, Bob convinced her to take ship to Australia, where she could stay in safety until he returned at conflict's end. And so Sybil Bungey arrived in South Australia on the steam ship *Nestor* in February 1942, moving in with Bob's parents at the house in Tarlton Street, near Brighton Beach.

On 10 March, 1942, Bob Bungey was awarded the Distinguished Flying Cross for services to the King and Commonwealth and, ten days later, half a world away, Sybil gave birth to a baby boy, Richard, at a private hospital in Glenelg.

For a year they were a family apart, lovers held together by the mail, Bob promising to Sybil that he would return as soon as the RAF would let him go. For everyone, Bob's skill as a pilot became more crucial than it ever had been before.

One day, Sybil went to the pictures in Adelaide, and saw Bob in a Movietone News reel. The narrator spoke of the 452 Squadron as heroes of the war, while the footage showed Bob and his pilots at their base, outside in the sunshine, smoking, laughing, shifting nervously in front of the camera, like ordinary boys would do. These were the bringers of death in this war – not machines, nor explosives, nor strange new weapons, but boys, their young lives commandeered by an ancient cult that sees make-believe lines on the earth.

In early 1943, Bob received word that he would soon be going home. He said his goodbyes to the boys he'd come to know as brothers, to the skies that had never deserted him, and the Spitfire to which he was as bonded as rider to his horse. For one last time, Bob strode over the clouds and the English countryside, alone between the world and whatever waited beyond. Then he brought her gently in to land, turned off the switches one by one, removing the straps and wires that tied to him to the war, and walked away.

On 4 May, 1943, Wing Commander Robert Bungey DFC came home to Sybil and the son he had never seen. The newspapers reported that a hero had returned, and the Mayor of Brighton celebrated his homecoming with an official luncheon in his honour. Bob would soon be posted to Mildura, to train young pilots for the fight against the Japanese. But the war – the death that waits on every moment – was over for Bob Bungey. He had survived.

Weeks later, on the morning 27 May, 1943, Sybil Bungey was lifting Richard from his cot when a spasm shot through her left side and dropped her to the floor. She had recently battled meningitis – a traveller's disease, they said – and some relic of the germ had remained in the blood to attack her heart. Doctors worked through the day but could not save her. Sybil Bungey died that afternoon, and nobody could say why. She was twenty-four.

The sky blew away from Robert Bungey's world. For three years he had survived the gory sorrows of the war, in the very patch of earth where it had raged the loudest. Yet it was here, in the town of his birth, further from the front line than one could be upon the world, that the war would choose to break him. And it would do it by obliterating the one cherished thing the war had given him.

At Sybil's funeral service, Robert Bungey saluted as the girl he loved was lowered into the ground at his feet. It seemed the right thing to do. She was as much a casualty of the war as the refugees that had streamed from towns and cities under Bob's own wings. He couldn't bear to be with anyone, the mere touch of another seeking his arm in sympathy was brushed away. It was alone that he had learned to cope with dreadful things – alone in the air, watching death come to friends, and enemies, too, who never were machines, never would be less than human beings in the minds of those who killed them, with lives more real and precious for every day that they were gone.

Bob walked alone along the Brighton shore that evening, the ocean and the pier, the sand beneath his feet, all where it had been when he was young and none of this had happened – the war, the death, the joy of love. He'd looked out from here a thousand times and dreamed of things, but never had he seen the sadness that hung from everything, the colours hostage to the sky, the hopelessness of the little waves that beat against the shore. It was everywhere. He could scarcely bring himself to breathe it.

For days on end, Bob drifted from here to there, from room to room, from the darkness to the shadow, moved by the people who came to help, but none of it meant anything. Not even little Richard was a joy, his tiny cries now shrieks of agony. It was all too sad to bear.

One night, as the others slept, Robert Bungey put his little boy into the pram and walked down to the beach. He did not wish to be here any more, on this heartbroken earth. He looked down upon his little boy, asleep under the night sky. What would become of him, with no mother's love and no father to protect him? Would he shuffle from one institution to another, deserted, hating Bob and Sybil for abandoning him, his heart reaching out for something never there? Would the desolation grow him into a damaged man? Would a better father not protect his boy from such a fate?

Bob said goodbye to the little one he had loved for all his short life, a love he cried into the air that night, and which travelled out into the sky forever. This world was not meant for pretty things, for soft skin, which Bob himself had destroyed from the sky. He was so sorry. He took out his service pistol, placed it against the little boy's head, and pulled the trigger.

Then Robert Bungey turned the gun toward himself, and put his world at peace.

In the same old house in Tarlton Street, just a short walk from Brighton Beach, an old man moves from room to room, where tokens of a war that raged in another century take pride of place on the shelves and on the walls. The pilots from the 452 Squadron have come to visit him from time to time – when the fly boys came, they talked for hours, about the flying and the fear, and the madness that came later. They shed a tear together. Everyone thought the world of his father.

When police came to the beach in 1943, they found Bob Bungey dead upon the sand, his little boy shot through the head beside him, the family dog protecting both of the bodies from anyone who came near. Incredibly, the little boy was found to be alive, the bullet having travelled through to the other side of his brain without affecting any vital parts. Doctors said it was a miracle.

Today, Richard Bungey limps a little, and his memory comes and goes sometimes, but that is all. He has lived a happy life.

There have been times when he has wished his mum and dad were there – when he married, he thought of them – but life has always been that way. Their absence is like the sky.

Richard doesn't hate his father. What war can do to a man's mind is something most will never know. It is not for us to understand, but to understand we never will. That's the nature of it.

But Richard does his best to know his father, and sometimes feels he does, through the clippings and the photos that he keeps, and the time he's spent with other pilots, who've told him things about the Bob Bungey they knew. He builds models of all his father's planes – the Spitfire and the Hurricane, and the Fairey Battle bomber – and he never misses Anzac Day, or a gathering in his father's name.

In the War Memorial in Canberra, the very Spitfire that Bob Bungey flew is hanging on display. Richard often dreams of sitting in it, feeling as his father did, in the very seat from which his father looked down upon the churning world.

He'd do anything, he says, to be closer to his dad.

THE MOTHER OF ALL LIES

Somewhere on the road between Queenstown in the west and Hobart in the east, one can see, just off to the right and up in the hills, the decrepit home of a family they say was so wild that the eldest boy lived chained to a flagpole in the front garden. This is Tasmania, the only state in Australia whose name does not trumpet with British colonialism, suggesting instead a type of exotica one might associate with islands of the Africas, or some gully of European subterrania wherein creatures similar to vampires dwell. To this day, inventive periodicals such as the Weekly World News *regularly favour Tasmania when choosing the seat of some fantastic yarn whose particulars of fact are best placed far enough away to render the checking of them impossible. In the Hollywood film version of* Doctor Dolittle, *Rex Harrison showed he meant business when he promised to pursue a mythical sea creature, if need be, 'from here to Tasmania', a place 'where only the brave and insane go'.*

As fate would have it Rex Harrison would come to know, intimately, a very glamorous woman for whom Tasmania was both an isle of salvation and a sink of inevitable doom, her decision to return late in life one that was not only brave and insane, but fatal. Upon her death awaited one final heartbreak from which her living self was spared, though her ghost, one might wager, is not ...

She was born Estelle Merle O'Brien Thompson in 1911, though her close friends called her 'Queenie'. She would later claim to remember little of her birthplace in Tasmania, and she never knew her Irish father, Arthur, whom her mother told her was away at sea, or in a hero's grave on the fields of the Great War, or lost to pneumonia just days before Queenie was born. The story changed with the seasons. The truth, Queenie knew, must be worse than them all.

The mother, Charlotte, was much darker than the child, who possessed a silky caramel glow that disguised her mother's Ceylonese blood. An unusually pretty girl, young Queenie liked to dress up and pretend to be people she was not – a trait peculiar, we are often told, to those with futures in the dramatic arts.

And then there was Constance, fifteen years Queenie's senior. 'Joyce', as her friends and family called her, wore her mother's darkness, and carried an invisible shame that had seen her banished to some distant institution. As a child Queenie had heard whispers of a scandal, but never the details of it. On occasion, Joyce would visit Queenie and Charlotte, though it was clear she was never welcome to stay, the stiflingly Christian society for which Charlotte groomed Queenie no place for her. It is not known whether Queenie ever knew Joyce as her own half-sister, only that they were related by a past the more glamorous girl would later disavow.

Though poor, Charlotte worked hard so that Queenie would want for nothing, securing her an education at a prestigious school for girls, where Queenie was accepted on account of her father having served in the war. Those who schooled with her recall a silent, sulking girl who played and dreamed alone, and never discussed her family. Girls less gifted by nature, but more richly rewarded by circumstance, punished Queenie's privacy with rumour. She was the mongrel child of some secret outrage, abandoned with a brothel's muck, salvaged from the gutter by some barren, scavenging Samaritan.

Queenie finished school at the age of eleven, her woeful marks more than any good school's reputation could bear, and slacked through her teens as a typist, a clerk, a switchboard operator. As a young woman she appeared in amateur plays, then professional ones, her striking looks opening doors onstage and backstage, from party to private parlour. By the time Charlotte and Queenie took a room in the fashionable movie district of the city, where marquees dazzled with stars from abroad, Queenie was known and popular amongst a twilight crowd who offered more than just love and friendship. When one of her many appellants promised to introduce her to a movie director in France, Queenie spied her escape from the land so far from the brighter lights, convincing Charlotte to escort her to Paris, their tickets afforded them by another of Queenie's infatuated suitors. The man made good on his promise, Queenie Thompson scoring a small part in Rex Ingram's silent film, *The Three Passions*.

Several more cameos followed, and, within a year, Queenie had taken a room in London, introducing the ever-present Charlotte to friends as her Indian maid – a ruse with which Charlotte was evidently happy to play along. Queenie wasted no time in ingratiating herself with the English cinema crowd, her beauty attracting the attentions of Rex Harrison, Leslie Howard and Douglas Fairbanks amongst others. But it was her introduction to Hungarian filmmaker Alexander Korda, a serious player in the Hollywood scene, which bore the most fruit.

In Queenie Thompson, Korda saw a true glamour star of American motion pictures. All she needed, he thought, was a new name, her history touched up here and there, to hide from view those troublesome details that just might frighten the thick and the ordinary, on whose money Hollywood so depended.

Her name would be Merle Oberon, after Shakespeare's fairy king whose spells, designed to lure others into love, would lead to so much chaos.

Merle Oberon entered the eye of the world in Alexander Korda's production of *The Private Life of Henry VIII*, the newly-christened star cast in the major role of Anne Boleyn, the tragic queen consort executed for high treason. The film won Best Picture at the 1934 Academy Awards, bringing Merle Oberon into the spotlight, the story of her life published in magazines and broadcast in newsreel reports, the details sanctified by fan magazines and Hollywood scriptures. It was said she was born of aristocratic antipodean stock, the death of her officer father in a tragic Tasmanian hunting accident seeing the child invited to live in the Bombay mansion of her rich and stately 'godmother', an intrigue of wealthy family members and stratospheric associates nursing the young actress through exclusive finishing schools in London and Paris.

In England, Merle's oddly maternal Indian maid, accepted the new version of history with no noticeable bother but, at home, Joyce reacted with ill-concealed distress. She had not been as fortunate as her movie star relation, a failed marriage leaving her with two young children and little to feed them, a severe stroke having crippled the entire left side of her body – a response, some said, to her anguish at being left behind, abandoned by the others in their quest for a more beautiful life abroad. Nevertheless she had followed Queenie's rise to fame as might an obsessive fan, her children watching perplexed as she returned from the local cinema both enchanted and destroyed, like a widow waking from impossible dreams. When she read of Merle Oberon from Tasmania, and the new life story that erased all that was, Joyce flew into what seemed a jealous rage. She wrote desperate letters to Merle and Charlotte, pleading for money, stirring memories, begging that she not be forgotten. Her mother replied to some of them.

Meanwhile, across the rest of Tasmania, news that the land had given birth to a star was greeted with great enthusiasm. Memories were recalled in lustrous detail, the island suddenly populated with midwives and doctors, school teachers and classmates, lovers and neighbours, all with tales of the young Merle Oberon remembered now with hand-to-brow relief.

The sullen, half-Indian peasant girl had won, it seemed, the admiration of her neighbours, and only by placing herself on the other side of the world.

Supernatural spiritualism finds the troubled woman as the worm finds the cadaver. Through her whole life, Merle Oberon sought audience with a pageant of spooks, mystics and veiled peepers in the dark, and she saw prophetic symbols in the shapes of clouds and people's names. She trusted the unknowable more than she did the world she walked upon, only too aware of how disappointing real people of flesh and blood could be. For Merle, the one grinding prejudice of which she often spoke, was a white-hot hatred for liars – of all the creatures that walked or crawled, she despised them the most. Their little fractures were the rifts that tore the universe apart. And of all the roles she took in life, it was the liar whom she portrayed the most convincingly of all.

In the 1935 film *The Dark Angel*, Merle played the role of Kitty Vane, a girl whose part in a frivolous pretense dooms three childhood friends to misery, salvation coming just too late when

Kitty finally reveals her true identity to the man she has loved, but left for dead, all her adult life.

Merle's curiously passionate performance earned her a nomination for an Academy Award in 1936. Joyce wrote to Merle begging that she might come over for the ceremony. The letter went unanswered.

Merle lost to Bette Davis who, in *Dangerous*, played a woman called Joyce, whose apparently jinxed existence is redeemed through an ultimate act of sincerity and sacrifice.

It was on a rainy day in 1937 when fate appeared to lose patience with Merle Oberon. Riding through the streets of London in the back of a chauffeured Rolls-Royce, Merle, running slightly late for a make-up appointment, snapped at the driver to step on it. As the chauffeur accelerated around a corner, the Rolls collided with a Daimler travelling in the opposite direction. Merle was thrown from her seat, her head striking a metal footrest on the automobile floor. She regained consciousness in an ambulance, immediately enquiring upon the state of her beauty.

For the rest of her days, Merle was forced to indulge a deception every time she faced the cameras, make-up smeared and lighting flared to hide the scar that lived above her left eye.

The accident scuttled the production of *I, Claudius*, in which Oberon was to star, and which many believe may have been one of the greatest motion pictures ever made.

A month later, Charlotte, who, as the ever-dutiful maid, had kept house for Merle in London all these years, quietly passed away from the effects of diabetes. Joyce was informed of her mother's last days via a letter from a nurse in the employ of Ms Oberon, the communiqué suggesting, ever so gently, that Joyce's constant, pleading letters had contributed to her mother's demise. The letter also made clear that Ms Oberon had troubles of her own.

Charlotte was buried in an unmarked grave in a cemetery in London, so far from home. Many years later, Merle employed an artist to paint Charlotte's portrait from a photograph, being sure to request that the skin be lightened to a more palatable shade.

In 1939 Merle finally acquiesced to marry Alexander Korda, despite having been in love with a procession of other men during their courtship, including David Niven, who could not remain faithful to her, and Laurence Olivier, who could barely stand her. It was Korda, after all, who had launched her career, and he could just as surely have smothered it.

Later that year, while stricken with the flu in Hollywood, Merle took a treatment of sulfonamide injections intended to battle the virus. She awoke in the morning, horrified to look in the mirror and see her face and neck a mass of sores that oozed vile fluid, the drugs having reacted with the make-up she wore every day. Her servants fell at her feet in tears. Friends rushed from nearby homes to see and stood with eyes wide and hands to mouth as Merle dashed this way and that, no point of the compass offering relief.

Alexander knew of a surgeon in New York who performed miracles at times such as this. And so, her face hidden from the world by a black veil of mourning, Merle flew to New York for salvation. There she was strapped to a chair while the skin on her face was frozen by carbon dioxide snow. A surgeon then ground her skin to bloody jelly with a diamond burr. For seven days after the operation, Merle lay with her hands tied to her bed so she would not scratch as the new skin crept and itched underneath the bandages, her food delivered through a straw. When the bandages were removed, the doctor declared the operation unsuccessful – it would have to be attempted all over again. Three times was this procedure repeated, until it was clear Merle could stand no more.

The make-up became thicker, the lighting burned hotter, to hide the permanent craters the experience left behind on Merle's face.

It was not surprising, then, that Merle found herself drawn to one Richard Hillary, a pilot for the RAF whom she met at a New York party in July of 1941. Only twenty-two years of age, Hillary had been shot down over the North Sea just the year before, his handsome face and athletic body charred by burning petroleum as he bailed from the cockpit of his Supermarine Spitfire. Hillary had endured months of painful operations and skin grafts that barely disguised his grotesque disfigurements, yet he carried himself with the dash of a young man who had nothing to hide and nobody to fear.

Merle fell for him instantly, no doubt spying parallels in their misfortunes. He had, after all, been born in Australia, and had spent his first few years in Sydney. Together they exchanged vague childhood memories of that land, like rushes from a film shot so long ago.

Merle ordered her personal publicist to organise a room at the Ritz Towers for herself and Richard to enjoy together in the coming months, a hideaway from the prying eyes of the press, or her husband. There they loved until the autumn came, when Hillary, still bound by his duty to the RAF, returned to England with a promise that he and Merle would be together again soon, their affair continuing through the seasons in letters so passionate and lurid that some censorial soul from later years saw fit to burn them all to smoke.

In January of 1943 Merle received the news that Richard, while on a night training operation, had flown his Bristol Blenheim into the earth.

The war was not yet over when Merle took the role of Kitty Langley in *The Lodger*, a film about a man with such contempt for actresses that he hangs their portraits with faces to the wall. Working on the film was a cinematographer named Lucien Ballard, who took a particular interest in Merle, inventing a special camera-mounted light that washed away her scars and blemishes. People said Merle had never looked more beautiful than in *The Lodger*. Merle divorced Alexander Korda and married Ballard the following year.

The marriage was not a happy one, plagued as it was by the flies of fame – the gossip, the prying eyes, the ongoing nuisance of Joyce and her letters, their dark, clingy poetry impervious to silence. Even Merle's maid, Vene, approached her employer for favours, begging Merle to help arrange a screen test for her daughter who dreamed of being a movie star. Merle organised for the girl to meet with producers, and Vene boasted to her friends of the future star her child would be. But the screen test was a failure, the girl no more than a pretty face, and Merle returned from a weekend in the country to find Vene had gassed herself in Merle's garage, her dead body lying on the front seat of the Rolls-Royce. Merle could scarcely comprehend that which some would do for fame.

By the end of the decade, her days as a glamorous leading lady clearly coming to an end, Merle's enthusiasm for the movie business began to fade. Her marriage to Lucien Ballard over, she began a romance with Giorgio Cini, son of a wealthy Venetian industrialist. With Giorgio, Merle journeyed far from Hollywood to Hawaii, Rome and the south of France. Giorgio talked to Merle of a future life together in Venice, far from the empty vulgarity of Hollywood, and for a time Merle saw a new world ahead. Close friends knew the couple to be engaged.

On a clear September morning on the French Riviera in 1949, Giorgio bade farewell to Merle as he prepared to fly home to Venice. He would be meeting her in Hollywood within the month, whereupon they would plan their wedding and future life. As Merle looked on from the airfield balcony, Giorgio's private plane rose into the sky then returned in a low pass, Giorgio waving his white monogrammed handkerchief so that his future bride could see. As a wing clipped the tops of the tall pine trees, the engine seemed to choke and sputter, the aircraft exploding in mid-air. Merle saw Giorgio's body on fire, falling from the sky.

Years later Merle reached out to Giorgio through a medium, who told her he was by her side, but did not recognise her.

It was in 1965 that Australia began to loom again on Merle's horizon. Now married to Mexican tycoon, Bruno Pagliai, Merle accepted a promotional invitation from Qantas Airways to be part of the inaugural flight between Mexico City and Sydney.

She arrived at Sydney airport to find a phalanx of reporters armed with questions about her childhood in Tasmania. Merle shooed them away with vague responses, as if there were something dark that dwelled within the answers she did not wish to give. Later, at a dinner in her honour, she told one reporter she had since visited Tasmania, then another that she had not. Others were surprised to hear her say her birth in Hobart had been entirely unexpected, a premature arrival necessitating the family remain there until she was an infant. Mention of her father – his name, his military rank, his death – drew instant curtains on the conversation. She complained to some that she felt ill. To all she seemed wary, disoriented, looking for escape. When it was suggested to her that she pay a visit her birthplace, she declared the idea ludicrous, then became most anxious to retire.

Merle Oberon had been in Sydney but seventy-two hours before she was on the plane home to Hollywood. But that was not the end of the matter.

In 1978, Merle received another invitation to visit the land that was her home, from those who wished for her to be the international guest at a television awards presentation. At sixty-seven, her marriage to Bruno Pagliai was over and so, too, was her career as a glamorous Hollywood actress. Her fourth and final husband, Robert Wolders, many years her junior, begged her to accept. He longed to see Australia, the place about which he'd heard so much. Wolders had been good to her – unlike her other husbands, he'd had no career that challenged Merle's, but simply lived to care for her. It was he who had urged her to respond to Joyce, to make it clear the pathetic letters were no longer welcome – an act which seemed to have, at along last, silenced the voice that could never let go. Wearily, Merle agreed to grant Robert this wish.

News that Merle Oberon was coming home caused great excitement in the city of Hobart. The mayor ordered plans to be laid for a grand reception in her honour, and a solemn blessing of the very house in which she'd been born. The newspapers reported on a sensational homecoming like no other.

In the coming weeks, one by one the local society fixers returned to the mayor with troubling news: proof of the existence of Merle

Oberon was elusive. There was no record of such a birth on the island, and no school in the state recalled her name. The death of her military father was not registered with any known authority, and there was no evidence of any such man, be he an officer or a sapper, in any of Tasmania's armed services. Nobody bearing the Oberon name had ever entered or exited the state by sea or air.

Suspecting that simply a name had been changed, and not wishing to disturb Ms Oberon herself, the mayor's office made enquiries with people whose Hollywood connections might yield some answers. It was then they discovered the depressing truth: there had never been a Merle Oberon from Tasmania. She was Estelle Thompson from India, or somewhere in Asia – it didn't matter. The story of her roots, the military father and the aristocratic lineage, had been invented by Alexander Korda and his Hollywood starmakers, who had chosen Tasmania because it sounded exotic and was so far away. In those early years, with so much being promised, Queenie Thompson had made a contract with an unfathomable lie that now hunted her to this very end of the earth.

It was too late to cancel the grand homecoming – that would be too embarrassing for everyone. And so it was decided that the show must go on, Merle Oberon cast as the clueless star in a production everyone knew was a farce.

Merle had been in a silent mood during the long journey to Sydney, and drifted through the television awards presentation as if she were tranquillised. When the presenter asked what she recalled of her childhood, she said she remembered nothing.

In Hobart, on the eve of her grand homecoming reception, Merle refused to leave her hotel room, sobbing quietly to herself, complaining of headaches and ailments of the mind. Puzzled, Robert Wolders could do little but convince her that he loved her as she wept at turns through the night.

The following evening, Merle moved toward her fate with the resignation of a prisoner ferried to the gallows. She said nothing on the ride to the Town Hall, and smiled uneasily as the assembled crowd welcomed her home with speeches, dedications, the artifice of familiarity. When Merle rose to respond, the expectant hush of the room seemed to become too much for her. She had spoken but a few words when her voice began to break and then fell silent. A compassionate applause ushered the tearful star from the podium.

What happened in the moments that followed will never be truly known. Perhaps Merle overheard something, some truth whispered out of turn, or saw it in the voiceless glances that conspired around her. Those watching Merle as the guests closed around say she simply bowed her head, as if praying to herself and, with little theatrical flourish, fainted into the arms of Robert Wolders, the only soul in attendance not playing a part.

The following day, Merle Oberon departed Tasmania forever, leaving the theatre that bore her name to be opened and dedicated by others. Upon her arrival in Hollywood, it was revealed she had suffered a heart attack from which she never quite recovered, surgery and convalescence stealing her life until Thanksgiving Day, 1979. Before she died, she told Robert Wolders she would soon see him again. For she would visit all of those she loved, and who truly loved her, in the afterlife.

There are people in Tasmania today who swear Merle Oberon was indeed from there. Their mothers, fathers, aunts and others knew her as a child, they say, or spoke with somebody who did. They present as proof the old canard that says good people never lie.

In Bombay, India, Merle's birthplace and true childhood home, lived a woman who lied for all of her days. It was a lie to protect a child from shame, a promise she kept to the very end. It was the shame of many a lustful father, and the kind of promise that could only be kept by a mother who selflessly loved her child.

The girl born Constance Joyce Thompson did not outlive her beloved Queenie for very long. Beside her bed, in a locked drawer, were letters and trinkets, jewellery and documents, memories of lives now ended forever. Amongst the clippings and poems never sent was a faded birth certificate from 1911, the parents of one Estelle Merle O'Brien Thompson inscribed as Constance Joyce and her father, Arthur Thompson.

The night before she died in 1981, Joyce claimed to have seen her loved and lonely child standing at the foot of the bed, smiling, her face more beautiful than anything that had ever flickered upon a screen.

A MELBOURNE TRIPTYCH

The tabloids tell of a world gone to hell, of crimes and sad dramas large and small for every tick of the clock. It is said the modern city is more violent and crazed than the metropolis of yesteryear. But the newspapers of old tell of times just as deadly and scandalous, particularly in the city of Melbourne, whose Victorian streets played host to daily sensations that would swamp our front pages for weeks.

What follows is an album of three such unpublished episodes from a single decade in a century long gone. One can walk the same streets where the tears were shed, though some of the dwellings are gone. The old Melbourne Opera House no longer stands, and students of the RMIT University Business School built in its place are likely ignorant of the bloodbath from which only time has spared them. The old Falls Bridge can no longer be walked, but a fine picture of it by Frederick McCubbin hangs in the National Gallery of Victoria, and superbly decorates the mind in preparation for the second tale in this little triplet. For the third, stroll from South Melbourne to Spencer Street and take a drink at the Waterside Hotel, then shed a tear into the Yarra River for lovers long gone and hearts never mended . . .

I

On the evening of Saturday, 21 July, 1880, the best of Melbourne society gathered at the Opera House in Bourke Street for a performance of *Les Huguenots*, a grand opera that told the tale of the St Bartholomew's Day Massacre during the French Wars of Religion. It was said the fourth act, in which the hero chooses honour over love, was one of the most gripping in the history of staged melodrama.

In attendance were three people whose lives, after this night, would never be the same. One was Mr J. J. Greer, an Irishman but recently come to Melbourne from England upon the steamship *Garonne*. A respected young man in his home country – his father was a Presbyterian clergyman in the county of Down, Ireland, and his uncle was seated in the House of Commons for the county of Derry – Greer, an accountant by trade, sought employment in the colony, bringing with him Mrs Greer, a statuesque Frenchwoman and quite the beauty, her loveliness turning heads wherever the couple went.

The third character in this tragedy was one Monsieur A. L. Soudry, a Parisian deputed by the Government of France to oversea his nation's court at the forthcoming Melbourne International Exhibition, for which the Royal Exhibition Building in Carlton Gardens had recently been completed. As the newspapers would later reveal, Soudry had been a passenger on the steamship *Garonne*, too, where the exquisite Mrs Greer most certainly came to the Frenchman's attention. Whether the strangers became intimate before landfall is not known, but what is certain is that, while J. J. Greer was seeking employment in Melbourne, his French wife and Mr Soudry were enjoying tea and passing letters, and perhaps indulging secret joys of which Greer was unaware.

However, by the time they were to take their seats at the opera house on that fateful Saturday night, it was obvious Greer had become suspicious. Seated in the dress circle with his wife, the young man barely watched the production, his agitated gaze drawn toward a certain Frenchman seated in the middle of the circle. Mrs Greer also appeared to pay little attention to the performances, her eyes directed at the same place. Those prone to gossip (of whom there were many on the fringes of the Opera House dress circle) whispered to each other about that which seemed most evident: that Mrs Greer and Monsieur A. L. Soudry had been intimate, and that the husband knew it. As the fourth act of *Les Huguenots* reached its climax, it seemed the stirring music belonged to the drama unfolding in the audience.

As the curtain fell before the fifth and final act, J. J. Greer excused himself from his seat and departed for the amenities, whereupon Monsieur Soudry seized his chance and, moving through the crowd, sat down beside Mrs Greer and entered into private – and, presumably, passionate – conversation.

Suddenly, J. J. appeared in the gangway behind their seats and, producing a nickel-plated pistol from his pocket, pointed it at Soudry's face and pulled the trigger. The loud report of the firearm was instantly drowned out by the sounds of women's screams and the shouts of men who rushed the scene. Greer pointed the revolver at his wife and fired again, the bullet ripping through her cheek and tumbling from her open mouth, her shattered teeth falling to the carpet as she dropped to her knees.

The panic in the house was deafening, and those who fainted – and there were many – were trampled underfoot, the crowd parting only for Greer as he hurried along the aisles toward the front of the stage and the exit beyond, firing another shot into the ceiling for no reason anyone could see. Then, as if realising that escape would mean little, Greer stopped, placed the gun to his ear and pulled the trigger, the shot echoing into howls of horror as Greer fell beneath a spray of pink mist, covering all who were near.

The dress circle looked like a butchery, blood and skin and bone and brain was spattered on the seats and carpet, and the smell of cordite drifted like some phantom in the air. At some point, J. J., still conscious, asked for water, then passed out. The assassin, the Frenchman and Greer's once-beautiful wife were ferried to the hospital with haste, through the crowd of many thousands who had gathered in the street outside. News of the most dramatic performance the opera house had ever staged had travelled fast.

In the days that immediately followed, the newspapers gasped at the 'tragedy', the 'extraordinary occurrence', 'one of the most remarkable that has over occurred in connection with the theatre in Australia'. But as the noise settled, and it became apparent that both Mrs Greer and Monsieur Soudry would survive their wounds where Greer would not, sympathies for the living began to shift to the dead. An inquest found the deceased had laboured 'under temporary insanity', but many felt otherwise, one newspaper speaking of the 'unfortunate and misguided perpetrator' as 'a most gentle amiable man' who had 'been deeply wronged'. Another reported Monsieur Soudry's expressions of sorrow for Mr Greer, adding: 'But if he had thought of that before, the trouble might not have happened at all.'

In October, a Melbourne coach driver assaulted Monsieur Soudry upon realising his identity, and when Mrs Greer boarded the steamer *Chimborazo* home to England, the ship's officers were so disgusted they turned the ship around and dropped her back in port, refusing to give her passage. Eventually, however, the disfigured Mrs Greer returned to the British Isles, never again the beauty who had once turned heads, and Monsieur Soudry to France, where he was relieved of his government commission on account of his 'adventure in Melbourne'. They never saw each other again.

J. J.'s heart had still been beating when one newspaper published an expectant and sympathetic obituary:

> *He came out for the purpose of bettering his condition with very influential introductions, and his prospects at starting from the old country were full of promise. They will be at an end in this world before this letter can reach you, and you will have heard of the death, by telegraph, of a fine manly fellow whose life might have been otherwise but for a foolish woman.*

The following year, a waxworks exhibition at the School of Arts in faraway West Maitland, New South Wales depicted, amongst Zulu kings and members of the Kelly Gang, the scene at the Melbourne Opera House. Greer was shown heroically, like a soldier firing the last shots in a battle all but lost.

II

It was no surprise to Sarah Williams on the night of Tuesday, 1 December, 1885, when her husband didn't come home for tea. He was rarely home for tea, or for anything at all, and when he was home he was drunk. That was the way of things.

She was many years younger than her husband, who was employed as a tailor in a Flinders Lane shop, and made a living as a soak in public houses after hours. He made good money as a tailor, and no money as a drunk. His work took him away from his wife and family, and the drink took away his money.

None of which would have been so distressing had Sarah been able to leave, to spirit herself away from the man she'd married and all the dreadful things that were married to him. But at thirty-five she was the mother of no less than seven of the man's children, the eldest only ten years old, the youngest but a year-old babe.

Little Alice had been sick for days, and Sarah had been driven spare. As the hours ticked by in the Port Melbourne home, the children crying for their tea, the husband nowhere to be seen, what little humour Sarah had evaporated in the stifling air. Charging the eldest to take care of the others until she returned, Sarah picked up baby Alice, made her way out onto Bay Street, and began the long walk to the city to find her husband and bring him home. She'd walk all the way into Flinders Street if she had to. She was furious.

It's over a mile from Port Melbourne to the bridges on the Yarra River, and at some point the weight of the one-year-old child would have begun to tell on the mother. By the time Sarah reached Falls Bridge, her arms would have been numb from pain. And it is here, in the very middle of the bridge, with the river running underneath, that Sarah encountered her husband, staggering home at eight o'clock.

An argument ensued, and all who strolled along the Yarra heard it, the voices raised high above the clatter of carriages and the gentle whoosh of the running river. After heated words, Sarah turned to make her way back to the house, her belligerent husband by her side. She urged him to take Alice from her, as she'd carried her the whole of the way. But Mr Williams refused – she'd brought the baby here, he argued, and she could take it back. It was not his decision to walk a mile with an armful of child. He was not so stupid.

At this, Sarah was heard to shout something, though her exact words would later be disputed. Some heard: 'Look what I will do!'; others heard quite definitely: 'I know I will suffer for it, but I do not care.' It scarcely matters. For Sarah Williams, out of her mind with rage, threw her baby over the parapet, the little bundle swirling through the night air like an autumn leaf, hitting the water with a sickly splash. Little Alice sank under for a moment, then bobbed to the surface, at the mercy of the river's current.

A gasp went up from all who saw, and for a time there was silence on the bridge. A baby's distant cry was heard, just for a moment, but then it ended sharply. The little bundle was then seen to sink into the darkness.

Mr Williams seemed to sober in an instant, dashing from the bridge toward the riverbank below. He and others leaped into the water, splashing hopelessly to where the baby had last been seen. It was a pitiful sight: Mr Williams, absent father, who cared more for drink than the lives of his own children, wading to his neck in the murky water, crying out to a child now far away and getting further still, lost to the river forever.

By now a crowd had gathered on the bridge, and many women were attended to for fainting. Mr Williams was dragged sobbing from the river before he drowned along with his daughter. A policeman arrived and arrested Sarah Williams on suspicion of infanticide. He also arrested her husband, on a charge of drunkenness.

At the watch house, Sarah claimed she had only been passing the child to Mr Williams when it slipped from her grasp, but the many witnesses denied her that defence. They were both locked up for the evening, in separate cells, pending investigations.

Drenched to the bone, and going through withdrawals, Mr Williams curled into a baby's shape beneath some blankets and sobbed himself to sleep. Sarah Williams sat indignant for a while, staring straight ahead, saying nothing. She had been alone for some time when the gravity of what had occurred began to weigh upon her, and she began to pace her cell, emitting tiny, anxious gasps each time her little baby's face appeared in her mind's eye.

And it was late into the evening when, startled by the thought of it, Sarah expressed her sudden fear for the others, the six children she had left at home. Policemen were dispatched to the house in Bay Street, where they found the children, crying all, a miserable little choir that bewailed two parents somewhere gone, and a little one who would now never be returned.

Found guilty of manslaughter, Sarah Williams was sentenced to death by hanging, a fate then commuted to two years in prison, and a lifetime to dream of her little girl.

To this day, Alice Williams is somewhere between the Yarra River and the sea.

III

At thirty years of age, Peter M'Quade, a plasterer by trade and a Scotsman by blood, was tall and handsome, muscular and passionate about things. His gut sank when he first spied Jessie Cameron, a fetching young brunette who had come to Melbourne – no doubt against her widowed mother's wishes – from the small mining town of Lal Lal, near Ballarat.

Attracted to the bustle of the city, where it was said the world awaited pretty girls, Jessie had found accommodation with a respectable working family called Evans, who lived in a residence beside the factory Mr Evans owned in Grant Street, South Melbourne.

Each day, Jessie walked to Spencer Street, where she was employed in a small hotel. And it was here, in the drinking holes and cafés at the west end of the city, that she and M'Quade met and fell in love. For a year or more neither one was seen in the fashionable haunts of the Melbourne streets without the other.

It didn't take Jessie long to learn that the very reckless dash she admired in M'Quade was also the devil of him. When drunk, or simply overwrought, he was prone to fits of temper that often boiled up into violence. More than once he had taken a swipe at her, usually out of fear she might be returning the glances he knew too well were being cast her way by other men. Whether M'Quade's suspicions were ever founded we will never know, but what is clear is that Jessie always forgave him his tempers, even if she didn't outwardly show it. Perhaps she believed such displays were evidence of his love, just as her withdrawals from him were products of her need to have him love her like a drug: the many times he'd knocked upon her door begging forgiveness, and she'd pretended not to care. Theirs was a love whose soundtrack was made of smashing bottles and slamming doors.

It was after one such episode that M'Quade showed Jessie his hand – he wanted to marry her, and would propose when everything was right. He had purchased rings, which he was paying off each week with portions of his wage, and had made arrangements for the purchase of the furniture and the renting of the cottage. For Jessie, it was too soon to speak of marriage, though she was secretly delighted she had charmed M'Quade to plan such things. As a show of good faith, she accepted the gold watch he presented her, as a promise of the marriage that would happen one day soon, when they were sure.

One Wednesday, 11 March, 1890, as M'Quade and Jessie strolled past Spencer Street Station, an engineer with whom the young girl was familiar smiled, a greeting she returned. M'Quade flew into a rage, and the couple fought all the way to South Melbourne. At some point along the way M'Quade, mad with jealousy, struck Jessie's face so hard it caused her cheek to swell.

By the time they had reached the door to the Evans family home, M'Quade was deep into his usual throes of contrition, pleading that Jessie forgive him, that he'd simply lost his mind because he loved her more than he could control. He became so desperate that he dropped to his knees and begged that they be wed the next day, so that petty doubts be laid to rest by the knowledge that she was, at last, his wife.

But Jessie was angry and wanted none of it (she also knew better than to give in so easily). She demanded that he leave, which only made him plead some more, the noise of his desperate sobs, and her heated insistence that he go, threatening to disturb the neighbours. In the end, if only to be rid of him, she agreed to receive him if he called upon her in the morning, when perhaps her mind had cooled, and she'd given things calm thought.

M'Quade arrived at ten o'clock, so distressed it seemed he hadn't slept. Once more, on Jessie's doorstep, he begged forgiveness and pleaded that she marry him. But Jessie's cheek was still red from his slap, and so she determined to teach the man a lesson, to ensure it was the last time she felt his hand upon her in anger. It was better, she told him, that it had happened before they were wed, when it would be too late for her to leave without disgrace. Now, however, she could do just that, and still be fresh for some other man who might want for himself a lovely young bride who would adore him.

At this, a look came upon the face of Peter M'Quade that Jessie would later struggle to describe. It was not a look of violence, or even anger in the common sense. It did not belong to Peter, or to anyone she had known before, and thus she couldn't name it, or ascribe to it a mood or a particular disposition. The very strangeness of it filled her with alarm.

As if sensing Jessie's fear, M'Quade softened and assured her that, even if she didn't want him, he would always love her, would wish her well, and would trouble her no more. His resignation was so touching that Jessie began to cry, and they held each other for a time, two lovers far too proud or hurt by some ancient thing to tell the other the truth. As M'Quade bade her farewell, Jessie wondered how long it would be before she would see him again.

But it was too soon the very next day to see Peter M'Quade marching resolutely toward her door, some time after noon. Instinctively Jessie hid herself within the house, pretending to be gone. But another boarder, unaware of the trouble Peter and Jessie had been having, allowed Peter inside. Unable to find Jessie, but convinced she was not far, he allowed M'Quade to wait for her in the parlour. After some time, M'Quade found himself alone and made straight for Jessie's room.

From her hiding place, Jessie could smell the drink on him; she could hear the temper in his breath. Overnight, some thought had nagged at him – an imagined lover, perhaps, for whom he had been sacrificed – and now he was in a fury. He broke open her jewellery box, tore through her drawers, smashed the gold watch, ripped her dresses, cut up her hats. Though Jessie dearly wished to emerge and ask him what was wrong, to allay whatever fears were making him crazy, she knew it best to stay where she was until M'Quade was gone. By the time he left, Jessie had only the clothes she wore.

Discovering the damage done within a room of his own home, Mr Evans insisted on calling for the police, and within a few hours M'Quade had been arrested, even worse for drink than he had been before. He was taken to the watch house, where various charges were read and docketed, and a customary search yielded a knife which he'd concealed in his trousers. He was then locked in a cell by himself. It was just past four o'clock in the afternoon.

One hour later, the officer in charge was in the yard when he heard a shot from the direction of M'Quade's cell. Throwing open the door, the officer found the prisoner lying on the floor, blood pooling beneath his head, a revolver in his hand. Somehow, they had failed to find the other weapon he had hidden.

A local doctor was called, but it was too late. Peter M'Quade would neither love nor trouble anybody again.

Hearing the news of her lover's death, young Jessie Cameron dissolved into such misery that even the police were moved by it. They tried to convince her that she had been saved – that this madman had carried a firearm, and had obviously intended to kill her for rejecting his advances. Pitifully she declared that, even to the last, she had intended to marry him. She had simply wanted to punish him, so that he might never hurt her again, and that they might be happy forever.

The next day, the papers reported that Peter M'Quade, while dying on the floor of his cell, had muttered the words: 'I loved her.'

THE PUGILIST

It's a warm November evening, and a large crowd has assembled in a hall in suburban Melbourne to witness a national title fight. In the centre of the room is the boxing ring, its emptiness speaking of an ominous tension, like a raised guillotine awaiting the life that will enter but never leave. Boxing literature hums with references to the dignity of the sport – the nobility of the pugilist and the graceful old gentlemen in his orbit. Words like 'finesse', 'poise' and 'bearing' are as recurrent in boxing airspace as they are in the ballet scriptures. But there is none of that here. A man in a hat and coat blows into a handkerchief – once, twice – swears very loudly, then looks at what he has done before folding it neatly and placing it back in his pocket. There in the ring is our boy, who raises an arm as his name is spoken, the crowd blessing him with hoots and hollers. He looks up briefly, with almost a smile, then returns his eyes to the canvas. If he is dwelling upon what brought him here, there is no sign of it. As the bell rings to begin these proceedings, one can see in his eyes the memory of a dream once abandoned, and now, again, within reach. But it's a dream that has come at a terrible cost . . .

He was born in a land that would descend into war, though he would know none of it, his life but a rumble of games and dreams and imaginings the men of war never see. His father was strong and strict, like the men from the police shows that appeared on the television, his mother pretty, like Sophia Loren, and gentle with he and his younger brother. His childhood was a vagueness of friends and enemies, places both real and improbable, too, catastrophes into which he would march as the hero, the touch of his hand and the land was saved.

His father and mother were both religious and passed their beliefs on to him and his brother. For all his young life, he had felt God watching him, marking his movements and judging his thoughts. One could not escape from the verdicts of God in the hideouts of youth, the imaginary caverns through which children burrow. God saw everything that others did not. Only God knew the truth over which others fought, and which grown men twisted and moulded to suit their own needs and ends. There was a fairytale about a man who whispered a secret into a hole in the earth, which grew to a tree with strong branches from which a flute was made, the instrument refusing to play any tune but the one that sang of the whispered secret from which the roots of the tree had grown. God was like that tree. He knew everything and, somehow, one's secrets would never be forgotten or erased.

He was ten years old when he learned his family would no longer stay in this land of strife. The nation was being torn apart, whole families parted to either side of lines that were drawn through streets and thoughts and beliefs. They would come to Australia where they had relations who told of a realm where the living was easy. It didn't matter to the boy where his life played out – it would go on forever. He would miss his friends but they would stay in his heart, where lines could be drawn by no man or machine.

Over seas for a day and a night he flew, the world turning under him like a giant ball of water that knew no end. It seemed they had circled the globe many times before the land came, a strange terrain with red slanting roofs upon houses that all seemed to have swimming pools in the yards. At the airport, policemen asked many questions and went through the family possessions as if in search of something wicked about which they'd heard. They found nothing. The boy was impressed with their uniforms and the way they remained so well in the control. He would like to be like them, he thought, when he grew up.

The family settled in a house in St Albans, on the western side of the city of Melbourne, where the people who walked the avenues seemed to come from all parts of the earth, from the Balkans and the banks of the Mediterranean Sea. It was strange for the boy to walk along unfamiliar streets, in the stifling heat, under a sky of a different hue, the very sounds that filled the air – the birds, the engines, the bustle of commerce, and peculiar insects that buzzed by the ear then away – from some world apart from the land of his birth. That he was amongst it made him feel different, too. What would become of him he did not know.

The young boy could not speak a word of the language of his new home, nor understood others when they uttered it, the letters that preached from the signposts and billboards like graffiti that spoke to others but himself. His native tongue, and all the thoughts that had given birth to it, were of no use here. It was like being a soldier in peacetime, all the wisdom learned on the battlefields, of tactics and how men behave under fire, suddenly worthless in a world where fighting was no longer done. Sometimes he'd catch a word here and there, and the expression on the face of the one who uttered it – a turn on the lip, the crease of an eye, a near imperceptible recoil from the one who heard it. He came to know the moods from which some words would come, and the tempers they would arouse in others. In those first few years, as a prisoner to a language he was yet to master, he learned more about faces than many learn in their lives. He came to know when people were to be angry or would soon break into laughter or tears. It was like being able to read people's thoughts, to tell the future through a look in the eye or a float of the hand.

In school he studied the history of his new country, how the land had been settled by convicts and thieves, of the gold rush that drove ordinary men to madness, and of explorers who perished for want of a drink. He learned of Gallipoli, where thousands of soldiers died so far from home, in the squalor of trenches and mud and tears, and he felt for them, for he was far from home, too. He learned the names of people long gone, who had lived to make Australia great: Cook, who discovered the nation and died in a moment of anger and fear and betrayal; Bennelong, who suffered and died in the end from not knowing to which society he was meant to belong; Kelly, who was hung by the neck as a bad man, but who went to the gallows convinced he was good; and Bradman, who buoyed the nation through hard times and war with his skill on the sporting fields. Like all boys, he wondered what he might do that would make his name live in the books of history, so that others might read of him after he'd gone.

One night, the boy, now eleven years old, went with his cousin to a gymnasium where she was being taught in karate, a Japanese system of combat designed by ancient families for whom knives and swords had been outlawed under threat of death. He watched as they kicked and chopped with their hands, the limbs of the body turned into deadly weapons. He had seen this craft in the movies, where opponents were dispatched with terrifying force, the sound of fists against flesh like gunpowder. At the end of the class, the man who taught them spoke to the boy, and suggested he might like to try. The boy didn't know if he'd be capable of it – he was shy, withdrawn, and lacked the desire to destroy. It seemed like a lot to learn. But he'd now mastered English and he hadn't known how – one morning, he had simply woken to find he was speaking and hearing it, as if some giver of knowledge had crept upon him while he slept and left the wisdom behind. Perhaps karate would be the same. If he dedicated himself, he would learn. And so he did, going several nights a week to the gymnasium, learning the tricks of the martial art and the mental control that accompanied it.

After some time, the man who taught karate suggested to the boy that he might like to try boxing. He'd been watching and had noticed the boy had an effortless style, his height and long arms natural gifts for a boxer, and his ability to predict human movement – the perception he'd developed as an immigrant boy – translated to a speed in combat that many boxers lacked. Once again, the boy wasn't sure. He'd never had an interest in boxing or wrestling, sports that seemed too aggressive for a quiet boy like himself. But the teacher insisted that boxing was not about hurting others, or being violent or cruel. It was a legitimate sport, and there were many great names who had practised the art and were worshipped as gentlemen by civilised society. He urged the boy to think on it. He had seen many young fighters come and go, and had trained many to become local champions. He insisted the boy had a future, and told him that, should he ever decide to give it a try, he would be happy to train him into a worthy opponent in the boxing ring.

The boy thought on it and began reading of the sport, of the fighters who'd become famous names in the world, and in Australia, too: Les Darcy, Lionel Rose and Tony Mundine, fighters much loved as champions at home. Perhaps, he thought, he might one day rise to a fame such as theirs, and be remembered as a champion of the four-cornered ring. Maybe this was to be his fate.

But there were names not recorded in the Australian scriptures, and our boy would never know of them. Like Jim Dawson of Collie, who died in the ring after a twelve-round thrashing in March of 1922, or Lawrence Chute, who was just eighteen when a cerebral hemorrhage threw the towel in for him ten years later. The boxing bibles did not record the name of Charles Oliver Johnson, the 21-year-old who was beaten to death in the ring in Leichhardt in the summer of '33, or Alan James Alcorn, just seventeen, for whom the world stopped in the fourth at Lidcombe one evening in April of '46. George Christie never fought again after knocking out Richard Jeffery forever in the first round of a fight at Cobden in '32, and Carl Rich never got over the sight of his friend, Raymond McNamara, sagging to the ropes from a fatal punch Carl had thrown in the second round of a four-round match in Dubbo in January of '28. Harold Roach in '31. Robert Pattison in '39. Albert Joyce in Melbourne in '28. These were the men for whom boxing became a fight for their lives in their final moments. On the night of 18 April, 1917, Tom Rowlston, just nineteen years old, had wept bitterly while being led from the ring by Melbourne police, the bloodied and lifeless body of Sid Lorraine being dragged from the canvas behind him. It had been nothing more than one good punch.

In a modern, peaceful society the sport of boxing is indefensible. It is warfare at its most fundamental and primitive. With the exception of hunting, no other game sees a result dependent on the injuries suffered by the loser.

The quest of the boxer is his opponent's destruction. Nobody wants to win by points – the boxer's ambition is to thump a man's face until his brain malfunctions. It's called a KO, and a history of them looks good on your record. For the loser there can be no sanctuary in the mantra that it's 'only a game'. Your destroyer was faster, fitter, stronger than you. Perhaps he was younger. He may have been smarter. He wasn't just a better player. In the old money – and boxing is an old money world – he was a better man. When George Foreman lost to Muhammad Ali in 1974, he spent the next year dodging faces in the street and cowering in corners while his wife did the shopping, convinced that the sales girls were laughing inside at the loser of a man within their midst.

Boxing is, too, the only sport at which people pay to watch a man be humiliated. Those who despise a player of tennis will not fork out to see her fumble straight sets – the spectacle of her pain will be distant, hidden behind the walls of her dressing room or her home. With boxing, satisfaction for the sadist is slick and instant. The man he hates will be seen to bleed from the eye and buckle at the knee. The man who so pompously trumpeted himself all week will sit like a baby on the floor of the pen, legs outstretched, dumb mouth agape, silenced, stopped. We may not know or care for the one who made him so, but we cheer him for braining the bully to a pulp. Any man who enters the ring is brave beyond belief.

And this is the world into which our boy stepped when, at the age of twelve, he began to train as a boxer, learning the art of the ring and the discipline of fighting. He learned how to hit, how to jab, how to guard. He learned of the upper-cut, the most powerful weapon in the boxing armoury, and how to unleash it with frightening speed. He learned how to move his feet like a dancer and hover his body like a threatened cobra, to duck and feint and sway to the rhythm of the duel, to make his opponent fear and misunderstand him. Boxing is a battle of the mind as well as the body, and the smarter man often beats the stronger.

And through all of this he learned the discipline of one for whom every movement counts, and for whom every exertion is potentially wasted. The fighter who punches in a rage will very quickly find he has burned his precious fuel. Every good fighter who has ever lived knows that you don't throw a punch unless it's absolutely necessary. Like the language he had mastered so quickly, boxing came to the boy like a history through which he had already lived, a gift that was known to the dark shadows of his soul, and just needed a light to reveal it was there.

He had only been boxing for months when his mentor suggested he was ready for an amateur bout. The boy became nervous – aside from sparring in the gymnasium, he had never fought anyone in the whole of his life, had never known the pain and the passion of a contest with another boy, whose fists and fury would be directed at him. And this would be in the ring with people watching, mistakes and humiliations there for all to see. His mentor insisted that he was ready, and that a fight would bring him experience which all good boxers required. Sometimes a loss is as good as a victory, for it's through our mistakes that wisdom grows. It would only be three rounds.

On the night of the fight, the twelve-year-old boy battled hard, losing on points to a boy much older and stronger than himself. He lost his next fight, too, and then the next fight after that. He began to wonder whether all of this had been for naught, whether he might not be too weak for boxing after all. His mentor insisted it was not so, that every fighter must lose before he can win. The best fighters in the world had been beaten.

The boy doubted it – he felt as a three-time loser does. But there was something he had learned in the ring, when those three fighters had been beating him soundly. He had learned it was suicide to show any pain, any doubt, any hesitance, any fear of the contest. It was when one showed such weaknesses that others would pounce through a hole in one's world, to ransack the strengths to be found inside. It was a truth of which all human beings were aware and which served them well in all walks of life. So he kept his doubts to himself and kept going. He was no quitter. He had hitched himself to a wheel that turned and might break and crush, but would not be abandoned.

The boy's tenacity began to bear fruit. He won his fourth fight, and his fifth, and his sixth. He began sparring with professionals, men who had fought hard and won against fighters with names on the circuit. At the age of fourteen he became the amateur champion of his state in his weight group. The following year he won a silver medal at the national titles, and then came the Australian amateur junior welterweight title at the age of sixteen. He began to shake hands with important figures in the smoke and shouts of the boxing world. His mentor was sure that, if he dedicated himself, he might fight in the ring at the Olympic Games representing Australia, the country to which he now felt like a son.

The Olympic Games. This was where champions were made and legends grew. He still felt that it was beyond him, surely – he had only been boxing a few short years. But some people are lucky like that – their destiny finds them in luck and mishap, or in the intentions of others. He began to dream of Olympic gold, of standing on the dais to the national anthem of the country that would love him as its own.

His training became more intense than before – hours of skipping rope and hitting the bag, of dodging at shadows and snapping from punches. He'd go to bed early and wake at dawn, running until he was sure his heart would burst. He watched what he ate and took care with his thoughts. His whole life became geared for a few minutes in a ring.

In his twenty-fifth amateur fight, the boy learned a lesson that would remain in his mind like a teacher for the rest of his days. In the second round he hit his opponent with a left that sent him collapsing into the ropes and staggering slowly to his feet. The boy knew that his foe had been broken and he adjusted his fight plan for the knockout that would surely come. Suddenly his opponent surprised him with a savage punch of his own, one that seemed to come from a beaten soul whose eyes were glazed and whose knees were weak. The boy had his lights switched out for a moment by the man who had seemed no threat at all. He would never forget this, how the dead can come back to life to hunt down the living, how those weaker can pull strength from the dregs of their rage.

One day at the gym, while punching the bag in preparation for the trials to the Olympic Games, something went wrong with a bone in his hand. He was hurt and had to stop. His right hand swelled with a life of its own. Days of packing his knuckles in ice failed to stop it. His mentor told him he'd have to quit for at least a few months, as injuries like this can end good careers. He would have to miss the Olympic trials. There would be other tournaments but the next were not his. The boy was heartbroken – his dream of an Olympic medal was dashed, and no training or fighting would bring it back.

Languishing at home, he began to wonder if it had all been worth it, the running, the skipping, the waking at dawn, the denial of things that other boys do. It had been his existence since he had first entered the gymnasium as an eleven-year-old boy with no life of his own. He wondered what the days might be like without all the discipline and hardship, the drive toward an impossible goal. Perhaps in this time he could try the life that the other boys lived and see how it suited him.

He had his first beer at the age of seventeen, and began to go out at night and see girls and indulge in the lights that had dazzled his friends through his own years of toil. He was so shy from the years of his solitary labour that meeting new people seemed almost as taxing as fighting. But he began to feel a joy in the world, an excitement that he'd been denied for so long. Slowly the boxing life fell away, lost in the cars and the bustle of the night.

He had been so committed to his sporting endeavours that he'd never given thought to what he might do out in society. A friend suggested that his fighting prowess, and the control he'd learned in the martial arts, might make him perfectly suited to security work. So he studied a course and graduated, getting work at nightclubs and bars, his quiet confidence popular with employers, his disciplined hand useful in controlling the drunks and the louts who frequented the night.

And it was at one such bar that he went to work on the night of 18 January, in the year of 2004. In the corner of the establishment was a small band of drinkers, men and women who appeared to be celebrating something. They were drunk. When the bar closed, the boy did his duty – he asked them politely to leave. One of the men didn't wish to. He became abusive, aggressive. An argument rolled out onto the footpath, with screaming women and shouting men.

Only later would the boy learn that the man was an Australian sporting hero, and that nobody ever told David Hookes what to do.

On 12 September, 2005, Zdravko Micevic was acquitted of the manslaughter of David Hookes. In the weeks that followed his acquittal, Zdravko spent his nights in the gymnasium hitting the bag, his old mentor, Louis Korica, giving him the keys, allowing him to punch out the fear and confusion into the nights. It took Zdravko eighteen months to decide to pick up from where he had left off. The newspapers reported he was cashing in on his notoriety by becoming a professional 'blood money' boxer.

The Bosnian boy who'd dreamed of being his new country's champion won the Australian light heavyweight title in November of 2008, but the newspapers, who so love Australian champions, weren't there to report on it.

JOAN OF ANTWERP

In western Victoria, not far from Dimboola, lives a small town called Antwerp, born in 1846 when George Shaw and Horatio Ellerman chose to graze their sheep in the lush, green fields. Ellerman named the area after his birthplace, the Belgian city of Antwerp, where, in the sixteenth century, citizens were tortured and murdered during the witch hunts led by Fernando Álvarez de Toledo. Australia was spared such cruelties, they say – according to the history books, there was never an Antipodean Inquisition. But take a closer look at Antwerp and you will find the echoes of such a thing, a soundless cry that drifts over the meadows, through the ruins of the church built by Moravian missionaries. Something terrible once happened here which, strangely, has been all but forgotten . . .

It was in the warm summer months that Ralph Vollmer, a 53-year-old pig farmer from Antwerp in western Victoria, decided his wife needed to be saved. Joan, four years her husband's junior, had been showing signs of mental breakdown, bounding through the fields naked, spouting foul language and generally behaving not like her old self. A friend later suggested Joan's behaviour might have been a response to her husband's recent descent into the unyielding world of charismatic Christianity – the only place Ralph ever took Joan, claimed the friend, was to church, where the constant mumbling to effigies of tortured men was enough to drive any sane woman to tear off her clothes. Naturally, Ralph didn't see it that way. He decided his wife was possessed by evil spirits.

He first tried tying Joan to the bed, but she escaped. He then locked her in the basement of the farmhouse, but she made such a racket that Ralph couldn't sleep. He decided he was left with no alternative but to send for his neighbour, John Reichenbach, who, when not tending the hogs and ducks in his own barnyard, was the leader of the local Christian fellowship to which Ralph belonged. Ralph and John writhed and shook together whenever the Holy Spirit visited upon them – surely, Ralph thought, John would know what to do.

Reichenbach, accompanied by his wife, Leanne, galloped hastily to Ralph's farm to deliver his own diagnosis, and was inclined to agree with Ralph – Joan was possessed, but by how many demons he could not say. A casual head count of spirits noted something close to ten – an abusive one, who appeared to dislike listening to the Bible; a theatrical type, who played at games and deals in an attempt to escape punishment; and a few others who were harder to identify, as they were hidden, and could not readily be seen.

John sought the advice of Leah Clugston, the 77-year-old leader of the church to which they all belonged. Leah had started her ministry after being expelled from Reverend Roger Atze's Lutheran Church months earlier, for diagnosing 'possession' in cases that ranged from heartbreak to the common cold. Hearing the details of Joan's behaviour, Leah concluded that the woman was most certainly possessed, and the Devil would need to be dealt with, for he was not welcome in Antwerp, where good Christians dwelled.

Armed with Clugston's prognosis, John Reichenbach read a few verses from the Bible to Joan and sternly advised the demons that, if they were to remain inside of her, they were in for some trouble. He then departed for a more pressing engagement, leaving his wife to keep an eye on things with Ralph.

With Leanne's assistance, Ralph got straight to work on his wife, tying her down and denying her food or water that might nourish the beasts inside of her. They prayed aloud to the heavens, God's word filling the air as the demons in Joan moaned and complained of hunger and thirst. For days this continued, the fiends becoming louder as their host became malnourished and dehydrated, Joan's protestations at the curtailing of her liberties clearly the work of evil spirits. She was becoming aggressive, the devils inside her making brave efforts to break her bonds.

Ralph cast out for the help of David Klingner, another member of the church who lived nearby. Ralph needed more hands as he sensed the devils were about to go on the offensive, and there was no telling just how strong they would be. David was happy to come and help in whatever way he could.

The trio redoubled their efforts, ignoring Joan's desperate pleas as they strapped her down harder, prayed incessantly by her bedside, deprived her of all nourishment and sleep, slapping her face whenever it looked like she might fall to slumber. Strangely, nothing seemed to be working, the crafty demons now causing Joan to sob and beg and abuse her attackers in turn.

That this was his poor, suffering wife, beset with a problem that might deserve tenderness and care, did not appear to occur to Ralph. As a Christian it was his duty to rid his wife of evil, like a surgeon saving souls by removing gangrenous limbs. They were not hurting Joan – they weren't dealing with his wife any more. She was a host to goblins that must be overpowered and destroyed, her body as the stockade of the very Devil himself.

It was time to call in Matthew Nuske, a golf course greenkeeper from Melbourne who, despite his twenty-three years on earth, was considered a veteran of exorcisms. Nuske took one look at the situation and instantly knew what needed to be done. He sent the others into town to fetch as much wrapping and olive oil as they could procure. When they returned, he blessed the oil and ordered them to douse themselves in it, while he circled the house seven times with the wrapping, making sure all windows and doors were sealed to prevent any passing demons from coming inside to join in the bedlam. He then ordered that everything belonging to Joan – every piece of crockery, every ornament and porcelain statuette, every framed picture and item of jewellery – be smashed to pieces with a sledgehammer, lest demons were hiding inside them, too, and that all of Joan's flower beds and greenhouse vegetables were obliterated so that no mischievous sprites might use them as camouflage while sneaking up on the house.

In the early morning hours of 30 January, Matthew decided it was time to get medieval with the confederacy of spirits he had identified as being inside Joan Vollmer. He harassed the demons, screaming at them mere inches from Joan's face, slapping the woman's head with the full force of his hand, demanding the furies inside of her come out and identify themselves. There was a big one named Legion, who was master to the outrage, and several others, including a mother and daughter duo named Princess Joan and Princess Baby Joan, who were likely, claimed Nuske, to stick together and make life difficult for anyone trying to purge them from their host. Their eradication would best be achieved, he claimed, by beating the spirits out of their hostage. Thus Joan Vollmer was lashed to a chair against the fireplace, her body turned from the north – the direction from which Matthew ascertained the Gorgons were approaching – her feet tied to wooden stocks. And then she was thrashed and beaten as the devils begged for mercy.

Joan fought back, but the Christians fought harder, responding to every violent outburst and kick of defence with assaults of their own from every point of Joan's compass. Her legs were kicked. Her face was pummelled. Matthew Nuske slammed her head into cupboards and walls, the poor woman's body becoming a blue bag of bruises that would surely show the devils inside her who was boss. The demons were clever – they tried everything, from fighting aggressively to sobbing and pleading in pathetic attempts to appeal to the Christians' sympathies. Sometimes, Princess Baby Joan was conscripted to beg Joan's attackers in a childlike voice that might have melted their hearts had they not been so wary of the Devil's cunning. Matthew spat in the child's face and sent his fist crashing into her ear. The Devil was told he was no match for the crusaders of God.

As Joan fought harder, a fight for her life, the abuse became so violent that, at one moment, Ralph was forced to leave the room, to avert his eyes from what he was seeing. While his wife wailed and howled in the room next door, Ralph consulted the good Lord for strength. God assured him – through Leanne, David and Matthew, whose voices the Almighty evidently found to carry more authority than His own – that what they were doing was right. They were not harming Joan. What they were doing was an expression of the greatest Christian love for her. Any ordinary person may have withered and died under the cruel punishment they were administering, but Joan was still alive, fighting with them, struggling like an ox. Her survival through the violence was proof alone that she was clearly being driven by demons of terrifying strength and resilience. His moment of weakness only fleeting, Ralph returned to the room to continue with the others. When Joan looked up at him, her sad eyes begging through tears for deliverance, Ralph refused to be moved by the forces of Satan. He smashed her in the face with the Holy Bible.

At last, the spirits appeared to be departing in the blood, urine and faeces that spilled from their host. By late afternoon, Nuske had ascertained that only Princess Joan and Princess Baby Joan had been bold enough to withstand the punishment, clutching to each other in Joan Vollmer's stomach, refusing to come out. The mother and daughter demons would have to be taught a lesson.

Joan was moved to the bedroom, where she was held down while Leanne Reichenbach was ordered to sit on her stomach and bounce up and down so that the devils might be persuaded to make a move. At some point it was established the spirits had shuffled on up toward Joan's chest, which came in for special attention, Leanne and Matthew taking turns pulverising her breasts while the other beat the woman about the head and neck. Matthew pumped on Joan's throat with all his weight and holy Christian might, extracting the demons like paste from a tube. Each time Joan closed her eyes in pain, Matthew poked them open with his thumbs, so that the spirits may see the heroic champions of God against which they would fight in vain. Ralph and David stood by, hollering verses from the Bible, raising their voices to extinguish the cries from a woman beset by the agonies of the damned.

After two hours, Princess Joan and her demon child were identified as hanging on tight to Joan's tongue. While the others held Joan down, Matthew Nuske cranked Joan's mouth open so wide that he almost dislocated her jaw, giving the spirits ample opportunity to escape. Like this he held Joan Vollmer for close to an hour, her tears and gurgling sounds proof that the demons were on the way out. Suddenly, the thrashing, tears and choking stopped. There was a loud, supernatural hissing and groaning that rose from the depths of Joan Vollmer's body until, at last, she was still, Nuske proclaiming to the relieved and exhausted brethren that the spirits had been defeated and had flown.

At this moment, several members of the congregation – Ralph Vollmer in particular – noticed that Joan had ceased to breathe, and appeared to be fired by no obvious heartbeat. Nuske declared the situation quite normal. Assuring the others that Joan would eventually be arisen if everyone prayed hard and patiently, Nuske then left the farm, as he had other things to do.

After a whole night of praying and laying on of hands had achieved no noticeable resurrection, Ralph cast out for the local Baptist minister, Roger Atze, for advice. Atze came straight over, whereupon he found Ralph, Leanne Reichenbach and David Klingner in the kitchen eating lunch while the body of Joan Vollmer lay decomposing in the bedroom, her fluids leaking from her body into the bedclothes and onto the floor. He politely declined their invitation to dine, instead suggesting they fetch the local constabulary immediately.

When authorities arrived, they found the trio praying in the kitchen while Joan's body continued to rot in the 40-degree heat. The astonished officers were scarcely relieved to hear Ralph proclaim that they were about to witness one of the greatest miracles they had seen in their lives when Joan would come strolling out of the bedroom a picture of health.

At Joan's funeral three days later, Ralph Vollmer had still not given up hope, his insistence that Joan would rise from the dead having attracted a large crowd of onlookers. Ralph had even come prepared with some clothes for Joan, just in case she felt the need to change. It was not until the dirt was being tossed onto the coffin that Ralph Vollmer was seen to break down and cry.

Ralph Vollmer, Leanne Reichenbach, David Klingner and Matthew Nuske were brought before a jury of their peers in Horsham County Court. A woman had been killed, and even ancient law demanded that people be held accountable for such a thing. But for the Christians, justice had already been done – the Devil had been chased from Antwerp by the servants of God, and Joan Vollmer was in heaven, her ordeal over. It was not really Joan whom they had abused, beaten and tortured to death, but Satan, Joan's helpless body but a vessel for his evil. There was peace on earth, they said. They were sleeping well in the knowledge they had done the Lord's will.

During a trial that lasted ten whole weeks, the defendants challenged the Christian court to renounce their belief that the Devil exists, as the Bible on which the court swore did attest. They called upon men of the cloth to declare it true. They quoted from the Testaments Old and New, citing exorcisms performed by Jesus Christ and Jews. They recalled the exorcisms of Loudun in 1634, during which nuns were seen to convulse so violently they needed to be slapped and abused and restrained. Leah Clugston shivered and shook in the stand, panting like a dog as she testified to being overwhelmed by the voice of God. They dared the judge, the jury, all, to deny their right to be good Christian souls who believe in the word of God as truth.

And it worked. The court found them guilty, but of manslaughter, not murder – Joan Vollmer had been tortured and killed by accident, not design, by four good Christian people who had sought to destroy the evil that dwelled inside of her. Ralph Vollmer received a suspended sentence while Reichenbach, Klingner and Nuske went to jail for no more than four months, and then they were free.

So ended the chapter on Joan Vollmer's killing, an outrage that belongs in the same dark book as Salem, Loudun, and Fernando Álvarez de Toledo. Only this didn't happen in sixteenth century Antwerp, or anywhere close to the dark ages at all. It occurred in Victoria – here, in Australia – in the year of AD1993.

The people who killed Joan Vollmer walk amongst us today, free, while devils lurk in you and me.

THE AGONY OF ARTHUR DACRE

Waverley Cemetery reserves one of Sydney's most spectacular ocean views for the dead, who don't appreciate it, and the bereaved, who tend to understand there is more to life than pretty pictures. Here lie the men and women who did their best to make Australia great, or at least more interesting: Henry Lawson, the people's poet; Edna Shaw, the matron of Crown Street Women's Hospital and 'the mother of 100 000 babies'; Oscar Eliason, the conjurer known as 'Dante the Great', whose magic powers were no match for a buffoon who couldn't carry a firearm safely; George Freeman, the original 'colourful Sydney racing identity'; and John Sands, who really was in the greeting card business (and whose outrageously priced paper tokens of sympathy came in handy, no doubt, for friends of his family in 1873).

There are two graves here that are probably overlooked by the historics, the gothics and the gravestone rubbers who glide through the grassy aisles day and night, and that they are ignored would come as no surprise to the couple who lie within them, though it would irritate them greatly ...

The acting profession was not always one so rich with rewards for its proponents. The earliest actors, of Ancient Greece, were made to wear masks when on stage – a fly in the soup for the thespian intent on public adoration – and the Roman theatre was cast mostly with slaves, audiences booing and throwing things whether the performances were bad or not. The Middle Ages saw the art of theatre virtually exterminated by the children of God, the Puritans adhering to the beliefs of such killjoys as John Chrysostom, the fifth century archbishop of Constantinople and perhaps the world's first truly acerbic theatre critic, who regarded the theatre as 'Satan's assembly' and actors as naught but 'men pretending to be women and soft-limbed boys'.

The coming of the Italian *Commedia dell'Arte*, in which players performed unscripted scenarios from life – the birth of 'situation comedy' – revived the notion of acting as a decent, if not particularly noble, pastime. But until the 1800s actors were still sentenced to a social standing not far above that of the prostitute. Even the most successful thespian was considered an urbane curiosity along with the strongman, the magician, the sideshow freak, the animals in the travelling zoo. It wasn't until the second half of the nineteenth century, when peddlers of the old histrionic style – the roar and the bombast – were embarrassed by the likes of Henry Irving and Sarah Bernhardt (who proved how close to the human heart a good actor could strike) that thespians began to be regarded as anything like the celebrities that they are today.

Into this diorama stepped Amy and Arthur James, better known as Amy Roselle and Arthur Dacre, actors of the English stage, both in their forties and yet to strike the artistic blow that would ensure their performances ring through the ages.

By all accounts Amy was quite good. Her father, a Glastonbury schoolmaster, had a love for the stage that far outstripped any actual ability, and he was notorious in London for paying cash to well-known actors for the privilege of being cast as villain to their hero. It's likely he greased similar wheels for his daughter, who made her London stage debut in 1871, having only just turned twenty. But Amy's acting talents were to make her a regular fixture in the London theatre scene thereafter, her specialty being the classics, in which she could always be relied upon for intelligent and effective work. She played Lady to Henry Irving's Macbeth and held her own, or at least did not embarrass herself. She was a serious player.

Contemporaneous portraits reveal that Amy was probably never accused of being just a pretty face. Her long nose, slightly bulbous chin, and eyes that seemed moments from sleep suggest that Amy's reputation as 'an actress of certain consideration', as one critic proffered, was undoubtedly due to her handy abilities on the stage, and not somewhere else. She was also well liked outside of the theatres, in the streets and parlours where ordinary people who actually existed spoke about things that were actually happening, impressing all she met with her good grace and fineness.

Unhappily, Arthur Dacre was not so well regarded. A physician by profession, Arthur Culver James was relatively new to the theatre, an apparent mid-life crisis in 1878 seeing him leave his wife and steam for America. He returned not as Dr James, but as Arthur Dacre, actor, having convinced himself that his gifts were wasted in surgery, where a good day's work rarely scored anything so nourishing for the ego as a standing ovation. He was a tall, handsome fellow, his eagle-like head and soldierly moustache giving him that certain military air that was fashionable in the day, and in that respect he was rather the opposite of his wife.

Arthur Dacre owed any prominence he enjoyed to the emergence in popularity of the matinee idol in the theatre of the late nineteenth century. Along with such heart-throbs as Harry 'Handsome' Conway, Harry 'Handsome' Montague and 'Handsome' Jack Barnes, the 'handsome' Arthur Dacre was less suited to respectable evening engagements, where women were accompanied by male partners and behaved with the requisite decorum. Arthur's realm was the matinee, where audiences consisted almost entirely of women of leisure, who could safely squeal and gush at the players without fear of their husbands rebuking them for such slatternly displays.

Arthur, of course, considered himself a cut above such frippery, but, alas, the critics did not agree. Even an obituary, published in the days after his death, saw the author admitting to 'erring on the side of kindness' in praising Dacre's acting ability, adding sheepishly: 'I know many critics think otherwise'.

Arthur's reputation in the London theatre scene was perhaps forever tarred by his appearance in 1883 at the Opera Comique production of *Musette*, a vehicle for a new, multi-talented 'comedienne' named Lotta, and a play so terrible that it made news on the other side of the Atlantic. The *New York Times* reported that 'a more painful scene, or series of scenes, has rarely been witnessed on the London stage', the audience moved to 'ironical cheers, applause in the wrong place, and even hisses . . . a storm of disapprobation, which waxed still more furious when an ironical encore was injudiciously responded to'. The crowd's reaction – 'an organized riot of the most determined kind', as theatre historian Erroll Sherson would recall years later – was so ferocious the play was stopped several times as hostile patrons were removed by police. The London critics sided with the audience – *Reynolds's Newspaper* called *Musette* 'a travesty of ordinary dramatic canons' and the *Pall Mall Gazette* cited the 'poor quality of the wit' as the reason for 'a very turbulent first night'. The *London Era*, after spending the first hundred words of its review lambasting the audience for its 'malignancy', proceeded to get stuck into the 'irredeemable rubbish' that had made them so malignant, taking particular aim at the play's female star, whose character seems just as repellent after one and a quarter centuries:

> *Lotta is petite; she possesses vivacity, and seems the very embodiment of mischief ... She acts with her eyes, her elbows and her heels. She tells us she can't keep quiet, and truly she is never still. She kicks, she nudges, she grimaces, she whistles, she sings, she dances, she plays all manner of indescribable pranks ... she doesn't blush to talk about that 'darned hole' in her stocking, explaining to her shocked hearer that she knows it is a 'darned' one, because she darned it herself ...*

But it seems not even a dreadful play with a frightfully irritating lead player could distract the audience from its disrelish of Arthur Dacre. The *Pall Mall Gazette* noted his very appearance 'was the sign for loud sounds of disapproval, a hostile demonstration which was repeated whenever he came onto the stage'.

The ill feeling toward Dacre was a direct result of the 'theatrical divorce' that had dominated the newspaper gossip pages earlier that year. The ugly stoush saw Dacre accusing his former wife, an evidently popular woman named Florence Owen, of appalling infidelities, the evidence of which was provided by a phalanx of private investigators Dacre had hired to follow her around for months. In return, Florence painted Arthur as an opium addict who flogged her frequently. The jury found neither charge had been proven, though the court ruled that it was Dacre who had deserted his wife, and not the other way around. The trial also brought to light certain facts about Dacre upon which many would later have cause to reflect – he was said to be prone to depression and the frequent 'nervous, excited state' which, on occasions in the past, had rendered him 'not fit to practice in his profession' as a doctor. He took opium to help him sleep, which caused him to be 'irritable in consequence'.

His flair for theatrics, it also seemed, was not confined to the stage. One evening, Florence testified, she and Arthur fought, her husband becoming so impassioned as to take her by the neck and pound her head into the wall. Later, consumed by guilt at having been so cruel to her, Arthur took a surgical scalpel and melodramatically swiped at his own throat. The half-hearted incision caused only a superficial wound, yet Arthur slumped in a chair and prepared for 'death'. Florence was forced to call a doctor to stop the bleeding.

Amy Roselle and Arthur Dacre were wed in 1884, and for some years Arthur endured the humiliation of seeing advertisements for his wife's upcoming productions on the same pages as his own 'Actor for Hire' spots in the classifieds. Toward the end of the decade, no doubt out of sympathy for her proud husband, Amy agreed to promote herself and Arthur as a double act. Amy's general popularity might be the reason Arthur began scoring the best reviews of his career – he was 'adequate' or 'gave general satisfaction' in this role or that. The *London Era*'s review of Charles Coghlan's *For Life*, in which they both starred, was typical: Amy's performance was praised as 'distinguished throughout by emotional power of the highest order', which 'laid hold of the hearts of the audience', while Dacre's was 'pleasant and agreeable'.

By 1890, the couple's fortunes had plummeted. Amy's refusal to take roles in productions in which Arthur could not also be employed effectively scuttled her career. A tour of America, where the couple hoped they might discover a new audience, was a disaster. Though Amy was well received, scoring glowing notices and front-page features in journals like the *New York Clipper*, Arthur's most prominent notice was a piece in the *New York Times* reporting his bitter falling out with the Ugly Duckling Theater Company, which had been kind enough to offer him work during his stay. The article quoted Dacre complaining that the roles offered him were 'most insignificant', and responding to claims of his lousy acting by calling them 'untruthful'. When Dacre was consequently fired, he accused the theatre manager of having cynically organised the entire disagreement, of using Dacre's good name to sell tickets at posh prices only to hire lesser actors at bargain rates.

Back in London, Arthur and Amy resorted to all manner of desperate chicanery to hide the scarcity of their audiences. A review in *The Stage* in May noted that

> . . . for these recitals the hall is placed in semi-darkness – that is to say, the lights are turned down and the blinds and curtains pulled to, a footlight arrangement in front of the platform and two clusters of gas lights at the back concentrating all the rays upon the faces of the performers.

The darkness, however, did nothing to camouflage Arthur's shortcomings as an actor, the eagle-eyed critic for *The Era* noting that 'Mr Dacre was, if anything, a little too vehement in Bret Harte's *Caldwell of Springfield . . .*'

Before long, Amy and Arthur were offering their services in health spas and private drawing rooms, and it was a despondent Dacre whom theatre critic Ernest Bowen Rowlands encountered one night at The Savage Club in London. 'He seemed very much worried,' Rowlands later wrote,

> *and he talked freely to me of the misery of his career, and hinted that were it not for the loving affection and bravery of his wife he would feel tempted to escape from it all.*

In fact, despite being 'surprised to learn the extent of his reverses', Rowlands found himself deeply impressed by Dacre's declarations of love for his wife:

> *No woman, this usually reserved man insisted, could equal her who had been a loyal and true wife to him, who had supported him in all his trials, and never flinched from his side when disasters accumulated and disappointments mounted up.*

It was some time in 1894 that Arthur and Amy announced to friends and associates that they would be making one last play for the success they deserved by embarking on a tour of Australia, a country that had developed a reputation as something of a last bastion for the artistically aggrieved. The American performer J. C. Williamson had saved his own career in 1874 by taking the production of *Struck Oil*, which had failed in America, to Australian audiences, record-breaking runs in Melbourne and Sydney launching

Struck Oil on a smash-hit tour worldwide. Similar experiences with *HMS Pinafore* and *The Pirates of Penzance* saw Williamson abandoning America altogether for the blue skies of the southern colony, leasing the Theatre Royal in Sydney in 1881 and going on to become Australia's foremost theatrical manager. Throughout the 1880s, scores of British actors, playwrights and entertainers of the stage returned from tours of the antipodes utterly refreshed by the admiration showered upon them by Australian audiences evidently gasping for fine entertainment from abroad. In 1891 Sarah Bernhardt's debut at The Royal had been received with a thunderous standing ovation heard all over the world, despite the entire performance having been delivered in French. For Arthur Dacre it must have seemed too good to be true.

After negotiating with Williamson for seasons in Melbourne and Sydney, Arthur and Amy set sail for Australia on 11 December, 1894. Before leaving England – 'hopefully, for good', as Arthur confided to a friend – he and Amy performed one final show in Cardiff, an evening notable for Dacre stepping through the curtain at the end of the performance and roundly berating the audience for not having shown their appreciation more enthusiastically.

On the eve of their departure, Arthur hosted a farewell banquet at his old watering hole, The Savage Club. Ernest Bowen Rowlands was amongst the 'gathering of poor Dacre's friends' that assembled to wish him well in the forthcoming venture. 'It was not largely attended,' Rowlands later recalled,

> *The dinner was not a success. It was, indeed, the most dreary function of its kind I have ever assisted at. Speaking in light of subsequent events, one might say that its gloom was prophetic of the terrible end of the guest of the evening.*

The Australian tour began cheerily enough, the Dacres – as the press was referring to them – being the special guests at a grand dinner hosted by Melbourne's theatre elite. They began their run in March, with a performance of *A Bunch of Violets* at the Bijou Theatre in Bourke Street, Melbourne. Despite good advance publicity and enthusiastic gossip about the couple in the newspapers, Arthur and Amy performed to poor crowds from the very first night. 'The Bijou was almost empty,' wrote a correspondent for the *Brisbane Courier* on 4 April. 'I am afraid the Dacres must be losing money nightly, as we were told that it was one of the fullest houses of the season.'

In June, they presented *Esther Sandraz* at Her Majesty's Theatre in Sydney, the *Sydney Morning Herald* praising Amy for her 'incisive' performance, and Arthur for his 'sound' work, but, inexplicably, audiences stayed away. They'd found other things to do, too, when Arthur and Amy appeared in *A Scrap of Paper* at The Criterion Theatre in Pitt Street.

By October, both were noticeably distressed by their failure in Australia. Letters to friends spoke of being 'broken-hearted' and 'unable to conjure up any hope'. They were occasionally seen sobbing together, in each other's arms, as if saying goodbye. More than once, the late night hours would find Arthur 'entertaining' his company with gloomy monologues about the hopelessness of life, and of his belief that he and his wife might end it all, together, should things not improve. Nobody took him terribly seriously. Nobody ever had.

But then a light appeared in the darkness. Their performance of *The Land of Moa* at the Theatre Royal in October scored good reviews and, night after night, the seats began to fill and the applause became louder. Though the success didn't warrant an extension of the season, the management of the Theatre Royal was encouraged enough to engage Amy and Arthur for lead roles in an Australian play called *The Silence of Dean Maitland*, a short season beginning on Monday, 18 November, two days after the closing of *The Land of Moa*. It was the most significant role of Arthur's career, and was perhaps the break they'd both been waiting for.

But Arthur Dacre was never one to let a good thing just happen. His customary pomposity, combined with some good old-fashioned stage fright, sent Dacre marching into the offices of Mr Russell Jones, a solicitor in Castlereagh Street, in the week before the play was to open. Appearing in a somewhat anxious and excited state, Dacre complained that the management of the Theatre Royal was trying to harass him, shouldering him with a part he couldn't possibly learn in the allotted time. Their plan, claimed Dacre, was to give themselves an excuse to fire him, thus sparing themselves the duty of paying his salary. It was just as the Ugly Duckling company had done in New York – use Dacre's good name to sell tickets to the public, then save money by hiring less significant actors. He demanded Mr Jones intercede on Dacre's behalf. When Jones refused, Dacre stormed out, declaring neither he nor his wife would be appearing in *The Silence of Dean Maitland*, nor turning up for rehearsal the coming Sunday.

By Saturday morning, however, the situation appeared to have resolved itself. Friends visiting Amy and Arthur in their lodgings at 129 Macquarie Street found them buoyant and apparently excited by the prospect of the new play. That night, the final performance of *The Land of Moa* was the most successful yet, both Arthur and Amy receiving standing ovations, the very first of Dacre's career.

Those who loitered backstage that night noticed Arthur and Amy holding each other close, deaf to all the applause in the world.

It was four o'clock on the afternoon on Sunday, 17 November, 1895, when Arthur's valet, Alexander Watson, arrived at the Macquarie Street lodgings. Arthur was still in his pyjamas, Amy was on the bed in her nightdress, a cloth over her face. Watson assumed they were simply feeling the after-effects of a very late night.

As he prepared to leave, reminding them that rehearsal was at seven o'clock sharp, Watson passed Amy on the bed and said goodbye. Amy raised her hand, but her arm drooped back to the bed beside her, as if she were half asleep, or sedated. She then muttered something he did not hear.

At the door, Arthur handed Watson a number of letters and asked him to post them. He then took a copy of the Holy Bible and asked Watson to place his hand upon it, imploring him to swear that he would tell the truth about what he had seen that afternoon. Believing this to be little more than another moment from Dacre's melodramatic cosmos, Watson did as he was asked and departed, thinking little of what had occurred.

Nothing was heard from Arthur Dacre and Amy Roselle for the rest of the afternoon. Then, at six o'clock, a sound like crockery smashing to the floor was thought to have come from inside the Dacre suite. Climbing the stairs with a dustpan and brush, Martha Hope, the head housemaid, knocked on Dacre's door and waited for an answer. There was nothing. Putting her ear to the door, Martha heard a low, guttural moan from deep within the room. She then heard a male voice sobbing, 'Amy . . . Amy . . .'

Martha knocked again, calling out Dacre's name. There was a brief silence, then someone appeared to be struggling to unlock the door. A desperate voice from within panted, 'For God's sake, burst open the door!'

Martha alerted the landlady's son, who repeatedly failed to force the thick wooden door, and eventually climbed over the verandah of an adjoining terrace, entering the room from the balcony. He dashed across the room, calling for a doctor, and opened the door to the hall, where a small crowd of maids and lodgers had by now gathered for the unveiling of a most dramatic scene indeed.

Amy Roselle lay upon the bed, a handkerchief clasped in her hand, the soft, white skin of her breast punctured by two bullet holes that leached little red rivers out onto the white sheets. From wall to wall, it seemed, the carpet was sodden with blood. The washbasin that stood at the side of the bed was awash with crimson, a razor lying next to the sink. And in front of the basin stood Arthur Dacre, actor of the English stage, his hand to his neck, his pyjamas glistening with his own blood.

The little crowd gasped as Dacre turned and lurched toward them, his eyes mad with a tortured, terrible look, his left hand clasped to his neck, blood pumping through his fingers in jets. He staggered to his knees beside the bed and, before dropping dead, gurgled, 'Oh, God . . . The agony! The agony!'

And that is how the curtain fell on Arthur Dacre and Amy Roselle.

The newspapers told of a 'painful tragedy', of 'pride, poverty, despair and death'. *The Star* in London was most dramatic of all, telling of a proud couple 'who went to Australia to star, and starve, and bleed to death in each other's arms'.

An inquest found Amy had been killed by Arthur's hand. Whether she had consented, it could not say. Left on the bed a blood-stained note had read: 'God let us die together, I thought there was a last shot.'

But the letters Arthur had asked Alexander Watson to post for him would prove to be more revealing. Arthur once again blamed the audience for a very lousy last scene. 'We have really struggled against this,' he wrote to one friend. 'My sweet wife has lived a noble, heroine's life, but talent and honest, hard work are the last things they want now . . . We have never failed in our duty to the public before. I have never missed a night . . . We are broken-hearted.'

Some whispered of foul play, of Arthur's jealousies, his past, and the unlikelihood that Amy would have complied with such a sad and ghastly end. But most, like Ernest Bowen Rowlands, took sympathy on them both.

'It is not for us to judge him,' he wrote, continuing on with:

> *It is the province of all to pity him, and, whatever may be said about him, against or in favour of him, one thing I can certainly and emphatically say is that, in his life, Arthur Dacre did fight in terrible earnest the battle of life.*

The theatres were empty on the day they buried Arthur and Amy, the streets of Sydney lined with crowds as the funeral cortege made its way from Macquarie Street to Waverley Cemetery for their final appearance. The newspapers said it was the largest funeral procession the theatre world had ever seen. Arthur Dacre and Amy Roselle had, at long last, drawn the crowds.

Not that he would have cared for such nonsense any more. In a letter to a friend, written on that fateful Sunday morning in

November, Arthur was anything but hi-diddly-dee in regard to the acting life.

'Take my last words of advice,' he wrote. 'Be anything – butcher, baker or candlestick maker – but get work at anything else than as an actor.'

THE LODGER

The outback town of Boggabilla, on the southern side of the border between New South Wales and Queensland, is not exactly oversold by the Tourism Australia website, where it is described as having 'little to detain the passer-by, although there is a motel, a caravan park and the Wobbly Boot Hotel'. The young ones beg to differ – in June of 2006, Boggabilla hit the international headlines when the London Times *regaled its readers with the tale of the ten-year-old boy who, with his six-year-old brother as passenger, set off from Moree in his grandmother's Holden Commodore just to see his granddad in Boggabilla, some 120 kilometres away. Reaching speeds of up to 96 kilometres per hour, he made it just over halfway before being pulled over by police, the young driver responding to the flashing blue lights by indicating and smoothly pulling to a stop at the side of the road. In every respect he achieved more than the star of our next story, who set the little town courthouse alight during the Depression years, with an adventure more desperate and deadly than the region had ever seen ...*

Nobody thought there was anything particularly strange about a man wanting to ferry his family by river to Adelaide, all the way from Goondiwindi. It was a long trip, about 600 miles along the Macintyre River, the Darling, then the Murray, but it could be done. The year was 1934, the Great Depression still forcing people to do desperate things. And Mr Gray seemed to know what he was doing.

They tried to tell him the boat was too small – 10 feet long, 4 feet wide and 12 inches deep – and that he ought to consider a larger one. Local fishermen said it was a difficult craft to manage, and had been known to capsize on occasion. But it was cheap, and they didn't have much money. Besides, the dinghy was called *Phar Lap*. That had to mean good luck. He told them his wife and children were all capable swimmers, except for the baby, of course. It was a lie.

Lillian was thirty-seven and not strong in the water. Roy and Phyllis, nine and ten years old, could dog paddle but that's all. Colin, the baby boy, would doubtless sink like a stone. But they had to get away, quickly, before anyone discovered what they had done.

They set off in the morning, travelling for about nine miles on the current. At nightfall they stopped and camped for the night, sleeping under the tarpaulin they'd purchased in town. It rained all night, and in the morning Lillian begged that they walk until they found someone who might allow them some lodgings, just until the weather cleared up. So they packed up their camp and the little band trudged across country as the rain kept falling, until at last they come to a station called Bloomfield. The manager, a man called Ross, agreed to let them camp in his garage until the weather was finer.

Ross warned Mr Gray of the risks on the river, which would swell with all the rain they'd been having. There were twists and dogleg bends that would better a boatman of experience. One doesn't think about water as an enemy, but rather a road on which one floats. The truth is that she is a serpent asleep, and she wakes and snaps and swallows when one least expects it.

Lillian became nervous – for herself, for the children. She wanted to turn back. But they couldn't go back. Not now. They had to keep going, at least until they got to somewhere safe.

On Saturday morning, when the sun finally shone, they made their way back to the banks of the river, where *Phar Lap* was tied and waiting for them. They travelled all day on the current, beaching themselves at dusk near the home of a man called McDonald, who took pity on the struggling family and allowed them to camp on his property for as long as they wished. In the morning, on 5 February, they struggled overland to Stuartville station, where they obtained food and clothes for the children, who had been complaining of cold. A man called Carrigan saw them there, looking miserable and frightened, the children clinging to their mother as the father searched in his pockets for money he didn't seem to have. He said they were going to Adelaide, where their prospects would surely be better.

With the few clothes and provisions their money could buy, they slogged back to the river, climbed back into *Phar Lap* and continued on their journey.

They'd been going for about four miles when the water became fast and bumpy, the little children holding tight to the sides of the boat as their captain did his best to keep their world stable. Up ahead, he spied a tree that had fallen from the northern bank into the river, driftwood having collected in an unstable pile that sat upon the surface, the current churning all around. On the opposite bank, a clump of tea trees hung over the river, their strong boughs reaching into the water like the arms of creatures desperate to snatch things from the water that passed. He rowed to the south bank, warning Lillian and the children to keep their heads down as they passed through the trees, lest the low branches catch them. But before he could negotiate a passage through, the boat began to turn in the current, accelerating down the river, impossible to control. The boat slammed into a low limb, and toppled. The children panicked and screamed. The boat turned over.

Gray grabbed Roy and Phyllis, clutching onto their clothes, their hair – anything to stop them from being washed away down the river. The current dragged all three of them under a branch, tossing them back to the surface on the other side. They grabbed hold of the boat, which had righted itself. Lillian was screaming for her baby. She tried to pull herself up upon the boat, to raise herself out of the water, that she might see little Colin, who'd been swept from her arms. The boat tilted under her weight, became swamped, and capsized again. Roy and Phyllis also lost their grip and disappeared into the current. Gray tried to go after them but Lillian grabbed him and pushed him under. She was reckless, panicking. He pushed himself from her – he knew that's what you had to do with desperate, drowning people, who will take you down in fright. But when he tried to swim back to Lillian she was gone, swept away in the merciless torrent. He hit his head on a limb and went under again.

When he resurfaced he struggled to the bank and climbed out. Where was Lillian? Where were the children? As he staggered along the riverbank in despair he cried out their names but there was no answer, no sign of them. They had all disappeared around the next bend. Perhaps they had all taken hold of the boat and were safe, or had all washed up further downstream. He shouted again and again, but nothing. He collapsed on the shore and cried. What had he done? The woman he loved. And all those pretty children. It was hopeless. He had to get help . . .

Had our tragic hero been a subscriber to the *Edinburgh Medical Journal*, he might have taken heart from the recollections of Dr James Lowson, former physician to the Governor of South Australia, who had been aboard the SS *Bokhara* when it sank in a typhoon off the coast of Sand Island in the Pescadores, Formosa, in 1892. One of only the handful who survived (148 perished, of whom eleven were members of the Hong Kong cricket team, returning home from a match played against the Shanghai Cricket Club), Lowson described the feeling of drowning in vivid detail:

> *I got clear under water and immediately struck out to reach the surface, only to go farther down. This exertion was a serious waste of breath, and after ten or fifteen seconds the effort of inspiration could no longer be restrained. It seemed as if I was in a vice which was gradually being screwed up tight until it felt as if the sternum and spinal column must break. Many years ago my old teacher used to describe how painless and easy a death by drowning was – 'like falling about in a green field in early summer' – and this flashed across my brain at the time. The 'gulping' efforts became less frequent, and the pressure seemed unbearable, but gradually the pain seemed to ease up. I appeared to be in a pleasant dream . . .*

Had Gray been an enthusiast of human history, he might have also taken solace from the fact that mankind's cruellest executioners tended to consider the punishment of drowning so tolerable as to be akin to a lenient sentence. The *Lex Cornelia*, a Roman set of laws passed by Sulla during his dictatorship from 81 to 80 BC, ordained that those who killed their mothers or fathers were to be sewn into a sack and thrown in the sea, but when word got around that drowning wasn't so bad after all, the punishment was amended so that the prisoner was forced to share his sack with a dog, a cock, a viper and an ape. By the sixteenth century, throughout most of Europe drowning was considered the most compassionate of official cruelties, usually reserved for women and criminals of a more sympathetic class. In Scotland in 1526, for example, a man convicted of petty theft and low-level sacrilege had his death by hanging commuted to drowning 'by the Queen's special grace'.

But Mr Gray was likely just a reader of the papers, and would thus have had an added shame to pile upon his burden. These were days when drownings marked the hours like the tickings of a clock, but they were days of heroism, too, the newspapers filled with tales of fathers sinking to their deaths in pursuit of their drowning children.

On Sunday, 6 February, 1916, George Crump, a farmer of Lara Lake, had been hailed a national hero after diving into rough seas to save his seven-year-old daughter, Ruby, who had fallen from a jetty. Both sank from view, the girl found later, waves rolling her against the sand, as her father's body continued on an endless, unseen journey through the deep.

On 19 February the following year, there occurred a tragedy near Inverell when a farmer named John Handshaw drowned in the Macintyre River – the same in which the Grays had perished – while attempting to save the lives of his two children. The three washed up downriver, their bodies appearing to those who found them as a family lying on the riverbank, their heads turned to each other as if asleep. The papers reported on a 'brave father's death'.

And on Thursday, 25 October, 1923, the nation was heartbroken by the story of a 'brave man's fate' at Yalgoo, two hours east of Geralton in West Australia. Fifty-nine-year-old Henry Molloy, who had a wife and five children and had not been in good health, ran a quarter of a mile in an endeavour to save the life of nine-year-old Walter Coyne, who had fallen into a sump near a railway dam. After diving into the flooded enclosure, Henry rose to the surface with the drowned boy in his arms. But the steep and oily walls of the sump made escape impossible, Molloy's young daughter reaching into the well to grasp her father's hand until they both became exhausted, Henry saying a tearful goodbye to his daughter as he let go and sank to the bottom.

There would be no such melancholy praise for the lone survivor of the Gray family tragedy. And the public was yet to hear all.

Allan Carrigan instantly recognised the distraught man who staggered onto Stuartville station, the Gray family having been there to fetch provisions but a few hours before. The woman and the children, the poor man cried, were gone, lost to the river.

News travelled fast across the countryside. Policemen came from Goondiwindi and Toowoomba, civilians and station workers from miles around. They converged on the river, at the place where the boat had last been seen, searching the bushes and the fields by the water, calling out the names of the children, while fishermen with boats and grappling hooks dragged the river from bed to bank. Black trackers waded through reeds and dodged snakes. Sometimes the current nearly got the better of grown men. As night fell, and police called off the search until morning, the dreadful truth began to sink in: Lillian and the children were gone, and nothing anyone could do would bring them back to life.

That Gray was a mess was understandable – he'd lost everything. While assisting searchers, he had frequently fallen to his knees, his face to his hands, and cried out in anguish. But police still had to interview him, to find out what had happened. Like everyone else they were curious as to why a man would put his family in such peril in the first place. That night, as the sad man spoke between fits of sobbing and moaning to a God who didn't care, the police began to learn the whole terrible truth, of a tragedy even more harrowing than it seemed, of the real reason the Grays had been going away, and the awful thing they had done.

Frederick James Gray, the nation would learn, married Lillian in 1920 in the English city of Bristol, where they had met. They came to Australia in 1928 with their two children, Roy and Phyllis, settling in The Valley just outside of Brisbane, where Frederick operated a milk vending business. It was a small enterprise with no room for innovation or advancement, but it was a business of which Gray was proud. When Lillian gave birth to another child, Frederick couldn't have been happier. The thought of his family, their little faces appearing in his mind as he worked through the day, made him smile and kept him going. In five years, he had never missed a delivery.

Some time in 1933 the Grays moved house, and a young stranger from across the street had assisted them in the moving of some of their heavy furniture. He was 27-year-old Charles Arthur May, a short man of medium build with red hair and a ready smile. May was a Londoner by birth and had come to Australia some seven years before, having moved from New South Wales to Victoria, then Queensland, in search of work. Gray had seen him before, when May had lived in a Brisbane flat to which Frederick had delivered milk. They became friendly and when May offered to help with the milk run, in exchange for nothing more than meals, Gray agreed.

May soon became friendly with the children and Mrs Gray and, after some time, he asked whether the Grays might consider taking him in as a boarder. Times were tough, and he could barely afford the rent on his one-room flat. It would be of great assistance to him, and perhaps he could help out with the business and around the home.

Fred and Lillian talked it over. It was risky, argued Lillian – they hardly knew anything about the man or his past, and to expose the children to a stranger in their home might be unwise. But the Grays were in financial hardship, too, and they could use the extra money. So they agreed to give May a try.

For a while things worked out very well, May assisting on the morning milk run and contributing to the home with food supplied through his ration ticket. Sometimes he'd help Lillian with the shopping, or provide what assistance he could to the children with their schoolwork, and read to them at night. He'd often return from town with something he'd purchased for the house from an auction sale. He seemed very determined to make a place in the family home for himself. Everyone grew to like him.

But as the stranger became more familiar with his surroundings, and more comfortable and confident of his place within them, he began to exude the manner of a master rather than a lodger: scolding the children for this or that, as if they were his own; making suggestions to Gray about his business, behaving like a partner, when he was no such thing. Gray had managed this milk run for years, alone, and he needed no talk of innovation from a meddling stranger. When Gray dismissed his ideas May became insubordinate, changing elements of the morning route without consulting his employer at all. Gray began to simmer, not always in silence, and there were several heated exchanges, May becoming a little less reserved with every angry episode. He began taking liberties, driving Gray's car into the town without permission, on one occasion taking little Phyllis for the ride, in the absence of consent from either Lillian or Gray. In his mind Gray imagined the stocky Englishman exercising similar freedoms with his wife. The idea made him hateful.

The matter came to a head one morning on the milk run, Gray exploding at yet another bold suggestion about the running of the business. There was a most intense altercation, Gray insisting in the end that the lodger pack his things and leave their house that very day. May returned to his old one-room flat across the street.

But the children were devastated. They had grown to be quite fond of him – especially little Phyllis, who cried and begged her father to allow May to come back. The whole family, it seemed, had become enamoured with the man. Reluctantly, and after cooling down, Gray approached May and offered his apologies, suggesting May might like to return on the condition he conduct himself to Gray's wishes. By evening, May was back in the Gray home, and on his best behaviour.

But it didn't take long for the rot to set in again. This time, it wasn't the business about which Gray became protective, but his family. He imagined May to be ingratiating himself too much with the children and, more worryingly, his wife. Lillian laughed. Her husband was being ridiculous, she said. Even if it were true, where would she fraternise with May, and when?

But Gray couldn't get the thought out of his head. May remained on his best manners – was even friendly and helpful on the milk rounds, where before he'd been meddlesome and irritating. But the more reasonable May seemed, the more Gray began to hate him. Sometimes he wished he could just make him disappear. He began to think unsavoury thoughts.

Then, one day, Gray returned from his afternoon milk run to find his family gone. There was no sign of May, and some money was missing. What liberty had been taken this time? A trip into town with his family, without even so much as consulting the man of the house? Or was it something else? Were Lillian and the children in danger? Confused, worried and furious all at once, Gray drove into Brisbane, searching everywhere, his imagination wild, all the while trying to calm himself down lest he found them and did something to May he might later regret. When day turned into night with still neither sign nor word, Gray realised he had to alert the police. Something was very wrong.

The police assured Gray they would find them. Every police station in Queensland was notified. If they were on the road, they would be discovered. They would call on Gray as soon as they knew.

At last, late one night, the police came calling at Frederick Gray's door. He was to prepare himself for a shock. His wife and children had gone willingly with May. They had purchased a car in Brisbane before driving to the small town of Texas, not far from Goondiwindi. There, introducing himself as Mr Gray and family, May had purchased a small boat, with which he intended to ferry the family all the way to Adelaide . . .

The bodies of Lillian and little Colin were discovered on 7 February, 1934, and Roy and Phyllis on successive days thereafter. In the weeks that followed, Frederick Gray sat in the courtroom in

Boggabilla and listened as May described how he and Lillian had fallen in love over the nine weeks he had been in the Gray household, how the children had become attached to him, too, and how they had all planned a new life in the south, far from Frederick Gray and his irritating ways. May had simply used Gray's name because he suspected the police would be searching for him, which is why they had chosen to travel by river. He had come to think of the children as his own and there would soon have been a new child in the family, had disaster not befallen them all.

The Coroner found that Lillian Grace Gray and her three children had drowned by accident in the Macintyre River on 5 February, 1934. Charles Arthur May was charged with vagrancy, and sentenced to twenty-one days in prison.

Frederick Gray went back to his milk run the very next day, delivering to homes as he always had. He told a local newspaper that work took his mind off his family – little faces which, if dwelled upon, just made him want to cry.

OF MONKEYS AND MEN

You will find the New South Wales hamlet of Dora Creek nestled amongst the dense bushland on the western side of Lake Macquarie. The Newcastle-to-Sydney train almost ignores the village as it passes overhead on an old iron bridge, the resulting rattle and clang being as much noise as the residents want to hear all day. Gone are the sawmills that once connected this parcel to Sydney by paddlewheel, and if there are memories of commercial ties to the city they are not visible. This is a place you might stop when you've had enough, when you care no longer for what the modern world has to offer, or to do something of which you feel the world may disapprove.

Dora Creek is the perfect setting for an old urban myth, which tells of a Nazi scientist who escaped to these parts after the war, continuing his experiments in a secret laboratory amongst the trees. As if to warn of such wickedness, two giant smokestacks from the nearby Eraring power station stand knee-deep in the skyline and can be seen for miles, like silent totems of a past civilization in a world where nature has reasserted herself. Of the people who dwell in their shadows, only a few can vaguely recall the fantastic tale that belongs to this place. They squint through security doors and murmur that it was 'a queer thing' best forgotten. Nearby, an old house still stands, the porch facing out to Pulbah Island as it always has. The occupants have never heard of the man who once lived there, or the thing that happened here . . .

On a winter's day in 1943, Doctor Henry Leighton Jones attended a medical conference at Newcastle Hospital in New South Wales. He was to deliver a paper in the afternoon, the first public disclosure of discoveries made from over a decade of research and highly experimental surgery conducted in his laboratory in the nearby bushland. But moments before he was due to take his place behind the lectern, a massive heart attack felled him from his chair, a room full of surgeons and medical practitioners unable to save him. On the floor lay the paper he was to have delivered, a document that promised to reveal the very secret of life, as illuminated by a man who dreamed his journey still had so much further to go.

He was born Henry Jones, near Cardiff in Newcastle, in 1868, and left school at fourteen, taking a job as a postal clerk in a mine at nearby Cockle Creek. When it was discovered the family farm was riding a coal seam, Henry used his share of the sale to travel to the USA where he studied dentistry and medicine at Louisville, Kentucky, graduating in 1901, and obtaining the necessary licences to practise in New South Wales by travelling to Great Britain, signing on at the Edinburgh Royal College of Physicians and Glasgow Faculty of Physicians and Surgeons.

During his time in America Henry dated a young woman named Leighton, a girl many years his junior. Why the romance dissolved is not known, but the encounter so affected Henry that he adopted the young woman's name into his own. Thus Henry Leighton Jones returned to Moss Vale in New South Wales in 1905, where he practised as an MD, dentist and pharmacist until accepting the position of Government Medical Officer in the Northern Territory in 1915. As a captain in the Australian Army Medical Corps, he saw action in the Pacific during the Great War, returning to Darwin after the Armistice to settle into a private practice that extended from Melville Island off Darwin to Oodnadatta in South Australia, from the back to the very belly of the nation.

These were vibrant years, the 1920s, and Leighton Jones was wealthy and in his prime, his social standing unmatched. Photos from the time show a handsome face gazing out with a confidence and a readiness to know. He rode through town in a chauffeur-driven Clement Talbot, though he was known to prefer the company of Aborigines, Chinese immigrants, and others from the fringes of decent society, who regularly rode with him on his shooting parties. In 1923, in a boat he built himself and captained with his own mind and muscle, Henry sailed to Singapore to attend the Congress of the Far Eastern Association of Tropical Medicine, where he established a friendship with the Sultan of Johore, who was to prove a very useful contact later in life.

Henry retired in 1928, purchasing a house at Eraring in New South Wales, near the mouth of Dora Creek, a place not far from the home of his youth. Here he preferred a private existence, the elegant, well-attired gentleman viewed by the locals as something of a remote eccentric. On hot summer days, children peered through the ferns to spy on Henry as he reclined inside a chair fashioned from an open fridge on his balcony, gazing over at Pulbah Island in the lake, as if waiting for ships that were promised to arrive. At night, local fishermen were guided to shore by the light that glowed from Henry's window as he read and lingered until dawn.

What thoughts entertained or tormented Henry Leighton Jones during these days and nights we can never know, but it's likely he dwelled, like most men of his years, on the question of how much time he had left. His had been a nourishing life, full of challenge and adventure, but he was alone, his memories to be shared with no one, a lifetime of experience and acquired instinct to be lost to the universe in his last breath. At sixty-one years of age, it was surely too late.

Perhaps this is why Henry became intrigued by the fledgling field of inquiry known as endocrinology, which proposed to study the rivers in the body that seethe in the young and dry up in the old. The Chinese had known of them for thousands of years, and the medical men of ancient Persia had noted the sour secretions that flowed from the bodies of the diseased and the aged. But it was only in the nineteenth century that European men of science had begun to grasp that the living body was a chemical factory forever in production, brewing tonics with such incredible properties that, if bottled and sold, they would be ridiculed as potions of hazardous magic, their bottlers lashed from town. The endocrine glands produced hormones, as they were now called, that stimulated growth, strength, even rage, each one with its own purpose, but all working in concert with a central conductor poised to respond to the body's every demand. It had been found that certain hormones fuelled particular organs and events, not simply as petroleum fuels an automobile, but as water fuels life. This was particularly noticeable with regard to the sex glands. In Germany, zoologists had noticed that when castrated, roosters did not develop combs or exhibit overtly male behaviours, but that when the testes were replaced, they returned to normal.

It was Henry's fascination with endocrinology that led him to open a book entitled *Life*, by one Professor Serge Voronoff, Director of Experimental Surgery at the College de France in Paris. It began:

> *The longevity of living creatures is in reverse relation to their organic perfection. The longevity of the mammals, in whose ladder of progression man stands on the topmost*

rung, is in direct relation to the duration of the period of growth necessary to complete bodily development. Thus the normal life-span of man should be from 120 to 140 years.

The book went on to explain Voronoff's theory of life being prolonged by the grafting of glands, both thyroid and testicular, from the young and healthy into the aged. So desperate became Henry to read more works by Voronoff, who could not speak or write in English, that he taught himself French by textbook and gramophone records. Thus equipped, Henry consumed 1923's *Greffes Testiculaires*, 1924's *Quarante-Trois Greffes Du Singe a L'homme*, and *Etude sur la Vieillesse et la Rajeunissement par la Greffe* of 1926.

And then, some time in 1928, Henry Leighton Jones packed his bags, jumped on a ship and hurried off to Paris to see Voronoff personally.

While serving as a surgeon on the Western Front during the war, where the English and the French casualties had been so terrible, Russian-born Serge Voronoff had tried to save young arms and legs by transplanting bones from the dead of the battlefields. Sometimes, when the bones of dead boys had been scarce, Voronoff had borrowed from the skeletons of horses and cattle, and had marvelled at the capacity of the human body to adopt the foreign matter as its own. Later, while working as the Khedive Surgeon-General in Egypt, Voronoff had noticed the premature senility and early death rate in eunuchs of the harem, and concluded that ageing was the result of a slowing down of endocrinal secretions, particularly of the sexual hormones. Voronoff believed that the testicles not only had a genital function, but also acted on skeletal, muscular, nervous and psychological development. His experience as a surgeon during the Great War had armed him with a knowledge of grafting and transplanting techniques, and he performed many experimental testes grafts in goats, sheep and bulls, the results convincing him this same procedure might have a rejuvenating effect on human beings.

By the early 1920s, in his laboratory at the College de France, Voronoff had been running clinical trials in which he had inserted slices of chimpanzee testes into the scrotums of aged men. The chimpanzee, asserted Voronoff, was wholly superior to man in regard to the quality of its organs, and devoid of those defects, hereditary and acquired, with which mankind was afflicted. The trial results, according to Voronoff, had resulted in a general rejuvenation of the entire system – improvement of the mind and memory, greater stamina, better hearing and eyesight, stronger hair and, most interestingly of all, a sharp increase in sexual virility. Voronoff was certain the treatment would lead to the prolonging of life.

As the decade progressed news of the treatment spread, and Voronoff was known to have grafted healthy testicles from the fresh corpses of death-row criminals into the scrotums of the willing and the wealthy. When it became clear that the eager old men of Paris outnumbered the lawless and immoral, Voronoff was forced to return to transplants from chimpanzees and baboons. His treatment was to gain him some celebrity in Europe and America, where Voronoff was seen both as a visionary and as a fraud, a pioneer and a leech on man's fear of death, his treatment cheered as triumph and carped on as little more than freak show placebo. The truth lay somewhere far in the future, or disguised by the swagger of bumptious old men.

When Henry Leighton Jones arrived on his doorstep, Voronoff welcomed more than just an enthusiastic pupil. So impressed was Voronoff with Henry's gifts as a surgeon that he invited him to stay and, for the next twelve months, the pair worked together to perfect the grafting technique.

And when he returned to Eraring in 1929, Henry came with Voronoff's English secretary, Nora Elizabeth Barrett, now Nora Leighton Jones, more than forty years her husband's junior.

In 1930, Leighton Jones carried out the first gland transplant in the Southern Hemisphere, grafting the testicles of a young scrub bull onto a pedigreed Jersey bull that had become lame in stud. The operation was a complete success, the Jersey bull going on to sire healthy calves. Leighton Jones was inspired to proceed with monkey-to-human grafts immediately.

Unlike Voronoff, who almost exclusively used baboons and chimps, Henry would insist on using only rhesus monkeys, which he arranged to import from the Sultan of Johore. The discovery by Karl Landsteiner and Alexander S. Weiner of the Rhesus factor in human blood was not to be published until 1937, and whether Henry was somehow aware of their work we do not know. Nevertheless the monkeys took up residence on Pulbah Island in Lake Macquarie, in view of Leighton Jones's front porch, where they would remain in quarantine before being moved to a cage in a converted water tower on Henry's own property.

Leighton Jones found a suitable clinic in nearby Morisset and gathered a team of local medics, nurses and assistants. In the local gazette he took out an advertisement that asked for volunteers. The Australia of the 1930s was a nation in a state of reckless subservience to the new gods of science and medicine – all manner of drugs were consumed on the orders of their respective labels. Children often had their teeth, tonsils or appendix removed for no other reason than to keep their otherwise hospitalised siblings company. The city-dwellers, awaiting connection to the world by sea and air, would soon become more cautious, but rural Australians were apostles to any treatments or trends that were blessed by the local medic. And so the letters poured in, from old men who wished to be young again.

The name of Henry's first prospect is lost to history, but enough is known to afford us the luxury of imagining his experience as he surrendered himself to such an uncertain encounter. As he did each prospect, Leighton Jones met the patient personally at the train station and drove him to his home, where he would remain for a week to be fed and waited upon by Henry's fetching young bride, the sound of caged monkeys gambolling outside his window serenading him to sleep in the evenings. Blood testing was performed with human and monkey blood cross-matched, for any human found to be not adequately compatible with any of the donor monkeys would be rejected. On the day of the operation, the patient endured the anxious half-hour journey from Eraring to Morisset in the back seat of Leighton Jones's car, the donor monkey sitting beside him as companion. Once at the clinic the monkey was anaesthetised with rag-and-bottle ether before the appropriate glands were removed and taken immediately into the next theatre, where Leighton Jones and the patient were waiting. The operation complete, Leighton Jones ordered that the patient remain at his home in Eraring for observation. After a week, if all seemed well, the gentleman was free to return to his new, improved life.

Word travelled fast about the miraculous operation being performed on those brave enough to dare. Women spoke of it over fences and wires. Men discussed it in the public houses. Newspapers mentioned it occasionally, a nudge and a raise of eyebrow palpable between the lines. The publicity assured an instant waiting list made up of ageing men from all over the region and beyond as Dora Creek became a modern Shangri-la to which the old men travelled and from which young ones returned.

The operations were not always testicular: some of the patients were women seeking pituitary grafts, whereupon glands were embedded either in the thyroid or the labia. One boy received thyroid, testicular and pituitary grafts, all of which were successful. Another woman received an ovarian graft, the talk behind hands in town being that she later complained of morning sickness.

As for the monkeys, who observed the comings and goings in town from their makeshift prison in the treetops, the price they paid for these vanities was death, not a single one of them surviving the procedures. Decades later, builders excavating the site of Leighton Jones's clinic were appalled when they unearthed what at first appeared to be the skeletal remains of so many children, huddled together in a common grave, as if cowering from some shared horror.

The coming of the Second World War closed the shipping lanes in 1939 and Henry Leighton Jones's supply of rhesus monkeys began to evaporate. While offered inferior monkeys from various zoos and circuses, Henry preferred not to risk it. He had performed over fifty operations, with no rejections of donor tissue, no litigations brought against him and, most significantly, many return visits from satisfied patients wanting the procedure repeated. Fresh in mind and will, but too old for the world that so valued the young, he determined to end the experimentation before some error, by his hand or God's, might haul the entire endeavour into the view of a displeased public.

Henry Leighton Jones had shunned publicity all of his life – only once or twice had he submitted to interviews for newspapers or magazines, and never had he been satisfied with what came of it. The last time, in 1938, he had agreed to an interview with a new magazine called *PIX*, which purported to be a reputable journal of august fact for the discerning reader. The resulting article, obsessed as it was with the sexual aspect of his operations, had greatly offended Henry, and so he determined to speak of his experiments no more.

Then, in 1943, a letter came from a representative of the British Medical Association, inviting Henry to deliver a paper on his work at a branch meeting at Newcastle Hospital in the coming winter. Henry had become accustomed to private life – to resting with Nora, watching over his children, looking out at the lake, replaying his memories – and, while he had kept in correspondence with many of his patients, the monkey operations had almost vanished for him like a boyhood hobby outgrown by the man. Henry wrote a return letter thanking the Association for the opportunity, but declined the offer, citing his desire for privacy and the privacy of his former patients.

When Nora saw the letter her husband intended to post, she raged at him. Here, at long last, was a chance for Henry to set things right, to see his years of work vindicated. All the years of silly publicity, raucous and sour, all to which he had foolishly submitted, could be slain with one wise stroke, and here was Henry refusing to take it. Henry begged Nora to consider the privacy of the patients, which was paramount to him, and which had been so violated by such outrageous articles and the scandalous talk they had inspired. Might not a room full of jealous medical minds threaten the same? But Nora insisted. What he was being asked to do was no more than every researcher in the world had done before him, what every scientific explorer *must* do in order to contribute to the quest for knowledge. All the experimenting and peering through microscopes would amount to mere fiddling in the dark, were one not to present those observations to the serious scrutiny of one's peers.

Reluctantly, Henry was forced to agree with his young wife. There had been little point in the whole enterprise if its lessons were to live and die in Dora Creek. Moreover, since that first trip to Paris in 1928, while Henry had been rapt in his own bloody theatre, the world had awoken to the serious implications of the work which had earned those like Voronoff such ridicule. European men of science had isolated and identified the hormone known as testosterone, its power no longer disputed, its synthesis winning two scientists the Nobel Prize for Chemistry in 1939. Others had shown that injected testosterone had androgenic and virilising properties on eunuchs, young boys and women. Steroid chemistry was entering its golden age and Henry Leighton Jones, working virtually alone in his bushland laboratory, had been a silent pioneer, unknown to the others with whom he'd kept pace.

And so Henry set to work on what was to be his sole manifesto. The records he had kept were vast and meticulous, the histories of both the patients and monkeys amounting to singular biographies of their subjects that would satisfy the most rigorous standards either science or literature could demand. With increasing vigour did Henry toil through the days and nights, his study becoming his entire world, the months passing without him emerging for anything other than bathing and meals. In correspondence to all of his patients, he informed them of what he was about to do, assuring them that their privacy would be maintained at all costs.

He had written of them in his paper but had replaced their names with a series of codes that only he could decipher. There would be no reason for any of them to ever reveal themselves, now or in the future. After all, at seventy-five years of age, fit and mentally sharp, Henry Leighton Jones was himself the best evidence for the veracity of his own treatment. For while in Paris, Henry had dared to submit to the procedure he had sought all those years to perfect. Now the father of a young daughter and infant son, he was proof that it worked, and that no age was ever too late. Soon he would show the world how.

It was a cold morning on 24 October, 1943, when Henry, his paper beside him in a leather case, waved goodbye to his family from the train at Dora Creek Station, on his way to Newcastle Hospital and the uncertain reception that awaited him there. Henry may have peered up from his newspaper as the train raced by Cardiff, the place of his birth so many years ago, before returning to the pages filled with advertisements – Beecham's Pills for the 'kindred ills' and Clement's Tonic that 'restores lost nerve-power and invigorates the system'. As his train drew in to Newcastle Station, Henry would have passed within sight of the Newcastle Town Hall where, just the evening before, the Bishop of Newcastle had spoken to the Conference on Religion and Life. 'Frustration,' he had preached, 'seems to be the dominant characteristic of all human undertakings. There is some perversity somewhere which tends to create evil out of good, and to deny to man the successes he craves, even when they seem most certainly to be within his reach.'

Nora Leighton Jones was devastated by her husband's death. There had been no warning – he had been in perfect health and in such fine spirits when they had said their last goodbye. To Nora, Henry had always seemed so strong she believed he would never grow old. That the very decrepitude he had so cleverly outfoxed would strike him so savagely, so finally, and at a moment so cruelly chosen, seemed to Nora like the work of some supernatural hand, a darkness that had watched disapprovingly over her husband's shoulder as he'd fiddled with fate, and whose wickedness must never again be tempted, lest the children be pursued by it, too.

Always concerned for the privacy of his patients, Henry had left instructions with Nora that, should anything ever happen to him, she must destroy the files pertaining to their operations, for fear that names and details fall into unreliable hands. It is said that a bonfire burned for three nights at the house by the lake, the old water tower, now empty of monkeys, silhouetted against the glow in the trees as Nora dutifully carried out her husband's wishes like the last disciple of a cult gone bad.

But there was one document that was better off spared, one that held within its pages Henry Leighton Jones's salvation. Out of respect, the British Medical Association had returned Henry's conference paper to Nora, unread, with a note pleading that she formally submit the document and, on behalf of her late husband, grant them permission to publish it posthumously. Here in Nora's hand was the instrument by which Henry Leighton Jones might be remembered, one last chance at immortality, and due acknowledgement from the scientific world.

But Nora was not in her right mind. Numb with grief and chilled by the superstitions that so often shadow an untimely death, Nora Leighton Jones tossed her husband's only testament into the fire.

So burned the legacy of Henry Leighton Jones, a man whose name would be lost in time, whose words and thoughts we will never know. All that remain of him are a few images frozen in a moment, a handsome face gazing out from photographs that would grow tired and withered with age.

A BOAT WITH NO NAME

On the banks of Lake Burley Griffin in Canberra lives a memorial to those who died on their way to becoming Australians not so long ago. Designed by school students, it's a touching tribute, a single painted pole with a personal message for each of the 353 who lost their lives. But a careful read of the plaque that introduces the outdoor tribute reveals that the SIEV-X Memorial 'remembers the 146 children, 142 mothers and 65 fathers who died on the refugee boat SIEV-X, at the height of the Federal election campaign in October 2001'. One might wonder why the relative proximities of polling days aren't similarly recorded on headstones, shrines, the stirring monuments of history. The fact is that the tragedy of the boat with no name is a tale rarely told without the aroma of political bias accompanying the narrative, and that in itself is a tragedy, though an insignificant one in the scheme of things, as you will see . . .

In 1991, Amal Hassan Basry's twenty-year-old brother was killed by an American bomb that fell on the city of Basra, Iraq. A few months later, another brother was executed for refusing to fight against the Kuwaitis, whom he saw as his brothers and sisters. Later that year, a brother-in-law was shot for having taken part in an uprising against Saddam Hussein's regime.

Amal's husband, Abbas Akram, had fought for Saddam in the 1980 war against Iran but that counted for nothing when he was arrested, along with two of his brothers, and tortured in 1995. Another brother-in-law was not seen again after police came and took him in the night. It was in 1997 that Amal and her husband decided to escape from Baghdad, spiriting their two children to the Kurdish zone in northern Iraq, before fleeing over the border to Iran in 1999.

They heard talk of a place called Australia, a land free from war, where people lived without fear. They called it the 'Lucky Country'. It was far away and getting there would be dangerous, but staying in Iran was riskier. Iraq had been like a prison but in Iran they were hated. Their children could not go to school, and real estate agents would not rent them property. Every knock on the door was a threat of deportation back to Iraq where they would most surely be killed.

It was decided that Amal's husband would go ahead first. If he were granted refugee status in Australia, his family would follow with ease. He flew to Malaysia, then travelled by boat to the West Australian coast, arriving in January of the year 2000. After eight months in detention, he was finally granted a temporary protection visa and allowed to settle in the southern city of Melbourne. He called Amal and told her of a city that was beautiful and free. The journey, he warned her, would be dangerous. But they both agreed it was worth it.

Amal knew they couldn't all get to Melbourne. They didn't have much money, and every step of the way would see hands extended for payment in such a clandestine enterprise. The eldest son, who was nineteen, agreed it was he who must remain in Iran. He would join them later. He'd found work and was safe.

And so, in July of 2001, Amal and her younger son, Rami, then aged seventeen, left the Middle East forever, flying to Malaysia before journeying by boat to Sumatra, where they were to remain until their boat was ready to transport them to Australia. They stayed in apartments with other families who were making the same journey. One, a woman named Alia, gave birth to a child in the time they were waiting. Amal befriended her, and helped deliver the baby.

After a time they travelled to Jakarta to meet with a man called Abu Quassey, who would help to smuggle Amal and the others to Australia. It was a lot of money – 500 American dollars, and it was almost all they had. But it was all that stood between them and freedom. It was a good boat, Abu said, with a radar and satellite, radios, plenty of food and modern amenities. They paid him the money and travelled by ferry to Sumatra, from where they journeyed on a midnight bus to the port of Bandar Lampung. The following morning they would be on their way to freedom.

Before dawn on 18 October, Amal and Rami, along with other women and children, were taken by dinghy from the beach at Bandar Lampung out into the blackness, where the boat that would take them to Australia was waiting.

As they approached the vessel Amal wondered if there hadn't been a mistake. This was not the modern craft Abu had promised. It was just an old fishing boat, made of wood, not much bigger than the bus that had taken them to the beach. There were hundreds more back on the shore, waiting to join them. Surely there would be another boat. But they were told this vessel was merely the one that would take them all to a much larger boat which was further out to sea.

It began to rain as the people crowded aboard; men, women and children of all ages from Iraq, Afghanistan and Iran. Women and children were crying, their men trying to calm them, as hundreds of people were squeezed into every space, in the cabin and on top of it, down in the hold, hanging over the sides. In the bottom of the boat were women and children. Men and their families stayed together, up in the open air.

When at last the boat with no name was full, the engine sputtered and the journey began.

After only an hour the boat approached some islands in the dark, and a few dozen of the passengers climbed from the boat. It looked too dangerous, they said. They'd rather take their chances fighting local authorities than the sea. Amal wanted to leave too. Her good sense told her this boat wasn't safe. But then she thought of her husband, and the awful life that had pursued her to here. She had to stay. It would only be a few nervous hours.

It began to rain and one male passenger began to make noise, demanding the captain of the boat turn back, or else they would all be drowned. But others became angry with him, and began collecting more money for the captain to convince him to continue. The captain declared the boat safe, and said they would go on.

The boat lurched through the ocean and rain with its cramped human freight, and for a time it felt as if they just might make it after all. Children pointed at a school of dolphins playfully racing the boat. For just one moment the ocean did not seem an enemy at all, but a friendly bridge to another life. People began to relax and talk of the lives that awaited them, and those they'd left behind, now gone beyond the horizon, which could no longer be seen for the rain that joined the sea and the sky as one great curtain of grey.

It was afternoon when someone shouted out that they were now in international waters. Then the engine stopped. There was frantic movement and shouting in the cabin. Men began to climb over others and head toward the back of the boat. Something was wrong. People covered their mouths and noses as the acrid smell of petrol mixed with the stink of seasickness. The engine was heard to cough, and again, but it refused to start. The motor had been drowned by the rain, they said. So long as it was started, everything would be all right. A crowded, unseaworthy boat will survive so long as it moves through the water. But they couldn't remain still like this. They would surely sink.

As if hearing this the sea began to heave, the waves becoming larger, longer, angrier, tilting the boat dangerously as they passed underneath. Children cried. All around, men began to look worried. The anxiety of more than 400 people alone on the sea bred its own sound, its own smell. Even the boat beneath them began to groan, like an old dog too frightened to do anything but lay down and die.

After an hour people began to say they were taking on water. For the first time, Amal noticed the boat sat deeper in the sea. They were sinking. Men began to bail water with buckets, then other men with their hands, fighting in vain against the ocean and the rain. A member of the crew shouted out that everyone must throw their luggage overboard. Hearing this, Amal became weak with fear. Their situation was obviously desperate. People were praying, reading aloud the Qur'an. A man who was fixing the engine clamoured over the other people to hug his little daughter, who was crying out for him, before returning to help with the engine. As the water rose underneath their feet, people began to scramble from one side of the boat to the other, trying to escape the creep of the sea, the boat tilting after them as they moved to one side, then another.

Amal looked up for her son who was sitting on top of the cabin with other boys. The boat listed sharply, and everybody screamed. Amal waited for it to roll the other way, but it never seemed to happen. Suddenly the crowd on the boat toppled over, like rubbish tipped from the back of a truck. For a moment the screaming stopped.

Amal was under water. When she came to the surface, the screaming was different. It was everyone – men, women, children, screaming in the water for their lives. The boat had gone under, and lurched again to the surface like some living creature. Pieces were falling from it, and for a moment Amal wondered how they'd fix it, so that they'd all climb aboard and be safe again. Then she watched as the boat rolled onto its side and sank, pulled below by the hand of God. She shook with dread as she realised their bond to the world in which people lived had just disappeared.

The cries of hundreds were piercing as people thrashed and panicked and drowned in the middle of the Indian Ocean. Children screamed for their mothers, their cries cut short as they choked on the oily sea that poured into their throats. Mothers wailed for their sons and daughters. Men cried out desperately for their wives. Others grabbed at the children of others and pushed them under, trying to stay afloat.

Amal took hold of a life jacket that floated by. A dead woman was inside of it. She held on, the waves lifting little scenes of horror into view before sending them away behind walls of water and sheets of rain: a man underwater lifting a child over his head. Something white spilling out of the nose of a crying boy. Women clutching onto their dead children, crying, or to strangers who struggled to escape. So many bodies, distraught men turning them over to look at their faces before crying on to the next. The fuel creeping in the water. People calling to God, vomiting, sinking into the deep. Faces rising to the surface, eyes and mouths wide, before retreating to the darkness below. A hand belonging to no one. A friend, holding onto a piece of wood, struggling to keep the bodies of all her pretty children floating around her. A father kissing a cheek, sobbing, before throwing himself under in despair. The dead eyes open to the rain. Hands clutching at timber, at bodies, at sky. A woman floating by, her baby attached by an umbilical cord.

Amal's son appeared at her side. He took the life jacket from the dead woman and helped his mother to put it on. She would survive for longer that way. They were both going to die, he told her. She said no, tried to keep his spirits up. He asked her to swim near him, so he could kiss her one last time. She pulled him to her, and he kissed her. Then the waves became stronger, and ripped him from her grasp. He cried out that he loved her, and would see her in paradise. Then he disappeared.

Amal saw Alia in the water, hysterical, her new baby dead in front of her. Alia vanished, but the baby drifted toward Amal, as if reaching out for the one who'd delivered him. She kept wishing him away, but the baby kept coming, drifting closer, needing her touch. She could stand no more and pushed him away and held on to the dead woman who floated with her, like a friend.

The cries became fewer as the sea silenced those who could not swim, or who hadn't taken hold of a buoyant thing – a body, a life jacket, a piece of wood. Where once they had been a mob suffering together, they were now spread apart, and cries that rose and fell with the waves seemed to come from far away. The rain kept falling on the ocean, bodies drifting into sight, then vanishing into a mist of grey. An eerie silence fell – a silence but for the thunder of the sea.

As night began to fall, Amal became thirsty. She could hear others crying out for water, and she saw some drinking from the sea. Every now and then she would feel a stranger's touch, and turn only to find that it came from the dead, their lifeless bodies floating away as if in search of the ones who loved them. Sometimes they seemed only to be sleeping.

The fuel and saltwater was making her ill and weak. But she held to the woman who had given her the life jacket. She kept thanking her, and promised not to forget her.

Fish began to bite at her legs. The cries of others became so distant. Amal was alone in the cold, dark sea. There was no moon and no stars, no difference between the sky and the ocean.

Through the long night, Amal drifted in and out of the world, both within and somewhere without time, her mind like a camera taking snapshots of a world that was water and waves and rain and death. She saw sharks circling, and she prayed for it to end quickly. A whale rose up beside her, as big as a house, spouting water high into the air that rained down on the ocean around her. She wondered if she was delirious. She clung to the dead woman, her only reminder of reality.

She saw lights in the distance, and could hear others calling out to them. She found other survivors in the dark, clinging to pieces of wood. Together they kicked toward the lights. They came close enough to see that the lights belonged to three boats. They heard their horns blow. They heard distant voices speaking a language they couldn't understand. Amal and her friends cried out to the voices but the lights and the boats and the voices drifted away.

As dawn broke on the ocean Amal was alone again. She had drifted in and out of consciousness. She was so tired, so thirsty. She had lost her boy. She clung to the woman. There was nothing else to do.

Suddenly a boat was there – a fishing boat. Someone jumped into the ocean to help her aboard. Amal clung to the body of the woman who had saved her life. She didn't want to let go, but she knew she must. She kissed her, thanked her again, and said goodbye.

On board the boat were a few dozen others, some of whom said they had seen Amal's son, alive, clinging to a piece of wood. Amal begged the captain of the boat to keep searching. Bodies and jetsam floated by. An hour passed. Then, miraculously, they found Rami. He was alive. When he was hauled aboard, Amal held him close, too terrified to let him go. For two days they wandered the ocean in the fishing boat, looking for others who might have survived.

When at last the survivors arrived safely back in Jakarta, they wept as they told of what they'd been through, and what they had seen. Fawzi Qasim had lost a brother and two of his children, drowned when the boast had capsized. Through the night he had held his other two children on his shoulders. One had died in the morning of thirst. Zaynab Alrimahi watched her six-year-old brother clinging to a plank, crying as he choked to death on seawater and fuel. Faris Kha Dem went to save his wife, then heard his daughter shouting for him. His wife told him to leave her, to save their daughter first. He swam to his daughter, who was being tossed in the waves. She shouted out for him once more, but water went into her mouth as she tried to call his name. He watched her sink beneath the sea. When he turned back to his wife, she, too, was gone.

Rokaya Satar had boarded the boat in Bandar Lampung with her husband and two daughters, aged five and two. When the boat had first listed, Rokaya's elder daughter had slipped into the water, her mother holding fast to her arms, until another desperate woman had stood on her child's head and pushed her below. Rokaya fell into the ocean clutching her two-year-old, but the same desperate woman, who could not swim, climbed upon them as if they were an island, pushing them under. When Rokaya came to the surface she found her husband, but both her daughters were gone. They cried out for the children but there were so many bodies, so much screaming. When they found their daughters both floating, their dead eyes open to the sky, Rokaya's husband began to choke with grief. He said sorry to his wife – he had brought her to this and he could not bear to watch her die, too – and disappeared into the sea. Rokaya saw the body of the desperate woman, her own lifeless children still clutching onto their mother, and drifted with them, like family, until the rescuers came.

Abu Muslim had seen a couple holding each other while in the water, crying, asking each other for forgiveness before they died. Hassan Jassem, from Basra, lost his wife and three children. He had known something would happen long ago. He kept coming home and kissing his children in their beds, knowing that, somehow, it could not last forever. He hadn't known what had given him that feeling. Now he knew. All through the night, dead people kept rising from the deep, tucking themselves under his arms like loveless children.

Amal's voyage to Australia continued. She was forced to wait in Jakarta while her application for a temporary protection visa to Australia was considered. At nights she dreamed she was asleep in the ocean, or stepping into a room where the dead were waiting. All she wanted was to be with her husband. In June, 2002, nearly eight months after the sinking, she was finally allowed to enter Australia, and Amal and Rami were at last reunited with Abbas Akram in Melbourne. It was a reunion tinged with pain and apprehension – a horrible thing had happened, and there was still a chance they would be denied the right to remain in Australia permanently.

The wheels of bureaucracy turned slowly and by 2005 Amal had almost lost hope. The life in Australia of which she had dreamed, and had nearly killed herself to reach, seemed to be wishing her away. Every morning she woke with the worry that she might be deported back to Iraq. She felt she didn't belong, here or anywhere at all. She became so depressed she fell sick, despondent, her husband and son seeming distant to her, as far away as they had been on that night when she was alone in the ocean.

But then, in May of 2005, came the news that Amal, Rami and Abbas Akram had been granted permanent residency in Australia. Their long journey to freedom was over.

One year later, on 18 March, 2006, Amal Hassan Basry died of breast cancer. She was fifty-two.

A GRIM FATHER'S TALE

Parenthood is one of the great incommunicable experiences, and so should it be, for nobody cares about a child quite like its parents – a fact of which many a mother and father seem painfully unaware. An American writer named Kent Nerburn described the encounter of fatherhood thus: 'Until you have a son of your own,' he wrote, 'you will never know the joy, the love beyond the feeling that resonates in the heart of a father as he looks upon his son ... And you will never know the heartbreak of the fathers who are haunted by the personal demons that keep them from being the men they want their sons to be.'

It's worth thinking about as you read the following account of a short life, a life about which very little is spoken ...

When the father received the call in October of 1992 to tell him that his boy had been seriously injured in a car accident, he wondered if this might not be the dreadful moment that everyone had been predicting for years. His boy had been troubled for the whole of his life, prone to falls from grace and fits of recklessness. For many years they had said there was no hope in this life for one so emotionally disabled, society being so full of perils that crush the weak so easily. The father had never believed them. His little boy, he had told them, was like an oak tree that would grow strong with age, and would learn to stand against the wreckers in the modern world. But things were different now and perhaps those people – the school teachers and the child psychologists, the gossips and the prying neighbours – had been right all along.

When he saw his boy in the hospital, unconscious and in traction like a fish on a wire, his heart sank to his gut. The boy had been in hospital once before, at the age of ten, when a firecracker blew up in his hand, but this was serious – his boy had suffered head injuries, his body battered and fractured at the ribs and the vertebrae. Perhaps now there really was no hope. It seemed so long since there had been any hope at all.

The father had worked on the wharves when his boy was born in 1967, in the same month of the Australian referendum that first recognised the constitutional rights of the Aboriginal people. It was going to be a better world. His wife and he were still in love. It was a hopeful time for a charming life.

Fatherhood changes all men, and it changed this man forever. The world became twice as beautiful and twice as frightening at once, the fears that whipped the man in his life now lashes that he felt upon the child's back, too. He wondered if more than just the physical features – the woof of his voice, the colour of his hair, the expressions he wore upon his face – might not be the only likenesses passed from father to son, but the weaknesses and foibles also, channelled down in a genetic string over which no one has control. The father was a quiet man, who thought dark thoughts like other quiet men. Might such shadows of the heart be passed on as scars that now live in the father's boy? These are the questions all fathers ask, and so it was with this man and his child, from the very first day until the bitter end and beyond.

The man nursed his boy as a babe, watched him grow – fed him, clothed him, wondered at the softness of his skin and the precious mechanics of his tiny hands that could do so little yet would do so much. At nights he would peep into his room, constantly, to see that nothing had happened to him in his sleep, or simply to examine the little boy's dreams. It all seemed so fragile – the helplessness of the child as he struggled to eat, to stand, to pound along the floor on hand and knee. That people in the street had a smile for the boy as he passed by in the stroller, or in his father's arms, was a joy he knew would fade. How strange it is that life, as it grows, becomes less precious in the eyes of the world.

At first the boy seemed a fast learner – he stood and walked before other children do, and he seemed to recognise things and people when they appeared on the television. But by the time the boy was in pre-school, he was showing signs of slowing down. Those who cared for him at this time seemed to find him difficult to manage – he was demanding and did not play well with the other children. His teachers had words with his mother and father – perhaps, they suggested, their child had special needs. The father found this a trifle melodramatic. He was just a child, and children should not be judged by the rule and rigours of adults, not until they are old enough to know better.

But when the boy entered kindergarten, in a large school with many pupils, it became clear that something was not right. His teachers insisted he was aggressive, and destructive with property belonging to others. He didn't seem to have any awareness of the other children around him, unless they were getting on his nerves. The teachers suggested he was socially backward and academically slow. They strongly recommended that his parents take him to see a child psychologist. Perhaps he was autistic, or something more serious. The father still thought it all an over-reaction, but he reluctantly agreed.

And so the boy was only six years old when he saw his first psychiatrist, who recommended that he be sent to a school for children with learning disabilities. They were saying that he wouldn't make it in society, that his mind was too divorced from the physical world, from the other children with whom he wouldn't play, or would, until he hurt them and they went away.

At eight years old it became obvious that he had major speech problems – some words in the language seemed completely beyond him, no matter how hard he tried to understand them. His emotional troubles and learning disabilities appeared to give rise to violent, frustrated outbursts that would steam from nothing as the boy raged against a world that made him struggle. The only joy he seemed to derive from school, said his teachers, were those moments when misfortune fell upon others.

The boy was transferred to a school well equipped to deal with children with developmental problems. The teachers believed him to be hyperactive, and the boy was placed on a special diet and medication the specialists believed might help. But things did not improve – they got worse. He ached through the days with no friends and no apparent dreams that anyone could see. His temper grew worse – he spat in the face of a girl in class, urinated upon another. He was caught torturing a cat, twisting its leg until the animal cried out. The teachers didn't like him; that was clear from the hostile comments they made on his school reports. They were doing their best. But schools aren't built to save troubled souls. They are factories designed to mould girls and boys into women and men fit for organised society. They have not the time nor the apparatus to dwell upon the broken ones. This boy was different, too sensitive for the machine.

The man asked his boy to say what was wrong in his world, and he replied that it was the other children, not himself, who were the trouble. They teased him relentlessly, he said, called him stupid and made fun of his voice. He cried and said he didn't want to go to school. He didn't want to face his tormenters any more. He wanted to stay home with his father, and live amongst people who loved him. The man felt for him. He didn't care about the other children – they were nurtured and loved by the world in which they thrived. His boy was special to him, and he would love him no matter which road he walked, whichever dark door he would choose to open. Any loving father would be the same.

But the boy now had a younger sister – a dream child, compared to her brother. She was happy, well-adjusted, needed no special care. Her brother became jealous of her, and sometimes that resentment took an ugly turn, the boy teasing her until she cried through the night. The father wondered what had gone so wrong with his boy, and what role he himself had played in its making.

He determined to try to stay close to his son, began taking him fishing, which the boy seemed to enjoy. Fishing was something that all men could do, young and old, rich or poor, wise or foolish. The look on his boy's face when he caught a fish made all the troubles disappear. One day, the boy would grow away from his father, as all boys do. But these would be times they'd remember forever, on a boat in the lake, with no troubled teachers or prying psychiatrists, or the people in the world who judge others against themselves. From a distance they were nothing more than a father and son, on the water beneath them that ran deep with wonders no man can see.

The man and his wife separated when the boy was just a young teenager and, like all men going through such things, the father worried as to how it might affect his children. But by now the boy had become involved with a girl of his own, an older woman who lived at a farmhouse nearby, and whom the boy said treated him well, like nobody ever had before. The boy had met her while doing odd jobs, and had come to help her regularly with her invalid mother. The father decided he must meet this older woman, and at first he was suspicious – she was so much older, almost like a mother to him, short and stocky, with a temperament like a military man. The father wondered what her interest might be in his boy. But theirs was a purely platonic relationship, built on friendship and a love of like things: animals, outings, life in the country. And she did have money, with which she appeared to spoil the boy rotten. Perhaps this was just what he needed – a friend, but not one who might fight for attention, like one of his own age. Someone older, wiser, from whom he might learn. She did seem to take a firm hand with him.

In the summer, the father accompanied the pair on a trip to New Zealand, during which his boy seemed relaxed and happier than he'd been in years. The father let his fears about the woman go. She was good for his son, he decided. He had best not interfere.

When the older woman's invalid mother died, the boy moved in with her, and became like a son. He helped her care for the animals on the farm – the miniature ponies and pigs, the ducks and the cats – and he followed the woman wherever she went, content to live her life instead of his own. The boy and the older woman began to become notable fixtures in the town where they lived. They were often seen driving the country roads in her car, or riding ponies together in the country fields. They shopped together, running the woman's errands, and the boy became known to her friends and associates. Most of them liked him – he was polite and well spoken, would stand in the background as the older woman went about her business. Some thought he seemed lonely, a lost child in an older woman's world. Others found him quietly amusing – an eccentric, of sorts, like his older friend, who wandered about with notes fluttering from her purse, buying mundane items in great numbers, her purchases always coming to $100 or more. She told one sales assistant that she was a friend of Rock Hudson, with whom she communicated on a regular basis. The young boy, on the other hand, liked the music of Cliff Richard and his favourite movie was *The Lion King*. They were an odd couple, to be sure. But odd couples make the world spin, moreso than those who seamlessly fit together, no trouble to the universe at all.

For the boy's birthday one year, the older woman shouted him a night at a grand hotel in the nearest city, showering him with gifts, spending hundreds of dollars on him, making him feel the day he came into the world was a very special one indeed. She also paid his fees for a course at nearby learning institution, so the young boy could get himself an adult education. When he told his father, they were both so happy they jumped up and down on the spot together. Life seemed to have finally turned out for the better, the boy having landed on his feet at last.

Then one night in 1992, on their way home from an outing, their car collided with another on a lonely country road. The older woman was killed instantly, and the boy left in hospital, in a coma, with head injuries that might stay with him for life. His salvation, it seemed, had come to an abrupt end.

As the father looked down at the prone and battered figure of his boy in the hospital bed, he knew that he had to come back into his life again. The boy had lost his only other friend, the one who had been like an anchor for him, who had turned him from a troubled child in a difficult world to a young man who flourished in the country. But when he learned that the woman had bequeathed her estate to the boy, he became anxious. His boy wouldn't know how to cope on the farm by himself. He'd be alone again, his thoughts left to wander to places where perhaps they ought not. He remembered the words a psychologist had once spoken, when he said it would be unsafe and unwise to remove the father's influence from the boy's world. He resolved to move into the farm with his boy and to take charge of his life. They could return to how things had been when the boy was a child, and they had gone fishing together. They could start again, by returning to the life that had once been enjoyable for them both.

While his boy was still recovering in hospital, the father retired from his job, moved into the farmhouse and began to attend to his son's future affairs. He sold off many of the animals, which he found to be in an unhealthy state. He reshaped the garden and painted the interior, which was mouldy and unkempt. He visited his boy daily in hospital, informing him of what he was doing. The boy seemed comfortable with the arrangement.

While the father was acquainting himself with the farm, however, rumours were whispered in the neighbouring estates. The boy had killed the woman deliberately, they were saying, and his friendship with her had been all about money. A nearby couple had once been passengers in the car when they'd seen the boy reach over and impulsively grab the steering wheel from his elder companion, almost causing an accident. In fact, since the boy had moved in with her, she had been involved in three motor vehicle accidents which seemed to have happened with no explanation – the car running into a ditch, or into a tree by the side of the road. The rumours were saying that, this time, the boy's habit of grabbing for the steering wheel had resulted in the woman's death.

To the father, of course, such a scenario was absurd. His own boy had nearly been killed, and he knew that his son had cared more for the woman than he did for her money. She had provided him with a life that was good because she was in it. There had been no reason for him to wish her away.

After several months of convalescence, the boy returned to the farm that was now his home, and to his father who was, once again, his closest companion. It cannot be known what they spoke about during that time – the sadness of the loss, perhaps, or the accident and how it occurred. Did he reveal to his father some dreadful secret, some answer to a riddle best left unsolved? Did the father realise something in his last days with his son, something that darkened his own life beyond all chance of light?

Telling nobody at all of what he was doing, the father busily planned for his own absence: altering his bank accounts so that his boy could access them, and organising for his son to be placed in the care of a trustee. Then, one morning in 1993, for reasons we will never know, Maurice Bryant tied a set of diver's weights to his waist, waded into a dam on the farm and slipped himself under the surface. It was a quiet man's death – his suicide note, left pinned to the wall of a barn, read simply: 'Call the police'.

The two people who had meant the most to him now gone, young Martin was alone.

THE CHOSEN ONES

The small town of Grafton in northern New South Wales is notable for its jacaranda trees, the blanket of purple flowers that falls gently on the streets and cars and lawns every spring investing the town with a prettiness rarely seen outside of Walt Disney's world. When Grafton is in full radiant bloom, it's enough to make one feel slightly mad, as if the machines and gutters of civilization have been defeated at last by an icing of love. None of this explains why the lords of the colony felt it necessary to construct one of the nation's strongest jails here, the Grafton Correctional Centre having housed some of the land's least trustworthy souls since its grand opening in 1893.

But petals and prisoners are not all that grow in Grafton's garden – in 1845, Dr Francis Campbell, a Belfast-born physician who distinguished himself as a tireless reformer of the nation's lunatic asylums, conducted extracurricular experiments that determined the loamy soils of the northern rivers region provided an ideal climate for the cultivation of hemp, and his notes on the matter can still be viewed in the National Library of Australia. Today, Grafton is the southerner's gateway to a hundred miles of purple haze that ends at Murwillumbah on the Queensland border. It is through such clouds that we must peer to witness the beginnings of a strange little performance that boasts so much more than its international cast . . .

It was early on the evening of 16 March, 1996, when Scott and Wendy Longley strapped their two children into their HQ Holden sedan and began the long trip home to Grafton. They had been visiting friends in Lismore, where they had spent the day shooting the breeze while their two-year-old son and his one-year-old sister had frolicked under the broad blue sky.

On their way out of town, they were lured to the drive-through of the local Hungry Jack's fast food restaurant, stopping in the car park to devour the burgers and fries and drinks of assorted effervescence. Why 38-year-old Scott and the wife eleven years his junior were so hungry after leaving the company of friends is a question upon which we can only speculate, and nor do we know what they spoke of as they dined that evening; the financial strain of living, the monotony of life in the country, the popular TV show *The X-Files*, which was enjoying its second season on the local network. Perhaps, just for a moment, they considered the smooth shapes of the burgers in their hands and, how, when viewed from a certain angle, they appeared as flying saucers might. Though possible, it is highly unlikely they fiddled their fries into shapes and symbols, like letters or numbers – dollar signs, even. We can know none of these things. All we do know is what Scott and Wendy told us happened next.

The family car was a few minutes shy of Casino when Scott spied the lights in his rear view mirror. They were yellow with an aura of white, and they'd seemed to come from nowhere. Presuming they belonged to an off-road vehicle the likes of which he was simply not familiar, Scott returned his attention to the road ahead. But the lights came closer, bearing soundlessly down upon the family car with great speed. Scott watched in alarm as the two lights merged together as one, then vanished into the blackness beyond.

In the passenger seat, Wendy was silently engrossed by the greenish white lights that danced along the road in front of them – hundreds of little stars that had fallen to make way for the Longleys, and were now keeping pace as dolphins under the bow of a boat. Wendy watched them, dazzled, for just a few seconds, and then they disappeared.

Wendy asked Scott if he'd seen them, too, but he had not. Nor had Wendy seen the vehicle behind with the headlights that had strangely merged into one. The mysteries of the lights stole their thoughts as their vehicle lumbered in and out of Casino, their children asleep in the back seat, oblivious to all that had occurred.

It was late when the Longleys at last pulled into the drive at the Grafton home and ferried the children to their beds. Wendy was perplexed when she looked at the clock – it was 9.30 pm, much later than they had expected to reach their destination. Somehow, it seemed, they'd lost an hour. Perhaps they had spent more time in Lismore than they'd thought, munching on burgers and fries. The problem seemed to trouble Wendy, who remained awake until midnight, many hours past her usual bedtime. Scott, too, found it difficult to sleep, sitting up on the couch until the early morning hours. He paid no mind to the follies that babbled on the television in front of him, but simply sat, mesmerised by the shapes that flickered in front of his eyes. Once or twice, he was snapped from his torpor by a voice he thought was shouting his name, but each time it turned out to be nothing.

At daybreak, unsure of whether he had slept or simply drifted, Scott roused himself for the morning run he had taken nearly every day for a quarter of a century. He had been jogging for only a few moments when he felt a sharp pain inside his left nostril, as if made by a hypodermic needle. He stopped and felt for blood, but there was none, and the feeling ceased after just a few moments. About halfway through his regular route, Scott became aware of a pain inside his shoe. He stopped and removed the shoe to find a blister developing on his right big toe. It occurred to him that, despite all his years of athletic exertion, he had never been troubled by such a thing before. He also appeared to be harvesting a frightful measure of nasal mucus which, once again, was unusual for him. Distressed and irritated, Scott abandoned his exercise and returned home, where he found Wendy and the children all suffering from colds, his son's nasal mucus like vines, while Wendy complained of a pain in her ovaries and a feeling of soreness down the left side of her throat.

In the weeks that followed it became clear to Scott and Wendy that something wicked had infected their universe. Both began to see strange shapes materialising in front of their eyes – black dots, white blobs and weird blind spots that came and went with the light. Sounds occurred from unseen machines and angry shouts from unknown voices pierced the night. Scott began to have dreadful waking visions, of aircraft crashes and sinking ships, body parts scattered over green fields and men in hard hats digging graves for corpses whose clothes were wet with blood. He'd lie awake for hours watching images played on walls or ceilings, or lighting up the dark inside the curtain of his own closed eye – shapes and scenes and information, an encyclopaedia of unknown history so vast he couldn't possibly recall it. When he did sleep, Scott would often dream of stars that came and went as he visited them in the cold of space, and he'd hear a voice, clear and close, telling him of dates and times and places, the meanings of them not at all clear. By day, he found he could walk the streets and know the general moods of strangers simply by looking in their faces. One night, as he sat in front of the television, he heard what he thought was Wendy in the kitchen, opening cupboards and turning taps. But by the time he had risen to investigate, the kitchen was empty and his wife was in bed.

Wendy became so disturbed by Scott's behaviour that she did what any loving wife would do. She picked up the local phone book and called the resident UFO expert.

Visitors from outer space are not unknown to Australian folklore. Indigenous Australians speak of the Wandjina, God-like creatures that descended from the stars of the Milky Way to spend the Dreamtime coaching earth people in the ways of the universe. Evidently terrible teachers, the Wandjina departed leaving no examples of their cleverness, nor instructions on how to manufacture so much as a prehistoric go-cart, let alone space ships in which we might tour the stars as they did. But ancient cave paintings in the Kimberley region of northern West Australia show the Wandjina as creatures with large heads, no mouths, big dark eyes and curiously futuristic garments, a radioactive glow depicted as emanating from their heads always. It is impossible to look upon these ancient drawings and not wonder.

In July of 1868, a surveyor was invited by floating beings to enter an 'ark' that had landed at nearby Parramatta Park in Sydney's west, and so began a national history of modern 'close encounters' that hit high gear in the 1950s, when flying saucers were all the rage thanks to motion pictures and Cold War science fiction. The beings at the centre of such events rarely varied from those depicted on the walls of the Kimberley caves: large black eyes, small or no mouth, silver suit, the telepathic timbre – a disappointing uniformity from a universe presumably teeming with life, the same cosmos that blessed earth with everything from mosquito to woolly mammoth. Unvarying, too, was the demeanour. Far from the evil aliens born in the mind of H. G. Wells, intergalactic visitors to Australia were almost without fail, courteous, almost fawning in their curiosity, the occasional prick or probe of a nether region a regrettable consequence of some awkward examination that simply had to be done.

That the celestial visitors routinely preferred to study those from the lower echelons of society is a fact not simply known to Australia but peculiar, it seems, to the entire planet, abductee statements often purring with implications pertaining to the general superiority of the chosen specimen – a quality so radiant as to be perceived by beings from other worlds, but consistently at odds with how the sample appears to be valued by its own species.

In 1994, a New South Wales woman came forward with an alien visitation tale that spanned three decades. It began when the woman was but a young girl, on a night when grey, bug-eyed beings in electric blue jumpsuits appeared in her bedroom for a telepathic chat. Similar visits continued over time until the woman was middle aged. On this last occasion, the woman was spirited to a nearby space ship for the obligatory adventures in deep gynaecology, under the watchful eyes of two statuesque male aliens, both charming and keen, and one comparatively dumpy female who appeared to be troubled by something like jealousy. Telepathically the males communicated their harmless intentions as they probed at the woman for several hours, the female taking no part in proceedings as she raged from one end of the saucer to the other. The males explained that they were simply taking some eggs from the woman's ovaries. The woman protested, but the aliens were persuasive. Apparently they were from a doomed planet whose decadent civilization had all but destroyed their own species, and her eggs would repopulate their world. They had chosen her especially for, throughout the whole of the universe, hers were the finest living qualities they had ever encountered. Before departing they urged her to trumpet their story to the world, lest her civilisation suffer the same fate as their own. The fools of planet earth were less than moved, only Melbourne tabloid *The Truth* showing the slightest faith in the woman's story, publishing it under the headline: 'Aliens Poached My Eggs!'.

For the experts, Scott and Wendy's story was intriguing, but it was next to useless without more information. Something had clearly happened to them on the road from Lismore to Casino and, to find out exactly what, the couple needed to undergo hypnosis, a dreamlike state from which the truth would surely be coaxed out of hiding. The Longleys were wary, but something had to be done, for Scott was getting worse. For the first time in years he had stopped running, and was watching an awful lot of television. Twice he had lost his watch, the first time finding it under the lounge, and then on the floor in the bedroom. And whenever the telephone rang, he would loudly declare that he had a rough idea of who it might be on the other end.

It was Scott who first volunteered to take the plunge, visiting a local Grafton hypnotist and allowing her to reduce him to a mumbling stupor. As the fascinated hypnotist took notes, Scott revealed aloud what he saw . . .

He was hovering over the family vehicle, which was parked by the side of the road. Looking down from a vantage above the road, he could see himself asleep in the driver's seat, with Wendy dozing to his left, their baby daughter asleep in the rear seat, belted in, and their little boy, still strapped in his baby seat, apparently wide awake. Scott watched helplessly as two alien creatures approached the vehicle from the nearby bushes. They were tall and grey with skin like snakes, tiny ears, small mouths and huge eyes as black as coal.

They approached Scott first, undoing his seat belt and lifting him out of the car. Scott was anxious, but not terrified – something told him he was not in grave danger. The aliens held him there for a time, as if unsure as to what they might do with him. Then two more aliens approached Wendy's door, opened it, carefully undid her seatbelt, carried her from the vehicle and stood nearby with similarly pregnant purpose. Meanwhile, a much smaller alien appeared and opened the back door behind which their daughter was sleeping. There followed some moments of confusion as it appeared this small alien was having trouble releasing the latch on the harness, but another alien appeared to render assistance, and soon both the baby and Wendy were being carried into a nearby field. From his position in the back of the vehicle, the little boy appeared to observe the happenings with no obvious signs of distress.

Scott was carried to the rear of the vehicle and placed face down upon the ground. One of the aliens then lifted Scott's forehead while another appeared with what looked like a supermarket pricing gun. As Scott watched from above, he saw the aliens press this machine into his neck, where it performed a soundless operation of unknown purpose. They then inserted something into Scott's right big toe, where the blister would later appear, after which they rolled him onto his back, pulled up his shirt and observed his abdomen.

At this point, Scott began to feel himself drifting down from his position above the vehicle, until he had merged with the vision of himself that lay upon the ground. He felt his own body return to within his power, whereupon he rose and stood to his full height. As Scott viewed the scene around him, he saw the aliens returning Wendy and the baby to the vehicle, being careful to latch their seatbelts as they placed them inside. In a field just a short distance away, he saw his son laughing and frolicking with an alien of compatible age and size. He turned to see one tall, gentle alien bend down through the door of the vehicle and plant a loving kiss on Wendy's cheek. Lounging casually against the boot of his car, Scott, politely but firmly, asked the aliens what the Dickens was going on.

They explained to him that they meant no harm, but had simply come to take samples for the purposes of study. The creatures spoke highly of the Longley family, expressing admiration for Scott's general outlook on life and his propensity for acts of kindness toward his neighbours. No sooner had Scott returned the compliment when he saw that the nearby field was suddenly full of all manner of aliens. He then noticed the spaceship, huge and coloured in gunmetal grey, hovering just above their heads.

The aliens announced their intention to take Scott alone onto the spaceship for further examinations. Scott protested, but the words had no sooner left his lips when he found himself naked on some manner of table, a phalanx of aliens by his side, scrutinising every part of his physique. Bright lights shone into his eyes and a mechanical arm with claws upon it hovered threateningly above his loins. He cried out that he wished to go home and, suddenly, he was back in his car, his whole family where they had been before.

They silently drove back to Grafton and, after putting the children to bed, Scott was surprised to look out the window of his study and spy a small spacecraft with two aliens inside, hovering above the garden. Through the window, Scott was told not to worry – the aliens were simply making sure the Longleys had arrived home safely. Having ascertained that everything was all right, the aliens bade Scott a fond farewell and returned to their mothership.

The hypnotist, having heard enough, awoke Scott from his hypnosis and revealed to him the story as she had heard it. Scott was amazed, but not altogether surprised. This explained everything – the strange sights and sounds, the lost watch, the languid hours in front of the television – and he felt so much better about himself now that he knew the truth. At Scott's urging, Wendy agreed to undergo hypnosis, too, and it was no surprise when the story she spouted bore a remarkable similarity to Scott's, though her memory was somewhat more vague. She, too, recalled being laid on a table, which was surrounded by aliens in great numbers, for whom she confessed to feelings of affection that were undeniable. She had no recollection of any formal examination, nor the peck on the cheek which was witnessed by Scott, but she was sure the sore throat from which she had suffered had something to do with her time in the spaceship.

Scott and Wendy's friends took these new revelations at face value, as did the various UFO researchers who were now showing a keen interest in their story. Some saw parallels between the Longley's experience and that of Betty and Barney Hill, the American couple who became famous in the 1960s for an abduction tale of similar quality. Others recalled the family Lutz, whose experiences in a haunted house in Amityville had reaped a bestselling book and a movie deal with all the trimmings.

Desperate to build upon the details of his experience, Scott searched around for fresh hypnotists who might be accommodating, and it was after three more sessions under the swinging pocketwatch that Scott's story began to grow like a germ.

Scott now recalled that the aliens had inserted a metallic rod into his right eye. There was little pain but, as the rod was removed and Scott's eye was dabbed dry with tissue, the aliens told him that what they were to do next would cause him some discomfort. Scott winced as the rod entered his rectum and rummaged about inside his pelvis. This was not, he recalled, a nice feeling. When the rod was removed, the aliens drew Scott's attention to a nearby pyramid made of glass, on the inside of which slept two foetal aliens, small and pink, no bigger than mice. Telepathically, the aliens told Scott that, yes, he was the father.

It appeared that Scott's fathering of intergalactic children had not been some mere midnight accident. As he looked out the windows of the spaceship, he saw that they were flying along an earthly coastline, then through a town, down a familiar street. Finally the spacecraft stopped and hovered above the house where Scott had grown up as a child. He could see children playing in the yard, and Scott hopelessly tried to call out to them. It was then that he realised one of the children was himself, at the age of four. With the aliens, Scott had travelled back in time, and was witnessing something he'd long since forgotten.

He watched as the alien took young Scott into his father's shed and conducted an examination. With the formalities complete, the alien asked Scott if he wished to go for a ride in a spaceship, to which the young boy responded with much enthusiasm. He was then levitated into the craft, whereupon the driver – no doubt concerned about safety issues – treated Scott to a pitifully pint-sized exhibition of intergalactic locomotion, the spacecraft moving a mere few metres forwards then backwards, left then right, before Scott was deposited back in his yard and the alien craft disappeared into the clouds.

The craft from which Scott was observing these reveries then flew through space and time until reappearing when Scott was eight years old. Again Scott watched as a scene from his past was replayed for him – the spacecraft hovering in the boy's backyard as a ramp descended onto the lawn. The same alien who had previously visited appeared, and young Scott ran toward him, the alien patting the boy affectionately on the head as a tender reunion was enjoyed by all. Once again, the old shed was deemed well enough for the purposes of a brief examination, after which Scott pleaded for another ride in the spacecraft, perhaps one a little more daring than before. But the alien declared they were running late, and there was no time for such folly.

Once more, Scott flew through time and space and returned to when he was fourteen. He saw that, this time, his father was there, observing the spacecraft with open-mouthed shock. Perhaps due to Scott's father's presence, the aliens thought best to stay away from the shed and do business with Scott inside their own vehicle. After some hours inside, during which he enjoyed a variety of games with aliens around his own age, Scott was told that at last it was time to go. Reluctantly rejoining his father on earth, Scott remarked on the wonder of the experience as he watched the spaceship vanish into the sky. His father, as if nothing of it had happened, told him to stop being so stupid.

The media is a shrine for the guilty and the heroic, a courtroom for the desperate, and a billboard for hucksters with something to sell. For the ordinary man and woman, there is no good reason to wish for media attention. The novelty of seeing oneself on the screen, or under bold headlines in a magazine, is a thrill of which average Australia tired long ago. For while the world forgets the news of the day as each fresh broadcast erases the last, a foolish exhibition in the glare of the media is never lived down by the fool himself. Why Scott and Wendy Longley chose to risk stepping upon the national stage to tell their story is a question that only they can answer. What is certain is that, in the autumn of 1996, Scott and Wendy knew something the rest of the world did not.

With the help of their newfound friends in the paranormal community, the Longelys began making overtures to the press at large. The organs of quality were less than enthused, the networks and newspapers of Australia accustomed to the bearded spooks who'd loiter in the foyers, manila folders bursting with papers that tell of one fantastic frustration or other. The Longleys, it seemed, were of a similar class in the cynical eye of the Australian media. But just as Scott and Wendy had given up hope, the phone began to ring. A weekly journal called *Woman's Day*, the highest-selling magazine in the land, sent a reporter to interview the couple about their ordeal, a photographer snapping a portrait so that Australia could see the stars of this story with their very own eyes. A morning TV program flew them to Sydney to record the telling of their tale, to be aired the same week the magazine would be published. The mass media, it seemed certain, would follow.

On the eve of their media blitzkrieg, Scott must have pondered the possibilities – the book deals, the motion pictures, the fame and fortune here and abroad. His was a wild old yarn, for sure, and there were doubtless many who'd dismiss it all as the ravings of a madman. But this was Australia, a land colonised by criminals whose greatest hero had charged police with an iron can on his head. Australians had always shown a certain fondness for the eccentric and the strange. His and Wendy's experience might well become the talk of the entire nation. After all, winter was but weeks away, and Australia had not played host to a single big news story for the entirety of the year.

On 28 April, 1996, the day before the Longley's issue of *Women's Day* hit the stands, a boy called Martin Bryant walked into the Broad Arrow Café in Port Arthur, Tasmania and gunned down thirty-five men, women and children. For the next few months, the Australian media babbled about nothing else.

In Grafton nobody knows what happened to the Longleys, only that they moved away. Presumably they're still out there somewhere. Their story looked swell in *Woman's Day*, and also scored a dramatic run in the Australian UFO Abduction Study Centre Newsletter that June, but there the public record of Scott and Wendy Longley and their adventure appears to end. And nobody has ever come forward with a sensible explanation for why their stereo kept stopping and the family computer played up so much, or why it was that Scott stopped running after twenty-five years, and spent so much time staring at the television.

FRIDAY THE THIRTEENTH

Of all the depictions of the terror of bushfire, none can match for sheer enormity and drama William Strutt's Black Thursday, February 6th, 1851, *a monstrous 106.5 by 343 cm painting that hangs today in the Cowen Gallery at the State Library of Victoria. Though events upon the earth constitute but the lower third of the picture, there is no sky in Strutt's hellish panorama, the heavens swallowed by a hulking wave of dark, angry red that threatens to tumble on a population in full-blown retreat. The scene at the foot of the wave is bedlam: wild-eyed horses bolt over cattle and sheep and dogs that stumble in the dust; a kangaroo lies upon its back amongst the bones of creatures long dead from drought; a man on horseback gallops with his wife held like a baby to his breast, his mouth agape, his eyes thrown back in terror of the deadly colossus that pursues them; women and children flee on foot, their arms thrown to the universe. It's histrionic in the romantic style, but what it conveys most perfectly is the sense of suddenness, of a battle erupted so swiftly as to have taken all life by complete surprise.*

But the saddest moment of Strutt's imagining can be found in the lower right-hand corner of the picture, in a pile of belongings abandoned: blankets and boxes; a bird in a cage; a kettle; a rag doll; an open book; a single boot; and amongst them a string of rosary beads, left behind with the things no prayer can save. All these memories, Strutt seems to lament, will be burned when the chaos has passed over, and this clearly troubles him. It is doubtful that many Victorians had laid eyes on Black Thursday *before it was purchased from a South Australian owner by the Victorian Library in 1954. In any case, those who lived through the fires of 1939 had no need . . .*

At the Robinson house in Barongarook, about 80 kilometres west of Geelong in Victoria, the family dog had been acting strangely, dashing to Mary's feet and staring up at her, as if troubled by something, before running off to a distance and wailing at some imagined devil. Mary's husband, John, thought it might have to be shot. Then, as soon as it had started, the howling stopped.

The distant fires were no doubt the cause of it. The Robinsons had been watching the smoke for weeks as it drifted by in the sky throughout the early days of February, 1939. John, a woodcutter who worked at a nearby mill, had been returning home each evening with news of the fires that were burning steadily in the region. They'd heard of the much larger blazes to the east, and it was difficult to tell whether the smoke that lingered over their home hadn't drifted through the air from the Rubicon valley on the other side of the state. Reports told of the air in Melbourne streets being polluted with haze. Perhaps they had nothing to worry about.

On the morning of Friday the 13th, the house rose as normal at seven o'clock. The eldest son, Jack, went to work with his father, leaving Mary at home with the children; fourteen-year-old Teresa, twelve-year-old Mary, ten-year-old Vera, nine-year-old Paul, seven-year-old Jim, five-year-old Tom and Gloria, just seven months old. The older children went about their chores, Teresa and Mary going down to the well at the end of the property to wash laundry, as they did each morning. If their mother was anxious it didn't show. But as the morning aged, the wind came hot from the north, the occasional ember travelling across the sky like some messenger from hell.

At about ten o'clock, Mary looked out the window to see her husband and eldest son returning from the mill. John was looking worried, saying it looked bad. The family had no wireless radio that might have furnished them with reports of the blaze, which way it was going and how strong it might be. They sent the younger children down to fetch the girls from the well, and they all gathered together in the house and prepared for whatever fate would deliver them.

By eleven o'clock the smoke was becoming thicker, and the heat stifling. Though the children were anxious, John and Mary remained calm. They'd been through fire scares before and they knew there was no need to panic. It would probably turn, or perhaps the rain would come. There was nothing to gain from frightening the children.

They were standing outside the home, watching the smoke surge through the trees, when embers began raining on them from the haze above. The mood changed instantly, John herding the children into the house and stuffing cloth into cracks under doors. Through the windows, the scene changed as if in a motion picture, the smoke so thick, the strange glow from not just embers but mature, airborne flames. Through the smoke, they could see flames waving from the tops of the tallest trees. At ten minutes to midday, with the whoosh of a fireplace blown into life, the house ignited.

The air at the ceiling exploded, and when John went to open the door of the house he burned his hand on the doorknob. They had to escape. With Gloria in her arms, Mary used her hip to help John force the door, and at last the family staggered out into the open, where there was nothing to breathe but smoke and ash. In a single, crushing moment, Mary realised she and John and the young ones were doomed – she could not move quickly with Gloria and the littler children, and she knew John would stay by her side. Thoughts came to her in fractions of seconds, in the time it takes for a match to ignite. She shouted at the older children to run for their lives, hoping they might make the top of the road.

Mary, John, Jack and the two littlest boys lay down on a patch of ground in front of the house, Gloria pressed into the dirt under Mary's chest, the house an inferno behind them, the doorway through which they'd just passed now a wide open mouth that spewed black smoke and flame as everything inside – oil and food and clothes, all the children's toys, their tennis racquets and schoolbooks, and all the paper treasures from many lives lived – became fuel in a furnace that threatened to swallow them all. The iron and wood cracked and fell and, overhead, a canopy of flame swirled from the trees on every side of the clearing in which they lay.

Mary held tight to Gloria, holding her head into the dust, lest her little eyes burn. She felt the shoes burn from her feet. The atmosphere was itself igniting, the oxygen mixing with gases from incinerated eucalyptus trees to create a combustible air that could barely be breathed. John was screaming at the children to stay down, that they'd be all right if they just kept still and didn't move an inch, his shouted commands drowned out in the roar of the furnace that was all around, and the terrible sound of falling trees.

Birds on fire fell all around them. Rabbits and kangaroos came to die, their coats scorched, their necks and limbs swollen. It was as if their dreadful little homestead harboured all that was left of life from a burning world.

And what of the children? Mary thought. The others who'd made a dash for the road – had they made it to safety? Little Gloria was unconscious now, from the heat and dust. Mary prayed out loud that she might never have faith in God again if her precious lambs weren't saved. For three hours, the family lay flat on the grass as the fire consumed everything that stood or moved above them, the sky an eruption from waist high to the heavens, each incandescent cloud of smoke harbouring its own crimson fire that boiled from within.

Only when the bellow began to die, the cry and crack of exploding wood drifting into the distance, did John crawl to his knees. The fire had spared them. John had to go in search of the others, making Mary and the other children promise they would wait until he and Jack returned. Mary promised, but begged him to please hurry. Teresa, Mary, Vera, and Paul would be terrified, wherever they were, and would need to hear his voice and feel his protection.

John and Jack stumbled to where they thought the road would be found, but all familiar signs, all of nature's markers and tracks made by man, had vanished in the holocaust. They called out their names, and called again, and again, but there was no answer. Then they found the road, the lifeless tan of the dirt path now the most vibrant colour on a smoking landscape. They followed it toward the top of the hill – if the children had come this far, they would surely have made for higher ground. John and Jack's hopes swelled as they noticed the state of the thoroughfare, which looked as if it had not been touched by flame.

When they found them, they were lying together, side by side, Paul and Mary, Vera and Teresa. In the furnace, they had assumed the same positions in which they had always walked to school, two by two, descending by order of age – the same little arrangement that had ferried them safely all of their lives. There were no marks on their skin, no grimaces of pain. Just closed eyes and open mouths, sleeping children laid down on a summer's day.

John and Jack staggered over the ashes toward the place where their happy home had once been. They were both sobbing as they crawled to Mary, who instantly knew. There was nothing to say. They wept in agony, the little ones too. Nobody was scared any more. The broken have nothing to fear.

John went in search of the well, to get water for the miserable living. The track had gone, charred to the earth either side of it, and it took him an eternity to find the well on this alien hearth. When he found it, the water he drew from deep in the earth had boiled hot.

The baby and the young boys sucked the dirty water, but John and Mary were both too deadened with grief to feel thirst. They found Nigger on what was left of the verandah, the dog burned to ashes. They had not heard him cry. He had known all along.

After some time on the blackened floor of the clearing, they picked themselves up and began the long journey to safety, wherever that might be. When they came to the bodies of their four children, John covered them with an old burned coat. He and Mary could barely bring themselves to leave them behind – they both wished they could lie down and hold them, go with them to wherever they were. But they had to go on, for the little ones.

John walked ahead with no shoes on his feet, the heat of the road burning the skin from his heels, his sorrow killing the physical pain. Every now and then, he would stop and sway, fall backwards, a new bolt of heartbreak and shock, fresh from the last, making the muscles in his legs wither and slack, so that all that upheld him was bone. Mary wished for herself some dreadful disease that would shorten her days. But she kept moving, one step, then another, propelled by the last, and the terrible thoughts she had.

Much later, when life was tolerable again, John would tell Mary of when he went to the well, and how he had sat himself down on a log and wept. A tiger snake had come from the hearth, reared its head, and then slithered away, leaving in peace the most miserable creature on the earth.

THE ART THE
WORLD FORGOT

On the grassy slopes of Sydney's Domain, just behind the Art Gallery of New South Wales, one will find two enormous matches side by side, one burned to a tinder and its partner yet to be put to good use. Not to be lumped in with the Big Banana at Coffs Harbour, or the Big Pineapple on Queensland's Sunshine Coast – over-generously proportioned attractions for the amusement of passers-by – the 'Big Matches', as they are correctly identified by the plain people, are works of art, conceived by Brett Whiteley in 1968 and completed in 1991. They go by the mind-boggling title of 'Almost Once', just to prove there's something going on here besides two giant-sized versions of commonplace things. In what may or may not be a comment on the natural forces against which Australian modern art has always struggled, the Art Gallery of New South Wales regularly forks out for cleaners to hose lashings of bird poo off these colossal national treasures, an expenditure for which the ghost of Mr Whiteley is no doubt grateful. Think upon it as you read of this sad little band of castaways, shipped overseas and far from home, at the mercy of currents best described as stagnant, their cries for help heard by few, and acted upon by none . . .

One day in 1964, an American man in a red sports coat, pork-pie hat and wielding a silver walking cane waddled into an Adelaide gallery in search of a bit of Australian art. It was Harold Mertz, an affluent New Yorker of a quaint disposition, who'd made his fortune in the magazine subscription trade. Mertz was in Australia with his wife, LuEsther, on a holiday, the couple having just farewelled a decade of extreme highs and lows. Harold's Publisher's Clearing House had made him a millionaire by 1953 but, the following year, his only son, Peter, had been killed in a university initiation gone wrong, students abandoning the eighteen-year-old on a lonely road in Pennsylvania, to be mown down by a passing motorist who didn't see the boy in the dark.

Harold's initial plan was to find a few pieces to hang on the walls of his New York office – pieces that might excite his clients while relieving his ever-cumbersome tax burden – but the more he saw of Australian art the more enthused he became. As he toured the little gallery in Adelaide, the seed of an idea sprouted in his mind: to assemble the greatest collection of modern Australian artists that the world had ever seen, and to take such a collection to America, where Australian art was quite the unknown quantity.

Mertz was no connoisseur of art. He was, by his own admission, a magazine man, who could scarcely tell the difference between a masterpiece and a muddle, but he knew what he liked: money. He was convinced that a collection of contemporary Australian art – the Mertz Collection, as it would be hailed – would be received with excitement in the Americas, would make him more millions, bestow upon him a new reputation as a cultured man of the world, and go a great way toward diminishing his enormous tax bill. All he needed was someone to assemble such a collection, a man who might be blessed with a better eye than himself.

Mertz had come to the right place. The gallery in which he and LuEsther loitered belonged to Kym Bonython, an ex-bomber pilot whose interest in the world of art had made him an acquaintance of near every Australian artist of note or promise – Arthur Boyd, Charles Blackman, Lawrence Daws, Pro Hart, and a young Brett Whiteley, who was busy making a name for himself in London. It could be said that Kym Bonython had an uncanny sense for that which would become fashionable. Years earlier, Kym had extended Sidney Nolan a few thousand pounds to buy a Kombi van so as to tour the countryside of Europe, in return for five paintings of Kym's choosing plucked from Sidney's studio. One of the five was a strange sort of painting – a weird landscape portrait of bushranger Ned Kelly, depicted with an almost naïve simplicity. Kym couldn't say why he liked it, but he did, and he took it. In the late fifties, he had helped to finance the national tour of a young Victorian art student whose stage act seemed to consist of little more than a quaint impersonation of a housewife from the Melbourne suburb of Moonee Ponds. He and Barry Humphries had been good friends ever since.

When Harold Mertz explained his plan to Bonython, the young collector was at first a little wary. Kym's experience with Americans had not been good – he was still trying to extract money from Hollywood actor Raymond Burr, better known to the public as Perry Mason, who had purchased paintings from Bonython for the actor's Los Angeles studio and was taking his time paying for them. But when Mertz flopped out his cheque book all those fears disappeared. Expense, said Mertz, was not a concern. He was prepared to spend upwards of $100 000 for around fifty pictures, or as many as Bonython could get for the money – the best of contemporary Australian art that earnest American dollars could buy.

It had always been Bonython's dream to take Australian art to America, to build profiles for his friends in the land of plenty and exalt the reputation of modern Australian art abroad. He agreed to assist Mertz, being careful not to dissuade the American by pricing his services out of the bargain. He proposed a modest commission for himself, and Mertz appeared delighted. And then the little man in the pork-pie hat bade him farewell and continued on his way.

Few Australian artists in the sixties, no matter how skilful with brush or fertile in imagination, could have painted an American dollar bill with any accuracy, the greenback as rare in local art circles as accolades from abroad. Thus news of Mertz's money, and Bonython's mission so funded, spread through the Australian art community like a benevolent virus. Bonython found himself picking up the phone to the cheery voices of old artist pals from whom he hadn't heard in a while, the calls apropos of nothing much, other than just to say hello . . . and to ask what Bonython was up to these days. Cantankerous brushmen, who would normally guard their dens like she-wolves against the leers of visitors, merrily threw open the doors to their studios whenever Kym Bonython and his American friend came calling, gritting their teeth into smiles as the strange little man in his strange little hat shuffled amongst their works, poking with his cane as he proffered his own clueless critiques upon this painting or that.

Bonython and Mertz traversed the nation and travelled abroad, haggling with dealers and hassling collectors, commissioning many originals especially for the collection, notably a self-portrait of William Dobell, which pleased Mertz greatly. The artists themselves were no less enthused than their American benefactor. While in

England, securing a few paintings from the London studio of Brett Whiteley, Mertz, Bonython and the young artist found themselves sharing a cab through the city, and when they passed a billboard for Heinz baked beans, Whiteley was heard to mutter: 'Mertz means money'.

Bonython warned Mertz that the costs were blowing out – what had begun as a few score paintings was becoming a goliath of canvases, neither Mertz nor Bonython able to reject any work that might be thrust before their eye. But such concerns were waved away by the American, ever excited as he was with the burgeoning assemblage of pictures being corralled in his name. It took eighteen months and half a million dollars for Bonython and Mertz to at last be satisfied that they had assembled the definitive collection of Australian contemporary art; 153 paintings, no less, by such notables as Dobell, Drysdale, Nolan, Boyd, Perceval, Whiteley, Tucker, Coburn and over seventy others – all the names that mattered, or would come to matter in the years ahead.

The collection was given a trial exhibition at the Adelaide Festival in 1966, where it was roundly commended by those who applaud with lingering stares and no clapping at all. But there were those who noticed that, regardless of the *importance* of the collection – the names on the canvases and the cachet implied – the Mertz Collection was perhaps one of the most joyless gatherings of images ever to be assembled in the name of a single nation. Of the 153 paintings, scarcely a handful of them were what any sane person would describe as a pleasure to behold. Apart from the odd eruption of colour from John Coburn, and the homesick sentimentalism that lingered in Russell Drysdale's lonely outback portraits, the Mertz Collection was a grim old memorial of misery, anxiety, violence and despair, picture after picture inviting the viewer to descend into an abyss or shuffle on in confusion: the sadistic psychosis of Whiteley's 'Christie' series, obsessed as it was with one of England's most appalling mass murderers; the wide-eyed dread of Boyd's spectral unfortunates; the dark pagan totems of Tucker; the ghastly desolation of Dickerson's lost souls in the bush; the eerie silence of Nolan; Edwin Tanner's bleak circuitry; Clifton Pugh's startled cats and hang-dog breasts, and the dead-faced women of Cecil Brack. The Mertz Collection, important or not, was such a panoply of abstract expressionism, asylum geometry and dropsheet soul that, had everything gone to plan, it might have laid waste to the Australian tourism industry for the next thirty years.

As the paintings shipped out for America in November of 1966, like miserable troops set sail for a war all but lost, one might have been forgiven for wondering whether all those cheerless faces peering out from the canvases knew something the rest of Australia did not.

The month of March dawned well on hopes for the exhibition, *Life* magazine devoting eight pages to the works, and the local press waxing with considerable excitement. Thus *Australian Painters: 1964–1966* opened to a packed crowd at the Corcoran Gallery in Washington DC. The US Secretary of State, Dean Rusk, showed up, as did Mrs Lyndon Johnson. Unfortunately so did the critics.

The *Washington Post* quoted Mertz enthusiastically extolling the virtues of Australia – 'that great island, so empty and weird . . . like nowhere else on earth' – and its works of art, which he swore 'could only have been painted in Australia by an Australian'. The reporter did not agree. 'Ironically,' he wrote, *the paintings on view at the Corcoran seem neither uniquely contemporary nor uniquely Australian. The show is filled with echoes of London and Paris and New York. Everywhere there are examples of what appear to be familiar American and European paintings of the past few decades.*

The *Washington Times Herald* concurred:

Generally speaking, the paintings are as provincial and limited in style as those from Peru and Yugoslavia shown at the Corcoran in 1966 ... The show as a whole is not unlike the type of national art exhibition you might have found in Toronto, Ottawa, Winnipeg or Montreal some ten or fifteen years ago, or that you would find today if you removed all the paintings which showed an American influence. (This influence has evidently not yet reached Australia; it's because of this influence that at its top level Canadian painting is much superior.)

One review lamented the absence of landscape painting in favour of works by the likes of Whiteley, 'a kind of cross between Francis Bacon and David Hockney', and the disappointing work by Sidney Nolan, 'with its lack of feeling for paint'.

Within a few weeks, the buzz dried up, the viewers slowed to a trickle, and the show at the Corcoran was over.

Mertz's original plan had been for the collection to remain at the Corcoran for several months before it embarked on a grand tour of the major galleries of the United States, including the Met, the Museum of Modern Art and the Guggenheim. But not one of those galleries showed the slightest interest in Mertz's sullen jamboree of Australian modern art. Even the smaller galleries expressed little enthusiasm, and in only edited versions of the collection at that – the works by Nolan and Dobell, chiefly. The collection began to be chipped away, divided, a few pieces spread over provincial galleries from one end of the country to the other. By the end of the decade, Harold Mertz found himself with a monstrous storage problem.

Losing interest fast in the world of art, Mertz approached the Australian embassy but there was little that diplomatic circles could do. At last, with the help of the US Ambassador to Australia, Ed Clark, Mertz found an interested party in the University of Texas, whose Jack S. Blandon Gallery was happy to take the collection off Harold's hands. And there the Mertz Collection might have enjoyed pride of place on the substantial wall space of the gallery. But, as fate would have it, only months after taking receipt of the unwieldy stack of Australian masterpieces, the university received yet another donation, this time from author, James A. Michener, whose enormous collection of Latin American art did not sit well amongst the morose canvases that gazed out from the Australian frames. Thus the Mertz Collection – the once-happy marriage of Australian art and an American dream – was consigned to the university basement and little by little, year by year, the revolving staff of the huge learning institution eventually forgot all about it.

Mertz went back to what he knew best – magazine subscriptions and oil wells in Arizona, confining his collector's enthusiasms to antique French furniture, Russian iconography and bottles of very old Scotch whisky, while his art remained, unseen in the dark, the big-eyed Boyds and the angry Whiteleys languishing in a dungeon for three entire decades, moping in a subterranean pit of oblivion, from Vietnam to Kosovo, Apollo 11 to Napster. An entire generation came and went, and Australia's most important collection of contemporary art played no part in it.

Some time in 1999, the bean counters at the University of Texas found themselves desperate for ways to bring the institution's balance sheet back into the black. Thumbing through the vast inventory of the university's holdings, an accountant came across the name of Harold E. Mertz, and thus the collection of Australian paintings that dwelled somewhere deep in the basement storage. For all sorts of reasons it was decided that these 153 pictures belonged back in the land from whence they had come. It was the only island on earth that would take them.

In June of 2000, the Harold E. Mertz Collection of Australian Art was put to the gavel in Melbourne by the auction house, Christies, *The Australian* reporting triumphantly that 'The Australian art market's time has come'. In his introduction for the auction catalogue, Kym Bonython, now in his eighties, seemed not to hear the dismissive American groan in the quote he attributed to Mrs Mertz:

'The last time I saw LuEsther Mertz,' he wrote, 'prior to her death in 1991, she said to me: "I always said to Harold – Harold, those paintings belong back in Australia".'

CROCODILE TEARS

There are many versions of the journal kept by Captain James Cook during his voyage along the Australian east coast in the HM Bark Endeavour *– copies made for the Admiralty and such – but the original, held in the National Library in Canberra, is the only one that tells the absolute truth about 6 May, 1770. On that day Cook noted his impressions of the local stingray population, recording the 'great quantity of this sort of fish found in this place occasioned my giving it the name of Stingray Harbour'. However, upon reaching Batavia, where Cook got his first chance to marvel at the strange plants Joseph Banks and Dr Solander had gathered along the way, he decided to change the record about what had impressed him many months before, running his pen through certain recollections and replacing them with others, until the new journal entry told of the 'great quantity of new plants Mr Banks & Dr Solander collected occasioned my giving it the name of Botany Bay'. It is false – it was not foliage that impressed Cook on 6 May, but stingrays – and this little white lie has been copied from journal to map to atlas for more than 200 years. Thus one could rightly say the gentle stingray was the victim of the very first journalistic whitewash in the history of Australia. In the month of September, 2006, likewise . . .*

Stephen Robert Irwin had never quite enjoyed the level of popularity in his home country as he had abroad.

Born in 1962, Steve inherited the Queensland Reptile and Fauna Park that his parents had founded in 1970 on the Queensland Sunshine Coast, renaming it for the world as Australia Zoo in 1992. Four years later *The Crocodile Hunter*, a television series that featured Steve rummaging through the flora of earth in search of creatures great and small, appeared on US television, the first episode showing Steve's soul being joined to the American people during the ceremony of his marriage to Terri Raines in her hometown of Eugene, Oregon.

Steve's sideshow demeanour – the deportment of a Boy Scout on a sugar hit, with the vocal delivery a hybrid of Paul Hogan and Richard Simmons – was a perfect fit amongst the robust caricatures of American television. But while comfortable with the bedrock of his conservationist platform, the majority of his countrymen found Irwin's public persona too chunky a cliché to be taken terribly seriously. To the plain Australian, Steve Irwin belonged on the same page as Jeannie Little, Big Kev, the Wog Boy – commercial apparitions of domestic stereotypes that were somewhat embarrassing when exported, his appearance on American TV doing no more for Australia than Yosemite Sam had done for Arizona. As Michael Idato of the *Sydney Morning Herald* would later assert, 'Irwin's international success sits in uneasy contrast to his popularity in Australia', the 'wildlife warrior' considered 'at best, a jolly Queensland curiosity' by 'an Australian audience which had, for many years, regarded his international success with spectacular indifference.'

But even this weary worm began to turn in the summer of 2003, the *Sun-Herald* columnist Miranda Devine finding it necessary to jump to the defence of the man she herself admitted had been 'widely regarded with benign condescension' by an Australian public now turning on him, comments Irwin had made in support of the increasingly unpopular Prime Minister, John Howard, 'alienating Australia's cultural establishment', the 'vilification of Irwin' in which 'letters pages of newspapers exploded with venom and journalists sharpened their poison quills' marking a shift in public attitude as, suddenly, the 'likeable, outback ocker became Irwin, the greedy "millionaire" Howard-lover'.

But this was nothing compared to what lay on the other side of Christmas. In a portent of what was to come, Irwin's year in the news ended with reports that he'd been slightly injured while wrestling a crocodile during a research mission in Cape York Peninsula, the *Daily Telegraph* reporting his lucky escape on 30 December, adding it had been 'just a matter of time before Steve Irwin picked the wrong crocodile to annoy'.

On Saturday, 3 January, 2004, the heavens opened upon whatever was left of Steve Irwin's Australian parade of goodwill, outrage exploding from the front pages of newspapers all over the nation after Irwin was filmed playfully dangling his four-month-old son, Bob, seemingly within reach of the jaws of a monster crocodile during a feeding show at Australia Zoo. Brisbane's *Courier-Mail* led the charge with a temper that would become all too familiar over the coming months, the headline: 'Irwin a "bloody idiot" introducing a page-one story littered with quotes from furious child welfare advocates and wildlife veterans claiming Irwin was 'addicted to the attention'. Within hours, the images of Steve, the baby and the monster were dominating the television news media, current affairs programs playing the footage in slow motion as threatening bass notes droned behind the concerned voices of shaken reporters. Radio shock jocks took off the gloves against Irwin with impunity – he was a 'buffoon', a 'publicity seeker', no better than the king of celebrity psychos himself, Michael Jackson who, a little more than a year before, had sparked anger around the world when he'd dangled his newborn baby son from the balcony of a German hotel room.

By evening Irwin was moved enough to grant an interview to Melbourne's *Sunday Herald* during which he and Terri, distressed but unapologetic, protested their love for their children and affirmed their belief in their way of life, Steve responding to the criticism with a vague threat that he may retire from public life altogether. Earlier in the day, however, the same newspaper had received reports from witnesses to strange events at Australia Zoo, where the clearly-defiant Irwins had marched their five-year-old daughter, Bindi, into an enclosure with three fully-grown elephants, crocodiles watching from a few feet away as the child was instructed by her mother to 'flail around and look helpless'. The Irwins were giving Australia the finger.

By Monday every available journalist in the nation had been mobilised to shovel more coal into a media fire that would clearly be the talk of the working week. Professors, psychologists and social commentators were summoned for their opinions and croc farmers expounded the unpredictable dangers of the beasts, while breakout stories reminded readers of the recent and numerous fatalities that had occurred in the jaws of the primitive reptiles. Family experts chorused their disapproval as the overseas networks and newspapers caught on, the *New York Post* howling at 'Irwin's Sick Baby Stunt', London tabloid the *Daily Mirror* dubbing it the 'Crocky Horror Show' and Animal Planet, the cable channel that broadcast *The Crocodile Hunter* in the US, releasing a statement saying it did not support any activity that intentionally put a child 'in harm's way'. Sydney's *Daily Telegraph* both predicted and rode the mood with the headline: 'The world thinks Steve Irwin's stupid – we agree', while the Adelaide *Advertiser* soberly editorialised: 'Good parenting is not about publicity'.

On Tuesday the letters pages were swamped with readers hot for their first chance to join in the noise, Irwin lambasted as a 'lousy parent', 'brainless', 'stupid', an 'over-rated clown' and 'an egotistical idiot' whose conduct was 'bizarre', 'stupid', 'revolting', 'an embarrassment' and 'on par with Michael Jackson's', his 'completely irresponsible behaviour' the product of a 'goose' who was 'carried away with his own charisma' and needed 'some running repairs on his brain'. A cartoon in *The Australian* depicted a grinning Steve Irwin in front of a crowd at Australia Zoo, dangling his terrified baby son into the clutches of a ravenous, lip-smacking Michael Jackson. The title of the cartoon read: 'Un-Australian of the Year'.

Fairfax could wait no further than Tuesday to reap the benefits of a tidal wave of public opinion, the late edition of *The Age* gently lecturing Irwin for his 'error of judgement' and his 'uncharacteristic churlishness in attempting to publicly defend his actions . . . It is still not too late for an apology'.

The next day, news of Irwin's apology broke but, for Australians, it was an apology delivered wholly in the wrong direction. 'Irwin apologises . . . to the US', sulked the *Daily Telegraph* on 7 January, going on to tell of how Irwin had apologised to his American TV bosses 'in a bid to save his lucrative career'. *The Australian* accused Irwin of 'telling his US producers one thing and his Australian audience another', the page-five story quoting Australian documentary maker Malcolm Douglas as saying he had repeatedly lobbied Queensland authorities to stop Irwin taking his children into crocodile pens. 'No' was the resounding answer to a *Herald*

Sun poll asking readers whether Steve Irwin should still be considered for Australian of the Year, and in the regular 'Hot, hot, hot and not, not, not' column in the Adelaide *Advertiser,* Irwin's name appeared in the list of unfashionable things not once, but twice ('he's so "out" that he deserves another mention'). The *Sunday Territorian* declared: 'Steve Irwin – that's Australian for Stupid', while *The Australian*'s Susan Mitchell caned Irwin for using his daughter as a prop for damage control during an American TV interview. 'In the face of constant questioning from NBC about whether in the light of public reaction he would do it again,' she wrote,

> *he ignored the question and instead asked Bindi: 'Who do you want to be when you grow up?' Bindi looked up into the eyes of the crocodile-feeder and said in an over-rehearsed sing-song voice, 'I want to be just like my daddy.' Irwin looked straight at the camera as if to say, 'See, I haven't done anything wrong. My daughter wants to be just like me.' Yeah, sure Steve, she wants to be stupid when she grows up.*

On 8 January, the *Herald Sun* published a column by Jill Singer entitled 'If he could talk, little Bob Irwin may say . . . Dad's a drongo', in which the author began by asking: 'Since when did anyone consider the man was in any way normal?' She went on to describe Steve Irwin as 'simple-minded', 'Neanderthal', a 'chest-beating reductionist', a 'dangerous dropkick' and a 'dill', before comparing Irwin's parenting philosophies to those of John Howard, 'who toughens up the babies of asylum seekers by locking them behind razor wire from the time they're born', and George Bush, 'who assures the world that Iraqi and Afghani babies must be bombed for their own good'. The piece also likened Irwin to Michael Jackson.

Two days later the *Weekend Australian* published a story by Leisa Scott in which she recalled an interview with Steve Irwin at Australia Zoo in 1999, one that had almost ended when the journalist light-heartedly criticised a segment from Steve's TV show in which Irwin had 'rescued' lizards from a bushfire that appeared to the author to be well under control, dramatic music booming as Irwin leapt through flames barely inches high.

'The moment I told Irwin I thought the scene was corny,' she wrote,

> *his wide-eyed enthusiasm crashed. He sulked, muttered something, then got up and walked away. He came back to tell me I'd hurt his feelings, before leaving again. Only the intervention of savvy wife Terri enabled the interview to continue . . . Irwin said I'd learned something few people knew about him: he was 'super-sensitive' to criticism.*

The article revealed a frail reality behind Irwin's on-screen dash and bluster: the hushed-up injuries suffered by Australia Zoo workers; the letters from wildlife experts complaining about Irwin's methods; the animals in Irwin's charge that had bitten TV personalities. Steve Irwin, it seemed, was 'poorly respected in the industry', a man who had 'sold his soul for financial gain and has finally been found out for the idiot he is', a thin-skinned creature who 'writes the most disparaging stuff about anybody who doesn't have the same philosophy as he does, but he hates it when people come back at him'. The public attraction to Steve Irwin seemed eloquently summarised by the words of Queensland psychologist, Virginia Slaughter:

People go to motocross to see a crash and people go to
Steve Irwin on the off chance, somewhere in the back of
their mind, that he's going to get his arm bitten off.

The furore had barely simmered down on 25 January when the recipient of Australian of the Year, an award for which Irwin had been nominated months earlier, was announced as cricket player Steve Waugh. Though nobody had seriously expected Irwin to be in with the slightest chance after the events of the previous weeks (the *Courier-Mail* had proposed his selection for 'Dill of the Year, more like', while the *Sydney Morning Herald* had suggested Irwin's nomination 'shows why the award cannot be taken too seriously'), Sandra McVitty of Beaumaris, writing to *The Age* on 27 January perhaps expressed a nation's relief that 'at least we have been spared the grinning image of Steve Irwin, and for that I am thankful'. It would later be revealed that Irwin's nomination had, in fact, been withdrawn, the *Courier-Mail* of 17 February suggesting that 'Irwin's withdrawal paved the way for Steve Waugh to win the award by default'.

On 21 February, *The Advertiser* reported that Polish-born swimsuit model Joanna Krupa had been personally invited to Australia Zoo after Steve Irwin had seen her scantily-clad pictorial in *Inside Sport* magazine. 'He's a top bloke isn't he?' the newspaper opined, adding that the Member for Port Darwin, Sue Carter, had recently called for the renaming of the Steve Irwin locomotive. On 14 June, the *Sydney Morning Herald* reported that Steve Irwin was facing 'a possible criminal breach of wildlife laws after allegedly clowning with whales and penguins while filming in Antarctica'.

'Croc hunter lands in the soup again' howled the Melbourne *Herald Sun*, quoting Irwin himself as saying: 'There's a lot of people out there who want me dead', while the *Daily Telegraph* reported Greens Leader Bob Brown's opinion that Steve was 'more interested in the danger of wildlife than its conservation'.

Suddenly a new open season was declared on the Crocodile Hunter as the letters pages rained abuse all over again. 'That boorish purveyor of pseudo-environmental TV schlock Steve Irwin is at it again,' wrote Martin Walton to the *Courier-Mail*. 'Crikey, not him again,' moaned Peter Wood to the *Hobart Mercury*. 'Maybe it's time Steve Irwin's animals were released back to their natural habitat and he put in their place,' Peter Guppy suggested in *The Australian*, while James Dagnall of Elizabeth Bay prayed to the *Sydney Morning Herald*: 'I live in hope that sooner or later – preferably sooner – one of the animals which Steve Irwin cavorts with will eat him.'

On 16 June, *Courier-Mail* columnist Matthew Franklin suggested it was 'time people stopped fooling themselves about wildlife entrepreneur Steve Irwin', who was 'not an environmental scientist' but rather 'a show business personality out to make a quid' whose entire persona was 'decades off the pace', 'irrelevant to modern Australia' and 'downright embarrassing'.

On the anniversary of 11 September, the *Courier-Mail* reported that Mick Pitman, a man who had been hunting crocodiles in north Queensland for decades, had received a letter from Irwin's production company demanding that he stop using the phrase 'The Croc Hunter' on his website, while a piece in *The Australian* on 28 October seemed to suggest Steve Irwin's popularity was going swiftly south, his latest TV special having been trounced in the ratings by *Kath & Kim*.

Irwin featured heavily in all end-of-2004 remembrances, Gary Tippet at *The Age* recalling the 'bloody idiot', the *Newcastle Herald* crowning him with the year's 'idiot award' and Rodney Chester at the *Courier-Mail* recalling Steve's penchant for 'blaming the media and citing that his forefathers died for democracy and for his right to be a goose'.

The mood simmered through 2005, David Dale at *The Age* wondering aloud on 22 January whether Steve Irwin 'could really be as dumb as he acts', adding that the very sight of him made most Australians 'nostalgic for Dundee', while a few days later the *Sydney Morning Herald* quoted a social scientist who suggested most Australians found Irwin 'not real'. Early March saw Channel Nine's switchboard light up with complaints after Irwin appeared to mistreat a python during an episode of *The Footy Show* and, on 21 August, in an opinion piece entitled 'We're just a nation of yobs', Peter Goers bemoaned the 'boorishness and anti-social behaviour' that had led to 'national heroes such as Shane Warne, Russell Crowe, Steve Irwin and Lleyton Hewitt'. The *Townsville Bulletin* cast doubt on his intelligence in 'Irwin out of order' on 24 August, while 22 October saw Damien Murphy at *The Age* including Irwin alongside Paris Hilton, Mimi Macpherson and Michael Jackson as evidence that 'worship of slim achievement has become a defining characteristic of modern life'.

If Steve Irwin had been longing for quiet, the year of 2006 promised his best chance yet: a round-up of weekly television highlights in the *Weekend Australian* on 26 January noted that 'even though Steve Irwin's fifteen minutes of fame must be drawing to a close, Animal Planet has a *Crocodile Hunter* marathon beginning at 9.30 am'. The following month, Dom Knight at the *Sydney Morning Herald* placed Irwin between Britney Spears and Michael Jackson on a list of 'loopy celebrities', while early May saw Steve

Irwin coming in fourth place in a question about the most 'daggy' Australian figure on Channel Nine's network game show, *Bert's Family Feud*. On 8 June, Sarrah Le Marquant at the *Daily Telegraph* asked why newsreader Jessica Rowe had topped a poll as Australia's most annoying celebrity 'when it's still legal for Steve Irwin, Mark Holden and Sam Newman to appear on screen'.

In an interview for the August edition of the *Australian Women's Weekly*, Steve Irwin explained that whenever he saw eight-year-old Bindi about to rough up her younger brother, Bob, he insisted she take her shoes off first.

> *I tell her, 'Bin, I realise you have to pick on your little brother, but take off your shoes before you kick him in the head.' That way, she gets to whack him and he doesn't get hurt.*

'Let's nominate Steve Irwin for Father of the Year' scowled the *Daily Telegraph*, while the *Sunday Mail* declared: 'Steve Irwin has yet again proved his "model father" status' . . .

Then came September.

To the *Townsville Bulletin*, Australia had 'lost one of its finest ambassadors . . . one of this country's greatest assets . . . a decent father and family man . . . a bloke we were happy to call our own'. To the *Daily Telegraph*, he was 'Our loveable larrikin' and 'our man wearing khaki in America', while the *Sydney Morning Herald* saluted 'a true hero'. For Steve, 'Family came first' according to the *Hobart Mercury*, and *The Advertiser* remembered Irwin as 'a man who inspired us all'. The *Herald Sun* remembered Irwin as 'a man whose family was paramount to all he did'. The *Herald Leader* in Newcastle confessed to having heard of the existence of some who looked upon Irwin with embarrassment, but added: 'It is safe, however, to suggest that those who were mortified by the conservationist in khaki shorts with his utterances of "Crikey!" were in a minority.'

The letters pages were absolutely wet: 'Suddenly, the world is a darker place', they cried, without the 'beautiful Aussie man', 'a once-in-a-lifetime shining light' who 'showed us the true meaning of love and compassion' and whose 'gift was his ability to hold on tight to his inner child'. 'RIP the real Tarzan' the pages wept. 'Why did it have to be Steve Irwin?', asked a younger reader. 'Why couldn't it be someone older like Sean Connery?' The proprietor of the Stingray Café in Nelson found it necessary to fire off a letter to the *Nelson Mail* stating:

> *After fielding numerous calls and enquiries, I feel beholden to our loyal clientele to advise that 'it's business as usual'... Although we are much upset at the death of that Ozzie icon, Steve Irwin ... We would like to reassure all Nelsonians, that this unfortunate event will, in no way, impinge or hinder the trade and service of the Stingray Café.*

Rightly concerned about the collective state of mind of its readership, the *Daily Telegraph* arranged an urgent audience with a psychologist who warned that 'parents should be open with their children about Steve Irwin's death and reassure them of their safety', while the *Herald Sun* strongly advised mums and dads against succumbing to the temptation of lying to their children and pretending Irwin was still alive. The *Daily Telegraph* passed on a US family therapist's opinion that mums and dads should down tools and wander about in the wake of grieving children, parents encouraged to 'follow their children's lead if they suggested visiting a shelter or the zoo'.

Prime Minister John Howard appeared to momentarily lose his mind when telling Parliament that Steve Irwin, the third person to have been killed by a stingray in Australian recorded history, had died in 'quintessentially Australian circumstances'. Kim Beazley's comments were so gutless they ought to be erased from Hansard.

The Australian Radio Network urged fans to 'wear something khaki today' in 'International Crikey, It's Khaki Day', while calls went out for a state funeral, usually reserved for those from the halls of public officialdom. And why not? 'Hero's death to rock youngsters in same way Di and JFK's loss affected adults' declared the *Gold Coast Bulletin*, a sentiment echoed by the *Daily Telegraph*, which proclaimed his death 'a landmark for kids in the way the deaths of John F. Kennedy and Princess Diana were for adults', his appearance on the DVD '*Wiggly Wiggly Safari*, in which he appeared with The Wiggles, presumably Irwin's 'Berlin Wall' moment. Child psychologist Dr John Irvine said it was more powerful a loss than that of the Princess of Wales: 'When Princess Diana died, it only affected adults. But this is widespread mourning.'

Columnists recalled the deaths of their own parents in vivid detail. Radio disc jockeys sobbed on air. Anita Quigley of the *Daily Telegraph* confessed she'd been crying for days, reporting on the fact that, even if you didn't like him much, 'you still watched Irwin' and then 'felt better for it'. 'We are one . . .' the column then tearfully chorused.

Meanwhile reports began to surface that at least a dozen dead and mutilated stingrays had been found on Australia's eastern coast, their tails cut off in apparent revenge for their presumed roles in Steve Irwin's demise. Authorities urged that such retaliations were 'not what Steve would have wanted', while the Hobart *Mercury* reported that Mick Pitman, the original 'Croc Hunter', had been swamped with threats and hate mail from people demanding he change his name or die. In *Zoo* magazine's weekly 'Hate List', the 'stingray that killed Steve Irwin' was filed between *Australian Idol* judge Kyle Sandilands and Zimbabwe president Robert Mugabe.

On 6 September, all Australian media went berserk upon receipt of the news that Germaine Greer, now living in England, had written a characteristically unsentimental column for *The Guardian* in which she articulated the very same views that the local media had been expressing for years: Irwin was 'a great Australian, an ambassador for wildlife, a global phenomenon', but also 'a superhuman generator of merchandise, books, interactive video-games and action figures'. Correctly pointing out that there was 'no habitat, no matter how fragile or finely balanced, that Irwin hesitated to barge into . . . not an animal he was not prepared to manhandle,' Greer catalogued Irwin's much-publicised misdemeanours before concluding that perhaps 'the animal world has finally taken its revenge'.

To the *Herald Sun*, Greer was 'shameful', a 'snake in the grass',

> *criticising targets in the homeland she turned her back on. Irwin never flinched in the face of danger but Greer's fangs are quickly drawn when she sees a target that cannot defend itself.*

The *Daily Telegraph* editorialised about a time when calling people names was popular in the Australian press. 'But we grew up,' the tabloid claimed.

> *We moved on. We came to understand there is more to*
> *life than the cheap quip, the mock indignation, the lofty*
> *declaration of one's own percipient superiority. Most did*
> *anyway. But not Greer.*

This was twenty-four hours after the same newspaper had published a photo of a dog muzzle with the headline: 'Germaine, try this muzzle on for size', the article presuming to speak 'on behalf of all Australians' while describing Greer as a 'batty loudmouth' and providing her London address and urging readers to 'let her know what you think of her'.

Letters pages frothed: Greer was 'bitter and twisted', a 'grizzled harridan', 'revolting', 'an embarrassment' whose 'time has passed'. 'The sooner she pushes off this planet the better the human race will be,' fumed one reader. 'It wouldn't be jealousy on the part of Ms Greer would it?' proffered another reader, adding: 'As far as I am aware, people actually liked Steve Irwin.' Future Prime Minister Kevin Rudd raised himself from his august seat and ordered Greer to 'shut up', while Queensland Premier Peter Beattie officially branded Greer's opinion 'untrue garbage'.

Pursued by *A Current Affair*, Greer, like Irwin before her, was unapologetic:

'I don't care what I'm being called,' she said.

> *I just hope I'm out of touch with what idiots are*
> *thinking . . . As far as I can see, quite a few Australians*
> *have been embarrassed by Steve Irwin – lots. Millions,*
> *possibly.*

And to this the *Herald Sun* scoffed: 'But when pushed, she was *unable to name anyone who had publicly agreed with her.*'

Here were the very same organs that, for the previous thirty months, had been unstoppable in their condemnation of Irwin: the greedy, attention-seeking buffoon, no better than Michael Jackson; the loopy, daggy, annoying and irrelevant yob; the sick, stupid, child-abusing, brainless and over-rated national embarrassment, who made Australia reach for the mute button; the brain-damaged, un-Australian, churlish, two-faced, manipulative, thin-skinned, simple-minded Neanderthal; the phony, lecherous, petulant 'drongo dad', purveyor of pseudo-environmental TV schlock who cared less for his kids and the wildlife to which he fed them than he did for his own greasy pocket. These same voices, from the very same pulpits, were now not only saying the very opposite, and decrying those who did not toe the new line, but *denying* their previous opinions had ever been held by anybody at all.

Had it ended there, September 2006 might still have gone down as the most pathetic month in the history of the Australian media's craven relationship with its audience, a rapport that is not concerned with an exchange of information but rather the conducting of a feral orchestra whose very spasms are forever writing the score.

But then, on 8 September, in the West Australian town of Gidgegannup, car racer, serial philanderer and accused wife-beater, Peter Brock – a man who had been ridiculed in the press when he claimed that crystals and magnets placed under the hood make an engine run much better than normal – overshot a corner and crashed into a tree . . .

GOODBYE MR RIVER

With its Spanish arches and foreboding bell tower, the chapel that stands at the heart of the Northern Suburbs Memorial Gardens and Crematorium in Sydney bears more than just a passing resemblance to the Mission San Juan Bautista, as seen in the film, Vertigo. Hitchcock's story tells of a man obsessed with a woman who is faking, her suicidal exhibitions merely an act designed to make him spring into action – a performance that ultimately proves to be fatal in one of the most abrupt endings in movie history. Life's like that – it ends abruptly sometimes – but unlike the movies, we are often left with little by way of explanation at the end. There are no narrators to attend our final scenes, or Bernard Herrmann scores to warn of that which lurks behind closed doors. But let us move away from movies and maestros and temples of ash, to meet with a gentleman in a bit of a pickle – an ordinary fellow, like you and me, but different, as you will see . . .

Mr River checks into his hotel room and signs his name in the registry book. Immediately his signature seems somehow strange to him, like an alien moniker scribbled in foreign hand. He is not alarmed at this. It happens often. Mr River is a thoughtful man, and unusual things tend to happen in the minds of such fellows. He brushes it away as just another moment in his life, and makes his way to the elevator.

Once in his room he moves around within it, making sure everything is in order. He had once been excited by hotel rooms, but no longer. In his youth, like all children, he had considered hotels as akin to amusement parks – make-believe homes with their make-believe comforts and make-believe neighbours, the hallways like make-believe streets of make-believe towns that would all be gone tomorrow. But now he is older, Mr River is no longer enchanted, the amusement park too familiar, too much like home. He'd been on all the rides a thousand times. It just isn't fun any more.

Mr River owns his own business and, like many businessmen, he travels often, moving around constantly from kingdom to country, state to state, peddling his goods to whomever might wish to purchase them. What his business is about does not matter here – indeed, the less said the better. There are those who look down upon his type of business, and it's true that he moves within a world of hucksters and creeps. But Mr River is not one of those. He is, in fact, one of the nicest men you would ever wish to meet.

He came to Australia from China, where he had grown up surrounded by maids and cooks and washers of his laundry, who all called the boy 'Master', despite him having no noticeable mastery at anything whatsover. His father was a businessman, too, and was successful enough to ensure that the family need never want for anything. His mother was of the demonstrative kind, prone to extravagant panic attacks, which occasionally required the young Mr River to call for the help of those who might save her. He would always remember such episodes, particularly the concern in the eyes of those who came running.

To say that the young Mr River was mollycoddled and spoilt would not be to trade in falsehood. Nevertheless, afflicted with asthma, chronic short-sightedness and a slight lisp, the young Mr River was not a confident lad, and in his schooling he did not excel, showing lower than average aptitude in mathematics and the sciences. But he was an affable boy who made friends easily enough, and enjoyed the same things as most others, joining cub scouts, learning Judo, and trying his hand at archery, at which he became passably accurate. He had once been excited to see his photo appear in the morning edition of the *China Mail*, the scrawny young boy holding his tortoiseshell cat, which he had entered in a competition. For the rest of his life, he would remember with great fondness this fleeting moment of childhood fame.

When he was twelve years old his father's business affairs brought the family to Australia, and the shy young boy from Hong Kong was enrolled at a good school in the northern suburbs of Sydney. His appearance and accent, foreign to the other children, saw him mocked and heckled, and pelted by tennis balls while walking in the playground, physically challenged by the tougher boys. On his second day at school, he decided he loathed Australia and detested the people within it, who were racist and rude. The day would come when he would call himself an Australian, too, but not before despising what it stood for. It is a story familiar to many immigrant Australians.

Again his scholastic performance was poor, and more than once were his mother and father called to the school to discuss his unsatisfactory grades, which told of a dim student – a 'dreamer', they called him – with little potential. He tried harder to concentrate on his studies, but it seemed that further education was beyond him. He dropped out of school at the age of fifteen, taking a go-nowhere job just to give himself the financial autonomy that people out of school were meant to have. For the rest of his life it was important to him that he be seen as independently intellectual, a book in his hand at all times – on buses and planes, in the office, in cafés – not simply so that others might see, but that he might see it so, too.

The future looked grim for Mr River, and if he'd been a horse only the foolhardy would have gambled on him making a success of himself. Nor would one have envisaged the spectacular end that would befall him, or have imagined from where it would come.

Mr River had not been out of school for long when he was offered a position in a fledgling business, one that promised great reward for anyone prepared to gamble upon it. It required no financial outlay from him that could be considered significant, only his time and effort, and the willingness to uproot himself for long trips abroad. With no other propositions on the horizon, he accepted the offer gladly.

The twentieth century was a time when people made money from things that didn't tangibly exist. Entire empires were built upon the notion that the very air was filled with mercurial prices that fell upon things, or flew from things, tossing them from the realm of precious to worthless and back in the twinkling of an eye. A tin of bullets or a jar of jam would suddenly be worth more or less, regardless of the fact that the bullets and jam had not changed their molecular structure at all. Men became very rich selling notions, or moving amongst products that were effectively invisible – market futures, intellectual property, the conveyance of ideas.

This was the field into which Mr River would stride and do very well for himself. It was not the type of reputable business that dealt in bricks and mortar – indeed, he and his partners were never to produce anything substantial. Not really. Theirs was a business that was more speculative in nature, its success or failure depending upon the fragile mercies and whims of the market.

Mr River's responsibilities did not call for physical toil – he did not taste the sweat in his sandwiches, as they say – or rigorous calculation, but rather the wherewithal to make the right moves at the right time. It is proper to say that Mr River's acumen in this department proved to be exceptional, and was duly applauded by both his partners and prospective clients. It was not long before the business was travelling very nicely, largely due to Mr River's efforts and his uncanny knack for encouraging the market to their own advantage. From where he had acquired these skills was not apparent.

In any case, within a few short years, Mr River and his partners were doing business with the market monoliths, whose tentacles stretched to lands overseas. He travelled the world, shaking hands with scum – and royalty, too. The wealth rolled in quickly and Mr River invested in cars and houses both here and abroad, in Britain, the Americas and the south of France. He purchased clothes to make himself fashionable and all the trinkets he desired. He funnelled much of his fortune into places where the authorities might not look, for that is what he had to do. Like many businessmen he used drugs to keep working, or simply to make his great life better.

Mr River's sudden wealth and power opened up the world like a mystical flower, and life would never be the same again. The day would come when he would acclimatise to the wonder of new wealth, to the point where it made him no more happy or sad than the air that he breathed. There would come a time, too, when he feared he could no longer distinguish between the real and the fraudulent, those who befriended him out of avarice, or something even worse. He even came to be suspicious of his own family, whose pride in his achievements sometimes annoyed him.

But Mr River was never to take for granted the joy he took from his job, which made him feel useful and wanted and loved. Every time he arrived at work he would marvel at a strange feeling that washed over him as he climbed the stairs, a sense of transition that he couldn't understand, as if each step was elevating him to above the powers of ordinary men. And each time he felt it, or thought of it, it made him want to cry.

It is said that boys from dysfunctional families grow into troubled men. Mr River was from such a family, which is all that needs to be said about it. In the boardrooms and foyers he showed no signs of it, no scars or emotional bruising could be seen. It was only behind closed doors that Mr River exhibited any emblems of a lingering psychological kink.

If Mr River had a weakness, it was for sex (assuming, as one may or may not, that desire for intimate contact with other human beings is a weakness). His need to feel loved was intense. There was nothing in this world that could distract him from a passing pretty girl, and no calamity that he wouldn't willingly invite if the prize was the pleasure of a young woman's attention. The satisfaction of this desire was paramount to him, triumphing over all else.

Where this urge had its genesis is hard to say. Some might claim Mr River to have been a romantic, but romance and sex in the twentieth century went together like horse and motorised cart. He wrote poetry, as textbook romanticists do, though his poetry was never terribly good, almost exclusively concerned with women and how they made him feel, the sentiments glued by words whose lazy associations seemed just fine to him – 'run' went with 'hide', 'hope' went with 'pray', and so forth. It was well that his verse played no part in his success.

His first infatuation had occurred when he was just a boy, a pretty English girl in his swimming class arousing something in him that he could neither control nor understand. One day, driven by an urge that seemed the work of some nebulous puppeteer, he had lunged toward her and kissed her, the shock of his own revolution sending him falling backwards into the garden, breaking his arm. It was a portent for what was to come.

It is fair to say that Mr River's relationships had never been what others might call 'successful'. He could meet women easily enough – he once fell for a girl whom he met at a bus stop, then another with whom he struck up conversation when they found themselves standing together in a corner store. Girls seemed to find something endearing about his clumsy charm and, in the end, his wealth ensured that women saw him as quite the catch indeed. But his ability to maintain relationships for any lasting period was not good. Thus Mr River bounced from one liaison to the next, his passion as the orb in a pinball machine, all bells and hoots telling of found destinations when in reality he was only passing by. Most women seemed to disappoint him in the end, and he them, each grand new enthusiasm coming and going, not one of them staying for long enough to really get to know him. The end was often marked by histrionic displays – one girl said goodbye as he writhed in agony on the floor of a hotel room. He wanted her to see how much it hurt him. It was emotional theatre he learned from his mother.

There was one, he believed for a time, that he might marry – a beautiful, dark-haired girl with plump lips, wintry eyes and a keen mind. Mr River first saw her at his place of work and was dazzled. He made it his business to make her acquaintance, and was delighted when he discovered that she was learning to speak Cantonese. This, he thought, was a sign. He was only twenty, she seventeen, and at first he believed he had found his soul mate with whom he might share the rest of his life. For many years she remained by his side, encouraging him as his business grew, observing his transformation from an uncertain boob to a successful man. But even she would grow tired of his dedication to his work, his carelessness with regard to her feelings, and she came to believe that her future was not to be with him. She was to remain friends with Mr River to the very end, and was the last girl in his life who truly, enduringly mattered.

When she went away, the women in Mr River's life became little more than ticket holders in a pageant of beauty queens, prostitutes and escorts in the respectable sense of the word. Women became sexual playthings with whom he re-enacted scenes he had read in the works of the Marquis de Sade and other pornographic literature of that ilk, episodes whipped into magic by alcohol and drugs. Sometimes, he'd arrange for one of these escorts to meet him in a hotel room as he passed through their town. Once an old flame visited him at his place of work, just to see how he was going. She was pregnant with another man's baby, but that didn't stop Mr River from asking her to have sex with him. Some people thought him revolting and, if those people thought it, those people were right.

It could also be said that, despite being a thoroughly courteous gentlemen to all whom he met, Mr River appeared to have no respect for the bonds between other men and women. For him there were no lines of demarcation, no boundaries that couldn't be crossed. A girl perceived as belonging to another – by marriage or any other cultural attachment – simply did not, where he was concerned. Such mores had no value to him, or so it seemed.

But in fact they had great value to him, and many was the time he would sulk or brood in ill temper over some woman who had paid too much attention to someone other than him. The shy boy from Hong Kong was as jealous and covetous as the next man. One could easily conclude that Mr River, far from being cavalier with regard to the laws of sexual conquest, viewed the world as does the lion on the Serengeti, taking great satisfaction from robbing his fellow male of his pride. He had always been competitive with regard to his fellow man, but it had been an easy contest – for all his adult life, he had been successful, wealthy, at the top of his game. This was about to change.

It was as he approached middle age that things began to go wrong for Mr River. One day, while crossing the street, he became involved in a quarrel with a motorist who stepped out of his vehicle and punched him to the street, shouting something about foreigners as Mr River's head cracked onto the bitumen. In the months that followed, he wasn't himself – he was irritable, a hostage to insomnia, and when sleep did come it was terrorised by nightmares. A visit to a neurosurgeon showed he had fractured his skull and possibly damaged his brain.

The business was now going badly, Mr River's touch for the market having deserted him. Deals soured, money hemorrhaged from his account. He tried to arrest the rot but the baffling wires and funnels through which his business dealings had travelled were so tangled even he couldn't fathom them.

An English woman with whom he'd become involved – a married woman, with a family, and for whom he cared no more than he had for any of the others – left her husband for Mr River, locking him into a romance in which his heart felt hostage, and engaging him in a protracted duel with the hostile man of the broken family, who was desperate to keep his home from falling apart. How the memories of the damaged home of his own childhood advised Mr River during these days of combat is a matter about which we can only speculate, but when the woman fell pregnant with Mr River's baby it became a matter of masculine honour. He lost interest in his business, embedding himself deeply in the woman's affairs and the custody battle between the man and his wife, convinced that an assault was being launched against a family that was now rightly his own and his reputation as a man. He became obsessed and irrational, kicking walls and tilting at windmills. He took drugs to calm himself down.

When his baby was born, the stakes became higher. At last he had somebody who would never leave him – a child who would always bear his name no matter what the future would bring. He began to imagine the cuckolded man trying to take this one piece of family away from him, too. And that would never do.

He began to consume drugs heavily, and his friends noticed that he wasn't coping. He'd call them in the middle of the night and sob like a baby about his lot. They gave him the best advice they could, but nobody seemed to understand.

In the summer of 1997, Mr River flew into Australia for business, the mother of his child remaining abroad, embroiled as she was in the courts with her ex-husband, who would not allow her to travel with his children, and thus Mr River's child, too.

At his last meeting with his old partners it was clear that he no longer wished to be involved in their enterprise, preoccupied as he was with the man he believed was taking his child. His eyes darted wildly when he spoke of him. There were those who said he was using heroin. Nothing he had once cared about seemed to matter.

Now we return to Mr River in his hotel room. He has been with friends but they have all gone home. His life is still good – he can travel anywhere, purchase anything, and there are millions who might wish to be his friend. But none of that matters in the still of night, the drugs wearing off in an empty room. Here he is not rich or powerful, famous or glamorous – those things do not exist when one is alone. He is the same bag of flesh and blood and bone as the spoilt little boy from the pages of the *China Post*.

He speaks on the phone to the mother of his child, who tells him her ex-husband has won. He then calls the husband and loses his temper, is abusive and small, while the man at whom he directs his fury is calm and composed, the winner in a game still contested by losers. He hangs up the phone in a frustrated rage. He drinks until his mind is a mess. He falls asleep, wakes in a panic. He calls the girl he met all those years ago, the one with the dark hair and the wintry eyes, who has always been there, whom he's loved all along, and cries as he tells her he needs her. She says she'll be there right away. What he does next is not his next great move but simply another histrionic moment, a wasted tantrum in a charmed life.

He takes the belt from a pair of trousers and makes a noose that hangs from the closing mechanism above the door that opens to his room. He places his head through the opening and allows his naked body to go limp beneath him. He does not intend for it to be permanent – for him, nothing has ever been permanent. He will wake up in a world where everyone understands, for the girl will arrive at the door just in time and realise how serious his tears had been. She will take charge and make all his troubles go away. It is what women do when they love you.

And this is where the story ends, a man in a make-believe home, with a make-believe name, stripped of all his fashionable clothes, a girl he loved knocking on a door that he would never open. Hours later, the hotel would record that Mr River had checked out.

The funeral for the man who so feared for his privacy as to have travelled by any name but his own was stage-managed by a celebrity fixer, his eulogy delivered by a jock from TV, who had hosted the opening of a casino the previous evening. Mourners arrived in limousines, in outfits charged to the dead man's estate. A pop star performed a song at the service, which was televised so the lumpenmasse could witness the misery. Friends and relatives sold their stories to the papers.

In the years that followed his business partners would raffle his position in the company on a TV game show, to some sap by the name of 'Fortune', no less. For the man so concerned for the legacy he would leave there could be no greater proof of his insignificance.

Most tragically of all, the mother of his child would soon follow him to the grave – through 'foolish and incautious' behaviour, they said – leaving his child to be adopted by the woman's ex-husband, his imagined nemesis, who changed the little girl's name to his own. The very nightmare he feared is complete.

There are those who say it was a sex game gone wrong, but there was never any evidence for it, save for the fact he was rich and glamorous, and such people aren't meant to be lonely, bewildered, or indulge in childish cries for help – performances tragically unseen, as those of ordinary men tend to be.

His memory lives on at the Northern Suburbs Memorial Gardens and Crematorium, his ashes dispersed to the four winds, his dysfunctional family scattering them as angry birds with a bag of seed. They bicker publicly to this day, beating down anyone who gambles to mention him without due reverence. Like the man himself, one dares not write his name.

It's a wretched shame. For in an industry made up of hucksters and creeps he was, in spite of all, one of the nicest men one would ever wish to meet.

VOYAGE OF THE SAVAGES

Scarcely a white man exists on Palm Island, a tiny tropical land mass between Queensland and the Great Barrier Reef. It is a troubled isle of some 4000 souls, most of them employed as their own worst enemies, some living in houses with as many as twenty others who drink and smoke and snort life to hell.

The island served most of the twentieth century as a penitentiary for 'troublesome' Aborigines from the mainland and, today, the local inhabitants care little for the dwellings or discipline that turned their paradise into a prison. The public buildings, cheap and efficient defence force constructs, eroded and tattooed with graffiti, squat amongst tall palm trees that wave in the wind like cheerleaders for the losing team. All around the island, rusted corpses of vehicles sulk in the foliage and litter the seaside, wasted machinery from government contractors left behind where they stopped, as if the war just moved elsewhere.

The only immaculate slice of the island is the cemetery, a decent trek from the township, where fresh flowers decorate ominously fresh graves, the surrounding grass clipped and respectfully maintained. It is apparently so because local men, sentenced to community service by the court, routinely request that they serve out their time there – not out of any particular respect for the dead, but because, should their wives catch sight of them cleaning up in town, they'll be expected to do the same at home. But there is one grave that is set apart from the others, deep in the forest at the foot of the mountain that built this island, whose head remains in a bonnet of clouds as if not wanting to see. If you part the bushes, you will find a clearing. There it lies, its occupant alone; but home at last. He is the star of our next tale, a dreadful saga which, like so many others, begins in the name of entertainment . . .

It was in early January, 1883 when a cutter could be seen to be drifting between the coast of Townsville and the nearby islands, relaxing its sails in the wind as it poked the shoreline, curious, before billowing off to some other stretch of sand that took its fancy. On board was Robert Cunningham, though he preferred R. A. Cunningham when being introduced. Nobody knows what the 'A' in his name stood for – he once signed 'Anderson', then later, 'Andrew', and he announced himself to others as 'Robert Alexander'. R. A. Cunningham was a man who moved swiftly, for whom life began and ended with the rise and fall of every curtain.

Canadian-born of Irish descent, Robert had briefly served with the Californian Infantry at the end of the American Civil War, rounding up rogue Confederates and hostile Indians along the Mexican border, though whether he ever fired a shot is not recalled. After the war, he haunted the San Francisco area as a theatrical impresario, showman and musician, an agent and warm-up act for travelling ventriloquists, spiritualists, captured wild Indians, impersonators and exhibitions of the bizarre. The minstrel's life drew Robert into the world of circuses and freak show entertainment, and in the late 1870s he toured Australia with the Taylor Family Troupe, 'Messrs Cunningham and Cameron's Great London Gaiety Company' providing musical accompaniment for ten-year-old Mattie Taylor, mistress of the banjo, and bird impression.

Australia was hungry for such entertainment from abroad and, for the itinerant Cunningham, this fresh land must have seemed a promising mine for a career that was nearing middle age with few bright lights visible on the road ahead. By 1883, he had made several journeys between Australia and California, returning to San Francisco each time to pay rent in advance before sailing again, usually as a preceding fixer for some touring circus or troupe of amazements, securing venues and arranging local talent while performing in any country hall that would have him. He had a fondness for the coastal settlements of the north, the public houses of which must have seemed to him comfortable reminders of the saloons of the Californian frontier.

Through his experience with the tent shows of America, Cunningham had come to be within the influence of the greatest showman of all, P. T. Barnum, a man famous for his travelling spectacles of wild beasts and bewildering specimens. Barnum enjoyed a decent living as a young man thanks to the lottery mania that had swept America in the early 1800s, but his career began in earnest in 1835 when he introduced to the American public one Joice Heth, a blind, toothless and completely paralysed octogenarian whom Barnum sold to the world as George Washington's nurse, still breathing at 161 years old. There followed a menagerie of mermaids and giants, albinos and pinheads, magicians and midgets, Siamese twins and touring performers from the continent, all displayed amongst the stuffed animals and human skeletons that dwelled under the roof of Barnum's American Museum in New York. This museum was a den of exotic madness tempered only by the inclusion of a 'Moral Lecture Theater' in which good Christians gasped at such living frights as 'The Drunkard' (an exhibit whose fate is lost to history).

When the museum burned to the ground in 1865, Barnum put his show on rails, the Great Traveling World's Fair thrilling the populations of every metropolis connected by train to the last. Employing hundreds of hands and containing countless ever-changing exhibits, Barnum's circus was a juggernaut, rolling on from Philadelphia to Chicago, Washington to Baltimore, regardless of cost, lost lives left behind with little ceremony as 'The Greatest Show on Earth' rumbled along to the next destination.

P. T. Barnum, a businessman who recoiled from physical work, relied on the keen eyes of travelling agents like Cunningham, who were handsomely rewarded for any curiosity that might be procured from their travels abroad. As Cunningham's cutter tacked and jibed in the waters that surrounded Palm Island, a letter from Barnum lay upon the desk of the American consul in nearby Townsville. It expressed Barnum's desire to exhibit to the American public 'all the uncivilized races in existence . . . those who possess extraordinary peculiarities such as giants, dwarfs, singular disfigurements of the person, dexterity in the use of weapons, dancing, singing, juggling, unusual feats of strength or agility, etc'. The letter promised a generous commission, and advised that 'I might send a special agent to your country for any specimens which you may bring under my notice'.

While performing in Melbourne in November of 1882, Cunningham had received an urgent telegram from Barnum's agent, one J. P. Gaylord, requesting that Robert might use his knowledge of the region to acquire for Barnum 'a number of the finest specimens of Australian Aborigines'. R. A. Cunningham had wasted no time in securing passage to the north, where he knew such specimens could be found.

The creep of northward settlement from Sydney Cove in the first half of the nineteenth century sent back word that the Aborigine of the upper regions was increasingly less amenable to the white man's advances, a notion at odds with the first reports from the voyage of Captain James Cook in 1770. Much of the northern expansion had been cratered with suspicion and misunderstanding, usually involving lonely woodcutters and their advances upon Aboriginal women, or hungry Aborigines tempted by the plentiful displays of ready food in the white camps. The results were frequently disastrous, building a mountain of distrust that remains today. By the time the port of Townsville was established in 1864, tales such as that of the Cullin-la-Ringo Massacre of 1861, in which nineteen white men, women and children were butchered in cold blood by central Queensland Aborigines, were widespread. Less popular amongst the whites, though probably well telegraphed between the blacks, were the massacres that tended to remain nameless, such as an incident in 1840 when Aborigines were blamed for a robbery at a local doctor's property in Ramornie, just south of the Queensland border. The commissioner for New England, George Macdonald, who just happened to be in the area with a posse of border police, was prevailed upon to sort the savages out, and did so by rushing a large, unidentified camp of Aborigines at dawn and blowing their brains out as they slept. Most of those who escaped waded into the Clarence River, where they were shot like ducks from the riverbank until the police ran out of ammunition, the corpses of their targets floating downstream to be spotted later in the day by the enthusiastic white settlement at the mouth of the river. Back at Ramornie, the victorious raiding party was met with some sobering news: a convict called Lynch had admitted to the robbery, blaming the deed on the blacks, he said, because he knew he'd be believed.

In October of 1874, the cutter *Albert Edward* arrived in Townsville with a disturbing account of the natives on nearby Palm Island, by the shores of which she had been briefly anchored. During the night, savages from the island had boarded the vessel by canoe, the crew being suddenly awakened by bundles of flaming bark being thrown down the hatches and into the cabin. The attackers were chased from the boat and all, black and white, escaped with their lives, but the apparent devilish cunning of the Palm Islanders convinced authorities of the need to be rid of them. The experiences of the southern settlers, combined with colonial wisdom gained while dealing with indigenous populations in India and Africa, suggested a continuation of hostilities would lead to little more than a protracted bloodbath. Thus a system of induced 'dispersal' was preferred over eradication by cold steel. When not arrested for petty misdemeanours, the natives of Palm Island and beyond were routinely seconded into the Native Police forces, or else recruited to work with pearling fleets to the north, their agility in the water proving useful, the lure of the white man's treasures too good to refuse. Within a few decades, Palm Island's native population had shrivelled to but a few dozen, many of whom spent their time in transit between their home and the paid work that awaited them on the mainland.

By 1883, Queensland Aborigines were well accustomed to being offered journeys on the white man's ships, from which they would normally return with tobacco and other riches. The shores of Palm Island were forever dotted with natives peering out at passing vessels, hoping for the sight of friends and family, lovers and the loved, who days before had waved goodbye and promised to return.

Cunningham's mission in the service of Barnum got off to a troublesome start in Darwin in December of 1882. Having corralled a group of five Aborigines for his purpose, he was about to embark the SS *Euxine* for Singapore, where J. B. Gaylord had chartered a steamer for San Francisco, when a local policeman familiar with the natives began to question Cunningham as to his intentions. Not satisfied that Cunningham's companions understood the full nature of the journey they were about to undertake, the policeman informed them, at which they immediately bolted into town. Word evidently travelled fast, and after eight more days Cunningham found he could hardly get a local man to speak to him, let alone agree to accompany him to the docks.

A frustrated Cunningham then booked passage on the SS *Hungarian* on its maiden voyage to Sydney, alighting at the port of Townsville where he felt he might have more luck. After making himself known to the proper authorities and the local constabulary – lest the Darwin experience be repeated – Cunningham then hired a cutter and began to explore the isles and inlets in the immediate vicinity in search of isolated camps of Aborigines, who might be more easily convinced as a group to come with him on a shared adventure.

Exactly how Cunningham came to convince his captives to accompany him will forever remain a mystery, though his exploits in Darwin suggest truth was no ally to his scheme. We only know that when Cunningham embarked a ship for Sydney on 22 January, 1883, he had with him nine companions: Toby and Jenny, from Palm Island, and their Little Toby, a boy of no more than eight years old; Tambo and Sussy, also from Palm, who clearly belonged to each other; Jimmy, a younger, more fiery Palm Islander; Bob and Billy from nearby Hinchinbrook Island and, also from Hinchinbrook, a tall young man whose name would too soon cease to be of consequence to those who might have recorded it.

Nor can we know how deeply the long journey from Townsville to Sydney alarmed Cunningham's freight. However, when it was discovered that the next steamer to San Francisco was several weeks from departing, forcing Cunningham to book a hotel room in the city and his savages a shack at the rear, it evidently became clear to some in the group that a future awaited them beyond their wishes. On 12 February, Cunningham posted a public notice begging for the return or capture of two Aborigines who had 'strayed' from his care. Within a week, Billy and Jimmy were found, hiding in the bush at Manly on the other side of the harbour, their desperation to avoid recapture resulting in their arresting constable being badly injured in the execution of his duty.

The resulting appearance of the fugitives before a Sydney magistrate may have saved all from their fate. Despite Cunningham's insistence that both were his willing companions, the authorities were not convinced, particularly when it was discovered there were seven others, including women and a child, awaiting transport to America. An inspector of the court reported that the captives 'do not appear to know where they were going'. Newspapers trumpeted the injustice of it, the *Sydney Morning Herald* reporting that the native travellers seemed 'very unwilling to proceed beyond Sydney', while the *Evening News* minced no words in accusing Cunningham of kidnapping. The matter was even raised in Parliament, where George Thornton, Chairman of the Aboriginal Protection Board, protested that the nine be released before they 'fret to death or destroy themselves'. But a telegram from Queensland's Chief Inspector of Police assured all that the natives 'went willingly, understanding their destination and terms of absence'. The court dropped all charges and released the detained into the care of their American master, the court noting that their captor at least 'appears to pay attention to their wants'.

The combined weight of Australian justice, government and popular press had been no match for 'The Greatest Show on Earth'.

Is it not impossible to imagine how the Aborigines felt as they languished on the SS *Australia*, their entire world having slipped below the horizon? What had Cunningham explained to them about the place toward which they were travelling, where it was upon the world, and how far away from home it would be? Did they know? Did they watch the heavens shift in the night sky and understand the meaning of it? Might they not have felt as contemporary folk were they to learn, while adrift in the black of space, that they were destined for another star?

The group arrived in San Francisco in late April of 1883, the shock of their arrival in the strange city, and their mandatory dependence upon their captor in such extraordinary circumstances, seemingly lost on a reporter who observed that the savages appeared 'perfectly contented with their present surroundings, and displayed the greatest confidence in Mr Cunningham, whose experience in acquiring them sounds more like a thrilling romance than anything'.

Within days, Cunningham and his human cargo were racing across America by the Union Pacific railroad. The captives, who'd never before strayed more than a few miles from their island homes, would no doubt have watched out of their windows in awe as the train rattled across the deserts of Nevada and the plains of Nebraska, whistling over bridges on the Missouri and the Mississippi rivers, through the prairies of Illinois and the metropolitan centres of the east. That no record is kept of the visitors' reactions to the scenes that flew past their eyes during the journey is a singular tragedy amongst many.

They arrived in Baltimore on Sunday, 6 May, the next morning leading a Grand Parade through the city, ahead of the Zulus, Amazonians and Hottentots, the Georgia Coons and the Arizona Piccaninnies, Redskins of the Klondike, Japanese strongmen and contortionists from India, crocodiles lassoed in the Siamese swamps by Russian equestrians, and, at the rear, the star attraction: Jumbo, the elephant.

In the afternoon, they all appeared under Barnum's enormous Big Top for a matinee performance, the Palm Islanders' world suddenly alive with weird animals, loud music, freakish sights and crowds made of so many people that a mere gasp from all of them would send a chill through the bones. They were made to throw boomerangs and perform ritual dances while Cunningham thrilled the crowd with rot through the bullhorn, introducing Sussy as 'Princess Tagarah, daughter of the Cannibal King of Northern Queensland'. A newspaper advertisement from the time gives us some idea of the temper of Cunningham's rousing narrative . . .

> *These are the only ones of their monstrous, self-disfigured and hopelessly embruited race ever lured from the remote, unexplored and dreadful interior wilds, where they wage an endless war of extermination, that they may gratify their hellish appetite . . . With bestiality, ferocity and treachery stamped upon their faces, their cruel eyes reflecting but a glimmering of reason, having no gist of speech beyond an ape-like gibberish utterly unintelligible to anyone else, they are but one step removed from brutes in human form . . .*

On the first day, 30 000 people came to look upon them. The newspapers wrote of the cannibals more often than they did of Jumbo, the circus's star elephant. For the next six months, P. T. Barnum's 'Ethnological Congress of Strange Savage Tribes' was the talk of the eastern states, and by the end of October Barnum himself had proclaimed it 'the most successful season ever known in show business'.

None of which mattered much to Tambo and the others, their cut of the fortune being the 'nominal' fee that Barnum had always promised. Nevertheless, in an interview with a newspaper reporter, R. A. Cunningham made it clear he had no reason to expect any grumbles of dissatisfaction from his performers. 'They have every confidence in me as their protector,' he said,

> *as well they may. They realize fully that their good behavior will be duly appreciated and properly rewarded by me, and, as they know I am the only one who can restore them in safety to their native wilds, they act accordingly.*

At the conclusion of the circus season in October, the islanders from Queensland embarked on a circuit tour of the 'dime museums', small theatres of the absurd and the strange that had sprouted across America in the latter half of the century. Dime museums represented the uncultured end of the entertainment arena, where authenticity was even less of a feature than it had been in Barnum's American Museum. For the most modest of fees (though a fair price indeed), crowds filed through to gaze upon mutants and monsters, mummies, zombies, fossilised fairies, reassembled cadavers and other such treasures of fiendish fantasia. (In the last surviving dime museum in Baltimore, which closed its doors at the end of the twentieth century, the most popular exhibit purported to be that of Abraham Lincoln's last bowel movement, allegedly taken from a chamber pot at Ford's Theater, mounted in a frame along with a discoloured certificate attesting to its authenticity. The stool was later tested and found to contain crumbs of a confectionary biscuit cooked no earlier than the 1920s.)

In Cincinnati, at Harris's Mammoth Museum, the Australians shared billing with Admiral Dot and Major Atom, 'the world's smallest character actors' (they'd been forced to incorporate impressions into their act after a surplus of dwarves flooded the sideshow circuit), and Irene Woodward, 'the Original Tattooed Lady'. Irene was said to have received her ink markings when she and her family were captured by Sioux Indians in the west, chief Sitting Bull himself agreeing to let them go if he could watch while Irene's father tied her to a tree and tattooed the suffering girl from head to foot. (She later admitted to having paid for her tattoos in a New York parlour, and that she'd rather enjoyed the experience, which 'tickled'.)

But it was in Philadelphia that trouble first flared, Sussy developing a fever so worrying to the other Aborigines that they were overheard by newspaper reporters cursing Cunningham 'for bringing them away to die in a strange country'. Sussy appeared to have recovered by the time the show reached Baltimore in December, by which time Tambo and Little Toby were sick, as was the tall young man with no name. By mid February, a reporter for the *Pittsburg Critic* was alarmed to find Cunningham ladling medicine into the mouth of a miserable Tambo, remarking that it was 'all I can do to keep them alive'.

On Saturday, February 23, 1884, as the troupe arrived for their next appointment in Cleveland, Tambo dropped dead on the floor of his hotel room. Sussy was shattered, refusing to eat for days, while the others ignored all demands to perform. Infuriated, Cunningham told a reporter he was having 'great trouble with the creatures and wishes they were off his hands'. Tambo, he said, had been 'the worst of the lot'.

A few days later the tall nameless man passed away just as Tambo before him. We do not know what became of him, as

Cunningham moved his miserable little band out of town before the press could get wind of events. There was another reason, too, for why Cunningham was wise to put some distance between Cleveland and mourning Aboriginals in his care.

As compensation for the performance that never happened, Cunningham had sold Tambo's corpse to the curator of the very dime museum in which the troupe would otherwise have appeared. Stuffed and embalmed, his wide eyes staring out from behind a glass case, Tambo would entertain the curious of Cleveland for many years to come.

The *New York Times* reported on the 'death of a boomerang thrower', venturing only that 'the American climate proved too much for him'. The *Cleveland Herald* went further, suggesting that Tambo was 'a victim to the mania for curiosity exhibitions which has raged in this country and Europe for the past ten years'.

Cunningham's arrival in England a few weeks later signified the end of his contract with P. T. Barnum, who had no qualms about releasing Robert and his ailing crew from their American obligations. Cunningham doubtless felt a change of scenery and climate might raise the spirits of his performers, the smaller venues of England and Europe, with their decidedly more sophisticated airs, promising a more intimate and peaceful experience than the cheap horror and sawdust of the Yankee tent theatres.

The European tour began in Brussels in May, where the Aborigines would spend the next month of their lives being visited regularly by local anthropologists, who remarked on the group's quiet intelligence. They also examined each member physically. Almost all, they reported, revealed the presence of tuberculosis.

From Brussels, the Queenslanders were shuffled to Berlin, where the savages were seen to be wearying of celebrity. Invited by Cunningham to observe the creatures relaxing during dinner at their own lodgings, journalists reported the foul tempers that flared as each new member of the press entered the ever-crowding room, the eyeball-rolling natives seen to 'down forks and knives with a gesture of obvious indignation and protest against the violation of their privacy'. Others noted misery in their eyes, and speculated on the reasons why, one report suggesting with some surprise, that the savages 'appear to deal with death much as we do'.

Later, on invitation from a resident professor, the seven Australians enjoyed an excursion through the Royal Museum of Berlin, their mood becoming cheerful at last as they identified various boomerangs, message sticks and other Aboriginal artefacts on display. However, the buoyant atmosphere was crushed in an instant by the sudden sight of a mummified Aborigine, wrapped in bark, the knees of the corpse drawn up to the chin, after the fashion of the burial rites back home. The collector who had donated the specimen had retrieved the body from a tree in Queensland, cutting it down and ferrying it to England. It is not impossible that someone in Cunningham's troupe may have known him in life.

The experience appears to have been fatal for Bob, who lay down and died in Chemnitz not long thereafter. Cunningham was forced to outrun the spectre of death once again, mustering his sickly and miserable band through Breslau, Nordhausen, Erfurt, Saxony, with small engagements along the way in restaurants and beer halls of varying size. Jimmy passed away in Darmstadt on the last day of May. Sussy followed within the month, 'Princess Tagarah, daughter of the Cannibal King of Northern Queensland', succumbing on the 23rd of June, 1884.

When Toby died in Paris in November, Billy, Jenny and Little Toby lost their desire to even entertain themselves. A French anthropologist who examined them found the three sick and despondent, Jenny deep in melancholy and Billy turning away whenever offered money. When asked if he could comprehend the notion of passing time (for of course the world did not begin to turn until the white man looked upon it) Billy began reciting the names of places from Townsville to Sydney, from San Francisco to Baltimore, from Berlin to Paris – every single city and shanty town they had encountered on their epic journey, which began when they were all offered a ride in a land so far away and so long ago.

The anthropologist recorded that Billy had misunderstood the question.

We do not know what happened to the remaining three of Cunningham's band. They toured some more – Scotland, Ireland, Russia, England – but there, reports of them go cold and thus the spectacle viewed through time must end. R. A. Cunningham later claimed to have returned them home from whence they came, but there is little proof of it – there exist no tales of tribal welcomes home, of warm embraces with old friends, just laments for the ones who took a trip and vanished into history.

One did come back to Palm Island, so many years after leaving it. In 1992, Australian anthropologist Roslyn Poignant found the body of a young Aboriginal male, embalmed, mummified, lying in the basement of a funeral parlour in Cleveland, Ohio. It was Tambo, and on 23 February, 1994, on the 110-year anniversary of his death, Tambo at last returned to his beloved Palm Island, to be buried at the foot of the mountain unchanged since he had last laid eyes upon it. His gravestone reads: 'In memory of Tambo, a brave voyager . . . may his spirit rest in peace.'

R. A. Cunningham, too, would come back to Palm Island, his cutter seen to sniff the breeze off Townsville in 1892. Days later, he would sail away to America one last time, his companions for the journey another eight brave voyagers, who waved goodbye to friends and lovers, and promised to return.

A FORK IN THE ROAD

There's an intersection in Canberra that, today, sees a freeway collide with a city thoroughfare, the junction flanked by office blocks and strict departmental edifices which see plenty of traffic passing between them, day and night. But it was once a lonely crossroads, back in the day when the national capital was not yet half a century old, nothing like the metropolis it is today. And something happened here – not an event that might bring down governments or alter the turn of the earth, but something that changed lives and futures in ways we cannot know ...

Peter Schinnick was only a young man on the night of 29 November, 1952. Stationed with the RAAF in the Australian Capital Territory, he used his leave to take in the night life Canberra had to offer, and meet the single girls who lived there. Perhaps one would become his bride.

One week before this night, at the Coronation Ball in the city, he had met a young girl, from Queanbeyan, in whom he held some hope. Twenty years old and a trainee nurse from the Canberra Community Hospital, she was blonde, beautifully proportioned and very pretty. She seemed interested in him. They had been seeing each other all week, the first seeds of attraction blooming swiftly. Peter had asked her to accompany him to a party on this very night, and she had agreed. Perhaps this might be the beginning of a relationship that would last them the rest of their lives.

Shortly after nine o'clock, Peter arrived at the hospital to pick her up, bringing an extra helmet so that she could ride on the back of his motorcycle. He found her standing by the road in a little black party dress, looking quite the sacrifice. She climbed on behind him, wrapping her arms around his waist as they motored off into the night.

Peter doesn't recall anything of what happened next. He learned most of the details later, in court, and from the newspapers of the day.

The couple had been riding for just a few minutes when they approached the Patent Office on the intersection of Kings Avenue and National Circuit. Somehow Peter lost control and hit the kerb at speed, both he and his passenger tossed to the side of the road, she tumbling head over tail, breaking bones and tearing skin.

For a time she just lay there, hurt and bewildered as the wheels of the motorcycle spun in the distance. She managed to turn her head to look for Peter. He was lying several metres away, face down, not moving at all. His body was contorted. She called out his name but he didn't respond. She thought he was dead. She panicked and began to cry.

The road was lonely on this particular night, and she began to worry that if she didn't do something they would both die before anyone discovered them. But when she tried to raise herself from the ground, her body stabbed at her from inside. She lay back down and waited. She was yet to learn she had broken three ribs and fractured her pelvis in several places.

In the distance she heard a car engine, and then she saw the lights. As the car approached, she cried out for help. The vehicle slowed, the driver looked, and then pulled to a stop.

A man emerged from an Oldsmobile Tourer and came to her side. He asked if she was all right. She replied she was hurt, but that she was more worried about Peter. The man left and went to her partner's aid, leaning over the damaged body, peering into his eyes. He would live, the man said, but he didn't want to move him. The best thing he could do was to take her immediately to the hospital and, once there, alert the ambulance, who would then come for Peter.

The man helped the girl to her feet, and a few times she cried out from the pain that creaked in her shifting bones. The man carried her to his car, placing her gently in the passenger side, before climbing into the driver's seat and heading for the hospital, leaving Peter behind on the side of the road, oblivious to the world.

They had been driving for only a few minutes when the man announced that he had to stop for a moment. It was only then that the girl realised the man smelled of alcohol. He climbed from the car and seemed to stagger into bushes at the side of the road, crouching in the shadows, his head between his knees, vomiting onto the ground at his feet. The girl worried that he might not be sober enough to drive.

After some time, the man returned to the car and they continued on their journey. But soon the girl noticed they were driving on the road to Red Hill, not in the direction of the hospital at all. She mentioned this to the man, who insisted that this was the way to the hospital. The girl replied that it was certainly not – she was a nurse, she said, and she knew very well that the hospital was in the other direction.

At this moment the car seemed to shudder to a halt. The man swore and said that the engine had stopped. He opened his door and stepped out, to see if there was anything he could do.

Suddenly, he opened the young girl's door and climbed inside, forcing her back in the seat. The girl began to scream, but the man put his hand to her throat, then picked up a spanner from the floor of the car, telling her that if she made another sound he would hit her. But she couldn't stop screaming – she was in such pain, and now she was terrified, too. The man became angry, bringing the hard object down onto the side of her head. She almost passed out, and she felt her own blood trickle down her neck. She stopped screaming, and began instead to sob.

The man lifted her dress and undid his trousers, huffing the smell of stale beer in her face as he raped her, every thrust grinding her sore and broken bones.

He finished quickly, and began himself to cry. He was sorry, he said, but she was just so pretty. If it was all right with her, he'd rather that she told nobody of this embarrassing moment. The girl promised she wouldn't. The man then composed himself, climbed from on top of her, made himself respectable, returned to the driver's seat and started the vehicle.

As they drove, he calmly asked her where she would like to go now. Through sobs, she responded that she wished to go to the hospital – her bones were still broken and her boyfriend still injured by the side of the road. He seemed disappointed, but drove her there all the same.

Upon arrival outside the hospital, he gently lifted her from the passenger seat and helped her to the side of the street. She cried that she couldn't walk, at which the man told her to wait while he went inside the hospital to fetch help. He returned with a policeman, who thanked the man for his efforts as he carried the weeping girl inside.

It was only while being examined that the girl managed to pull herself together for long enough to tell the story, by which time her rapist had been and gone. An ambulance was dispatched to the scene of the accident, where Peter was found, still unconscious, as he would remain for the next three days.

Police fanned out in search of a man fitting the description of the rapist: dark hair; olive skin; medium build; mongrel. It didn't take long for Canberra authorities to find their man.

Twenty-four-year-old Vincent George Dixon had racked up no less than forty convictions between the years of 1938 and 1947, including larceny, assault, injuring police, drunkenness and absconding from prison institutions. In September of 1947, his sister had bitterly wept in court as she told of how Vincent had tried to rape her just weeks before, beating her savagely as she'd tried to escape, her newborn baby under her arm. Vincent had claimed no memory of the event, arguing that he'd been drinking 'plonk' with 'cobbers', and couldn't possibly have done it, being that he'd been so drunk. The judge had sentenced him to eighteen months' jail.

During his trial for the rape of the nurse, Dixon, who claimed he was so drunk he couldn't remember the evening at all, pled innocence from every possible direction as the evidence piled up against him: he had never been at the scene of the accident or seen the girl in his life; the man on the cycle was the one who'd had sex with her; someone else must have come along while he was vomiting in the bushes and raped the girl then; he'd had sex with her, yes, but it was consensual. His lawyer also argued his client's good character, noting that Dixon had alerted the ambulance and ultimately saved Peter's life, not to mention the assistance he had provided the girl with after the fact, which was very kind of him.

On Wednesday, 24 February, Vincent's lips were seen to tremble as Justice Simpson sentenced him to death by hanging. The following day, authorities destroyed the shack in which Dixon had lived, a grader flattening the earth until all evidence of his existence had disappeared.

Peter Schinnick eventually recovered from his injuries. He went on to serve in the RAAF against the Communist insurgence in Malaya in 1958, and later married, had three children. He doesn't think about the nurse often, he says. He last saw her outside the court house, sobbing, traumatised, so he left her be. He doesn't know what became of her – whether she recovered, married, had children of her own – and he never spoke of her to his own family, or of the thing that happened on that lonely road in Canberra so many years ago.

Children tend to believe their mothers and fathers were always betrothed, that there were never others who might be there instead, but for circumstance – an accident, a fork in the road, a broken date. They seldom spare a thought for the brothers and sisters they share, who pass them daily in the street, bound not by blood or law, but fate.

LOST CHAMPION

An old photograph in the National Library of Australia shows a parade of Sudanese military men passing down Sydney's George Street in 1885. In the background one can see very clearly an establishment called Foley's Hotel, a charming old saloon that doubtless drowned many a tear and housed many a daytime lurker. It belonged to Larry Foley, a former bruiser from a Catholic gang that prowled the streets of Sydney in search of the enemy – notoriously, in 1871 he went hammer and tongs with Sandy Ross, leader of a Protestant gang, in an organised street fight that lasted 71 rounds before police broke it up. Larry grew up and went legit, operating his establishment as both public house and temple of war, in which men fought titanic bare-knuckle duels that launched careers and ruined handsome faces.

Wives and mothers must have cheered when the wreckers knocked it down in 1908. Eighty years later, the Royal Australian Historical Society erected 101 green plaques around Sydney, celebrating historic places, people and events that had once been. One such plaque, on the footpath outside what is now the Strand Arcade, celebrates Foley's Hotel, an icon that has never really been forgotten, which is more than one can say for the national treasure about whom you will now read . . .

Montague James Furlong was born in Sydney on 22 July in the year of 1868. We know little of his early days, save that he was an apprentice plasterer before discovering he was good with his fists. These were bare-knuckle times, and Jim Hall, as he would call himself, was only too pleased to take the gloves off for man, woman or beast. It was said that a drunken Hall once struck a man in The Rocks, then the man's wife for interfering, finally backhanding the couple's child for crying out in defence of his parents. Whatever the truth, the magistrates of Sydney were well pleased when Jim began fighting professionally in 1886. Hall mostly fronted up for scrappy duels in Foley's Hotel, a pugilist's pub in Sydney's George Street that was affectionately known as 'The Iron Pot', on account of the sweat that dripped from the walls when the nights steamed with drunken roars and fighting fury.

Jim, a six-foot middleweight, showed that he had some mettle – on his third professional show, he fought to a draw with Mick Dooley, a one-time heavyweight champion of Australia, and in January of 1889 he held his own for five rounds against Bob Fitzsimmons, an ex-pat Kiwi who was widely regarded as the toughest around, and who would go on to thrill America as one of the greatest fighters the world would ever see. It was the beginning of one the most intense and anticipated rivalries in the Victorian boxing era, the watershed of which would arrive on a rainy winter's night in New Orleans in 1893.

But it was on 8 May in 1889 that Hall first made the crowds stand up and take notice, knocking out middleweight title-holder Edward 'Starlight' Rollins in the twentieth round at Sydney Stadium. Jim Hall had come from nowhere and beat a bona fide Australian champion. Those who doubted the result were astonished two months later when Rollins, having demanded a rematch, was knocked out again, only this time in the fifth. Before the year was out, Jim Hall's record was a litany of carnage: Jack Malloy, knocked out in the fifteenth round; Herbert Goddard in the fourth; Jack Slavin in the tenth; Herbert Goddard again, this time in the third, and in the third once more when Herbert was foolish enough to come back for another thrashing twenty-one days later; Eddie Welsh in the fifth; Pablo Fanque in the fourth ...

But it was Bob Fitzsimmons who was considered the fighter for Hall to beat. With a record of twenty-four wins – including one against a younger Hall – one draw and just four losses, Fitzsimmons was Jim Hall's ticket to the United States, where purses were plentiful for fighters from the colonies. Jack 'Nonpareil' Dempsey, the Irish-American Middleweight Champion of the World, who had been beaten only three times in sixty-five bouts, was on notice that either Hall or Fitzsimmons would soon be sailing to take his title. Exactly which one of the two Australian fighters it would be was an even bet.

A bout was arranged at Foley's on 11 February, 1890 and what happened that night remains a mystery to this day. Fitzsimmons claimed that Hall had promised to pay him to take a dive, thus clearing Hall's way to America to fight Dempsey. It's an unlikely scenario – Fitzsimmons was proud and, like Hall, on his way up, as keen as any to have a shot at a world title. But Fitzsimmons was known through his career as unscrupulously honest and gentlemanly – in the early 1900s, while staying at the Hotel Windsor in Melbourne, Bob, drunk and rowdy, was knocked out by a hotel guest named Charles Salter after making a rude remark to some ladies, and it was a contrite Bob who knocked on Salter's door in the morning to congratulate him for doing the right thing. Hall, who had no such gentlemanly record, swore to his dying day that he beat Fitzsimmons fair and square. What is known for sure is that Fitzsimmons went down for the count in the fourth round, and Hall was declared the winner. What is also certain – because Fitzsimmons never stopped bleating about it – was that he never received the £75 that Hall had allegedly promised him for hitting the canvas. Whatever the truth may be, it's fair to conclude that Fitzsimmons was outfoxed by his opponent, the controversy leaving both victor and vanquished itching for a rematch, so as to show the world who was the better man.

By all accounts, Jim Hall was an impressive physical specimen, a fact to which the *Washington Post* would dramatically attest:

> *When in his prime, Hall was one of the handsomest athletes that ever stripped between the ropes. Over six feet in height, broad of shoulder, taper of waist, thin in the flank and beautifully proportioned, he might have stood for the ideal model of an ancient Grecian sculptor. His features were regular in outline and, like that other Adonis of the modern era, James J. Corbett, bore scarcely a trace of the many battles in which he engaged. Jim Hall carried no 'tin ears', for the very good reason that his cleverness enabled him to avoid such disfigurement. A remarkably brilliant boxer, his cat-like grace and agility, combined with a thorough knowledge of ring craft and the ability to think and act at the same time, made him the perfect specimen of the brainy glove artist.*

Jim Hall was also a shocking drunk, incapable of keeping his temper from boiling over into violence and alcoholic rage. Everything had been set for him to sail to America to meet Jack Dempsey when, on the eve of his voyage, Jim decided to pass the hours farewelling friends and strangers alike at a local tavern. After drinking all day, Hall found himself in an argument with another patron. A fight broke out, the terrified drinker defending himself against the furious Hall in the only way he thought would be successful, by pulling a knife and lashing at the hands that flew toward him with cracking speed. Hall beat his assailant to a pulp, but not before the knife gashed his right hand wide open. Fleeing the law, Hall bolted for his boat, but his hand was bleeding so profusely the captain of the vessel would not allow him on board. Hall's American invasion was thus postponed.

While Hall was recuperating, Fitzsimmons seized the chance to leap into Hall's ticket against Jack Dempsey, steaming to the United States with his story about his organised loss to Hall and the unpaid £75. On 14 January, 1891, Fitzsimmons took Hall's place in the fight with Jack Dempsey for the middleweight title in New Orleans, shocking the nation by giving Dempsey a hiding, knocking him down no less than thirteen times and begging the champion to quit before more damage was done. He finally convinced him with a knockout in the fifth round, Fitzsimmons carrying the bloodied 'Nonpareil' to his corner.

Hall was furious at the news of Fitzsimmons' victory, sobering up for long enough to take ship to America, where news of his imminent arrival was telegraphed to a nation still buzzing from the bruising Fitzsimmons had given the 'unbeatable' Dempsey. The *Chicago Tribune* announced the coming war on 24 January, 1891:

> *Those who witnessed the Dempsey–Fitzsimmons fight at New Orleans are loath to believe that there is a middleweight in the world who can whip Fitzsimmons. Australia possesses such a marvel in the person of Jim Hall, who stopped the lanky Bob in three and a half rounds . . . He has whipped*

every middleweight of note in the colonies ... Hall is now on the Pacific Ocean on his way to this country to earn, if possible, the title of middleweight champion of the world. While the fact he has defeated Fitzsimmons has been denied, all the Australian papers give him credit for the performance and it is, no doubt, correct. When he arrives in San Francisco he promises to make it interesting for aspiring middleweights.

And make it interesting he did. On his first fight in San Francisco in February, 1891, Jim Hall knocked out middleweight Alec Greggains in the very first round, and later won on points against the well-regarded Tommy Ryan in Chicago, the *Manitoba Daily Free Press* reporting that 'it was evident almost from the start that the Chicago man was outclassed by the big Australian'.

Hall was immediately taken under the wing of Charles E. 'Parson' Davies, a Chicago boxing luminary whose stable included black fighter Peter Jackson, whose colour was the only reason he wasn't the heavyweight champion of the world, and James 'Gentleman Jim' Corbett, the reigning heavyweight champion who is credited today with having transformed boxing from a sophisticated brawl to a genuine fighter's art. Davies was not a man to be trifled with – a well-connected Chicago hustler, at handshakes with the Windy City's notorious underworld, he was perhaps one of the few people who might have been capable of keeping Hall's constitutional recklessness on a leash.

In just a few months, however, while touring Detroit with his fighter, Davies found Hall drunk one morning and angrily told him to go home and sleep it off. Hall didn't take the advice, appearing later in the evening, drunker still, in a bar in which Davies was entertaining associates. A boisterous argument ensued,

Davies keeping his cool while Jim Hall raged and abused, poking his finger into Davies' chest and generally making a prize nuisance of himself. Frustrated by Davies' composure, Hall threw a haymaker and Davies snatched a lemon knife from the bar and stabbed Hall in the neck, missing his jugular by millimetres, growling at the stunned Australian, 'Next time I'll make a sure job of it'. Hall responded by opening his shirt and daring Davies to plunge the knife into his heart, then accused the Chicagoan of cowardice as Davies escorted the drunk and bleeding fighter to the local hospital. It was the end of their association.

On the rebound, Hall was taken in by the Manly Art Institute in downtown Beloit, Wisconsin, a tight boxing outfit run by trainer John Kline, who saw great potential under Hall's wild demeanour. Both Kline and Hall knew all fights were meaningless unless Hall could be seen to beat Bob Fitzsimmons and put the simmering rivalry and the controversy of the Australian knockout to rest. Thus a showdown was scheduled for late in 1891 in St Paul in Minnesota, one newspaper reporting that

> *the bad blood between the fighters is almost as much of an incentive as the big stakes (a whopping $12 000), and a sport who is in the confidence of both men said he believed that they would be willing to get together even if the stake money were withdrawn.*

Hall trained as hard for Kline as he had in his life, abstaining from booze, he told the newspapers, 'except for the occasional touch of claret'. The nation geared up for what was being touted as 'one of the fiercest battles ever fought by middleweights in this country'. But the enthusiasm was no match for the Governor of Minnesota, who hated boxing with a passion. On the day of the fight, he instructed four companies of National Guardsmen to surround the amphitheatre at St Paul to stop the fight from happening.

It took Kline another twelve months to reschedule the fight, during which Jim Hall passed the time by drinking hard and brutalising a succession of boobs stupid enough to climb into the ring with him. He knocked out Bob Ferguson in Chicago in the fourth round, Owen Marley in the fourth at Dubuque, Iowa, and Joe Tansey in the fourth at Oshkosh, Wisconsin. In Chicago, he downed Mike Boden in the fourth, Al Fish in the third just ten days later, and Jack King in the fourth a month after that. In April, 1892, Jim presided over a month-long slaughterhouse that – the quality of the fighters notwithstanding – has never been bested in the calendars of professional boxing history. Beginning in Ariel, Philadelphia, he knocked out three separate opponents within six days: Jack Flood in the very first round, Jack Houghey in the second two nights later, and Mick White within seconds of the opening bell three nights after that. A week and a half later, at Niblo's Theater in New York City, Chris Cornell fell to the canvas unconscious before the end of the first round and, four days after that, in the same venue, Jerry Slattery was lucky to last the one and a half rounds that he did.

Unable to find anyone of repute who seemed terribly interested in climbing through his ropes, and infuriated by newspaper reports of his 'spectacular inactivity', Hall sailed to London to fight Ted Pritchard for the British world middleweight championship. Jim knocked Pritchard out in the fourth round, returning to America with the British prize belt.

But it was the fight against Fitzsimmons everyone was waiting for, the deep rooted hostility between the two fighters having been slugged out in the pages of the national newspapers for months.

Fitzsimmons alerted punters to the 'whipping' he'd given Hall in the early days of the younger Australian's career – along with gentle reminders of a certain outstanding £75 debt – while Hall branded Bob a 'turncoat' and a 'traitor', a reference to Fitzsimmons' imminent naturalisation as an American citizen, a change of national allegiance that evidently rankled Hall.

At last, 'the most anticipated fight of recent memory' was scheduled to take place in New Orleans on the night of March the 8th, 1893, for a purse of $40 000, the largest the American ring had ever seen. In the weeks leading up to the big night, the newspapers were unanimous about Hall's 'great shape' for the bout, and many tipped Jim to win it. The opinion of the *Chicago Daily* was typical:

> *It had been the general impression in this country that anybody who could hit Fitzsimmons could whip him, as many believe he will not stand punishment. This is, however, problematical . . . For all that, Hall will probably be returned the winner. He can punish anybody and knows Fitzsimmons' weak points. He has the skill to reach them, too.*

Much of the credit for Hall's standing was given to John Kline's disciplined and rigorous training of the wayward pugilist, and the papers reported upon frightening wagers being laid by the nation's top betting men, almost all in Hall's favour. But Hall appeared to be 'not in the best of shape' when he arrived in New Orleans on the morning of 6 March, a somewhat sour mood noted by journalists as he alighted from his train. 'Hall was not happy,' wrote one reporter, 'and he said so.'

On the morning of the fight, a curious notice appeared in the pages of the *Chicago Tribune*, the short piece telling of how Hall had been seen to jump in a carriage after lunch and drive hastily away with fellow fighter and big drinker, Charlie Mitchell:

> *Hall said they were only going to dinner and would return in a few minutes. Kline had Hall's work laid out for him for the afternoon, commencing at 3pm, but in the absence of Hall the necessary training had to be postponed. Poor Kline walked around the hotel as restless as a newly-caged tiger, and watched the clock as the hours sped away . . . At seven o'clock this evening, Hall had not returned and Kline was still walking the floor wiping the perspiration from his brow . . .*

Rain pelted down on the night of 8 March, 1893, as 4000 people crowded into the Crescent City Club in New Orleans, Louisiana. Celebrities, politicians and the luminaries of the boxing world packed the auditorium; Bat Masterson, Wyatt Earp's one-time offsider, now a boxing aficionado and freelance sports writer, acted as timekeeper for the event.

To some, Hall's strut before the bell seemed arrogant – the cock-a-hoop swagger of a conqueror before the fight has been won or lost. Word got around that he'd asked the Crescent City Club officials to show him proof of the certified cheque that was to be presented to the victor. While it has never been suggested that Jim was drunk when he entered the ring that night, his adventures with Charlie Mitchell the previous evening had doubtless left him with a shocking hangover and, for Jim Hall, there had only ever been one remedy for the shakes and tremors, the anxieties of withdrawal. Hall knew that this was the fight of his life, the moment that would prove his bombast to be either based upon truth, or mere shouts from the shadow of a boxer who wished to be. He would have needed all the courage he could get.

The bell rang for the opening of the first round, and it was Fitzsimmons who threw the first punches – two left upper-cuts from which Hall escaped unscathed. For two rounds the pair traded blows to the body and hits to the head, each winning punch immediately answered with an equally ferocious response. Fitzsimmons came out in round three as the aggressor, but then Hall landed two heavy lefts to Bob's head, followed by a right upper-cut that made Bob grab for his opponent and hold on in a clinch at the end of the round. Hall appeared to have his man where he wanted him.

Then began round four. Buoyed by his bashing of Bob in the closing seconds of the last round, Hall charged from his corner and straight into an arcing right-hand from Fitzsimmons, 'a blow that will shine on the pages of the history of American pugilism', according to the reporter for the *Chicago Tribune*, who was ringside. His praise went on:

> It was a right-hand swinging blow, full on Hall's left jaw and low down where such blows count fast. Quick as a flash it caught Hall and literally lifted him up and backwards. He fell straight back as dead, out as ever a pugilist was. But for the felt beneath the canvas his head would have suffered as it struck the platform heavily. It was a terrific punch and for a few seconds Hall lay still and quiet and scarcely seemed to breathe. The crowd and Fitzsimmons thought he was dead.

For a few minutes, all celebrations were on ice as Hall's team worked furiously to revive him. No amount of water or the shaking of limbs brought any sign of life to the prone figure. It was a nervous Bob Fitzsimmons who came up with the correct prescription, dousing Jim's face with whisky until the beaten Australian at last opened his eyes. Jim appeared to weep as he was dragged through the ropes, Bob Fitzsimmons waving an American flag high above his head as he marched victoriously around the ring.

In his dressing room, Jim assumed the position of the loser with haste, bursting open bottles of wine as he sobbed to reporters, barely able to believe that he'd lost. 'If I should whip Fitzsimmons a dozen times now,' he cried, 'I could never recover my reputation. I don't know what I will do now. I hadn't figured on losing, and have made no preparation for the future.'

Eleven days after his loss to Fitzsimmons, newspapers reported on another beating Hall was to suffer, this time in New York. After being denied entry to a bar, a drunken Hall picked a fight with a cab driver who refused to ferry him to another drinking house. According to the *Washington Post*, Hall was 'thrown down, kicked and pummeled by the enraged cabman until he cried for quarter'.

Licking his wounds, Hall took a steamer to England, where he believed a successful London campaign might rejuvenate him for a triumphant return to America, so that he might put the past behind him.

In London, he happened to discover a bar that was run by a former heavyweight champion of England, Jack 'Paddy' Slavin, who had relinquished his title the previous year. Slavin had been born in Australia, too – in Maitland, the same town from which

Les Darcy would hail – and he could more than keep up with Hall when there was any drinking to be done. Slavin was generous with Hall, whose thirst was deeper than his own pockets, but all Hall saw in Slavin was an opportunity to repair his damaged standing – if he could defeat a heavyweight champion, the humiliation he had suffered at the hands of Fitzsimmons might evaporate, and he could return to America to pick up where he had left off. He began showing up nightly in Slavin's establishment, dressed to the nines in a silk hat and a flashy coat, toasting the bar to the day when Paddy Slavin would have the courage to meet him in the ring. Night after night, Slavin resisted, until the insults became too horrid to bear and Paddy finally agreed to a duel to be fought at the National Sporting Club in Covent Garden on the night of 29 May, 1893.

The bookmakers backed Slavin at five-to-one, the heavyweight's bulk tipped to triumph easily over Hall's comparatively lithe frame. And for the first few rounds it appeared their expectations would be met, Slavin charging at Hall who bolted around the ring, seemingly desperate to escape. Newspaper reports tell of the assembled crowd 'booing scornfully at Hall's apparent cowardice'. The pursuit ended in the fourth round, when Hall suddenly turned and smacked Slavin square on the jaw, the former heavyweight champion tumbling into the ropes and down. Slavin recuperated, only to be floored by Hall again, who now seemed to have been playing possum all night. For the next three rounds Jim picked his friend to pieces, before finally slugging him down and out in the seventh.

Hall's win caused such a sensation in London that the call went out for a rematch with Ted Pritchard, from whom Hall had taken the British middleweight title just a few months before. Hall put all doubt away by dispatching Pritchard with a savage knockout in the third on 13 June, 1893.

What should have heralded the beginning of a return to form for the brilliant but unruly boxer from Sydney was, in fact, the beginning of the end. Hall's victories over Slavin and Pritchard made him an instant celebrity around London Town, and he became a permanent fixture in the late bars and early openers, getting into fights almost nightly, relying on the kindness of friends to bail him out of trouble when the sheen of celebrity began to wear thin. The word in boxing circles was that Jim Hall was a talent lost to himself, a drinker first and a boxer next, a loser who'd won a few, but that was all.

He returned to America out of shape, cap in hand, his reputation as a defeated fighter only reinforced by news of his behaviour in England. No promoter or trainer was willing to touch him. Jim's decline was rapid – his first two ranked fights of 1894 were against novices, Billy Woods and Henry Baker, both to whom he lost on points. In 1895 the only fights Jim Hall fought were with the law, a doctor from Louisville suing Jim for 'maintaining guilty relations' with his wife, and police arresting him for raising hell and assaulting patrons at a Cleveland Hotel. Joe Choynski, a fighter with a good record, agreed to fight Jim in Queens, New York, on 20 January, 1896, knocking Hall out in the thirteenth round. On 10 August, 1896, Jim was about to fight Steve O'Donnell in New York when he was arrested ringside for a massive debt of unpaid rent owed to his landlord and the fight was called off.

The ghosts of old rumours seemed to rise from the dead when, in October of 1897, a bout with well-ranked Charles 'Kid' McCoy in Philadelphia was called off by the referee when it became patently obvious the fight had been rigged in Jim Hall's favour. Two months later, Frank 'Paddy' Slavin took his revenge, knocking

Hall out in the seventh round during a fight in Quebec. In March of 1899, Jim was let out of jail to fight Charles Lawler, Hall having been picked up the night before for public drunkenness, and it was said he was too sauced to know when he miraculously knocked Lawler out in the tenth. Hall's last fight – his last roll of the dice – was for Joe Choynski's light-heavyweight title in September. With only three months to go before the century, and an era, would be over, Jim was knocked out in the seventh, complaining that he wanted to 'sleep in' as his handlers tried to lift the dazed fighter from the canvas.

Hall survived for a time on past glories, which lived on in the minds of the toughs and no-hopers of Chicago and Cleveland. But by the mid-1900s, he was a patient in a charity ward of a Chicago hospital. He was thrown out on the street when it was discovered he'd been sneaking into the Cook County morgue next door late at night, pinching jewellery and other valuables from unclaimed corpses to sell for drinking money.

His last payout came from a Chicago surgeon named Rahde, to whom Hall sold his skeleton for $150, the good doctor assuming he'd be able to collect on the deal within a year or two. Within days Hall was back, having drunk all the money, and insisting the price was now double or nothing. When Rahde complained, Jim let fly with the final knockout of his career.

On 11 March, 1913, newspapers reported that Jim Hall, 'a former well-known pugilist', had been found dying of tuberculosis in a hovel in Neenah, Wisconsin. Four days later, on the 15th of March, Jim died in the state sanitarium, the *New York Times* noting that it was 'twenty years ago last Saturday that Hall was knocked out in the fourth round by Bob Fitzsimmons in New Orleans'.

There ended the story of Jim Hall, a man who lost one fight, and so lost them all.

In 2006, Wisconsin boxing historian Bill Schutte found Jim Hall's grave at Oak Hill Cemetery in Neenah, the plot marked with no headstone or plaque to tell of who lay below. An admirer of Jim's had arranged for his burial in 1913, but had been careful to leave the grave unmarked, lest certain surgeons from Chicago came in search of Jim's bones.

With his own spare cash, Schutte purchased and then laid at the head of Jim's grave a small headstone, a black granite block inscribed with the words: 'Prizefighter'.

WHEN THEY ALL FEARED CLAUDE BATSON

The bushranger reserves a tender place in the Australian heart, celebrated in song and legend more so than any of the nation's law-abiding fathers. Frederick 'Captain Thunderbolt' Ward, committer of over 200 crimes, has a museum in his memory in the New South Wales town of Uralla, and is remembered by a number of roads and highways that bear his name. John Fuller, aka Daniel 'Mad Dog' Morgan, was distinguished in a 1976 film starring Hollywood big-shot Dennis Hopper. And of course there's Ned Kelly, who has soaked up more celluloid, canvas and printer's ink than any single creature in Australian history. But there are no such memorials to the man in this next tale, who terrorised a town for just five days back when the century was young – no monuments, no records, no mention of his name. It's as if he's been erased, not for the horror, but the shame . . .

Claude Valentine Batson first came to the attention of the world when he assured authorities he had an answer to the problem of Australia's rabbit plague. Representatives of the government took him seriously enough to gather one day on a hillside near Jingellic on the New South Wales side of the Murray River, to see the contraption at work, Claude offering nervous explanations as rabbits wandered in and out of warrens, unperturbed by the apparatus that seemed to block their way.

Twenty-three-year-old Batson had lived in the region for his whole life, and was regarded as a simpleton, his peculiarities noted by locals who'd known him for many years. A loner who attached his affections to nobody with any particular zeal, Claude moved from home to home, sometimes boarding with families or old women. He could not read nor write well, a fact about which he was sensitive, and he was prone to develop the odd grievance against folk for the slightest of reasons – usually, some said, for imagined persecutions. But it's true many mocked him, openly, convinced his apparent stupidity was an armour that rendered their ridicule painless. Others pitied him – he'd been badly treated as a boy, they said, by parents who had since disowned him. Claude himself never spoke of them.

It was on the eve of Christmas in 1923 that the people of Jingellic began to notice Claude acting a little more strangely than usual – nothing at all alarming, just odd utterances regarding abnormal plans. He'd surprised an elderly female resident, who knew Claude well, with the announcement that he had decided to become a bushranger, a dream in keeping with his oft-mentioned detestation of the rich. He was seen reading a Deadwood Dick, a 'penny dreadful' periodical that featured men with superhuman powers raging through the cities and across the lands. Another local fellow began receiving visits from Batson every day, Claude calling in to bid him goodbye, as he was moving, so he said, to lands in the north. This continued for weeks, a daily farewell in the absence of any evidence at all that Claude was going anywhere.

On the morning of Sunday, 10 February, 1924, Claude Batson paid a visit to Charles Barber, a 43-year-old local who had employed Claude from time to time on his farm on the Victorian side of the Murray River, opposite Jingellic, and was a good friend to him. Claude visited Barber regularly, and often took meals there on the invitation of Barber's wife, who had always shown Claude kindness. Staying at the Barber home at this time was sixty-year-old Thomas King, a tobacco grower from out of town. Claude did not like King – several weeks before, Claude had been enjoying a meal at Barber's home when he was crushed to hear Mrs Barber ask King to help her with the dishes, a duty she usually reserved for Claude himself. Claude began to simmer, imagining he was becoming an unpopular character in the Barber home.

On this day, Claude Batson arrived at the house just before eleven o'clock, his rifle under his arm. It was a fine, sunny Sunday, and he told Charles Barber he intended to go fox hunting. The Barbers were packing a hamper of food. Claude inquired as to the meaning of it, and was told the family was preparing to enjoy a picnic by the banks of the Jingellic Creek, on the New South Wales side of the Murray River.

Batson appeared to sulk – he would have liked to have come, too, and he complained that he hadn't been asked. Charles Barber told Claude to stop being silly – he was not a permanent member of the family, and if the Barbers decided to go on a picnic, or take a trip in the country, or go on a journey to the moon, it was not necessary that they seek out Claude first, just to make sure he wasn't going to feel left out. Claude's eyes narrowed. What of Mr King, he asked – was he going to the picnic, too? Yes, replied Barber, as was David Sheppard, who owned a farm nearby the creek.

Claude began to behave most peculiarly indeed, moving from one side of the room to the other, lifting things from shelves and mantels, fingering ornaments and framed photographs, the look of a man in mischief as he inquired as to where the picnic was to be held, and how long it was expected to last. After a time he took a seat at the kitchen table, and began to clean and oil his rifle and two revolvers. Charles took little notice, but when he entered the kitchen to find Batson nailing pieces of leather to the soles of his boots, he couldn't help but ask what the devil he was up to. Claude replied that the leather strips would prevent his feet from slipping. Only then did Barber notice that Batson's hands were shaking.

It was noon before Mrs Barber emerged from the bedroom, announcing to Claude that they intended to leave for the picnic soon and would like to lock up the house. Batson muttered something, gathered his weapons and then left. He was last seen walking up the road with his guns in the direction of the hills.

The picnic party had only been gone from the house for a few minutes when Claude emerged from the trees, having remained in hiding until he was sure the coast was clear. He entered with a key that Charles Barber had given him – he was trusted in that way. Once inside, he proceeded to tear the house apart, throwing clothes from drawers and food from containers. He paid particular attention to the property of Mrs Barber and Mr King, leaving the personal possessions of Charles Barber practically untouched. He did, however, avail himself of a bottle of whisky and half a bottle of claret, which he sat down and drank until there was no more drinking to be done.

Oblivious to the events that were taking place within the walls of his own home, Barber, along with his wife and Mr King, joined the other members of the party on the bank of the creek, near the house of William McGrath, all enjoying the afternoon sun with glasses of wine, tobacco and pleasant conversation.

An unusual thing occurred when King, in the process of lighting a tobacco pipe, appeared to set off some sort of explosion within the apparatus. The entire party turned to look at him, King staring down at his pipe with a perplexed expression on his face. Suddenly, the front of King's shirt seemed to rapidly change colour, a deep crimson spot appearing underneath the front of his collar, then spreading to his shoulders and belly. The man sat still for a moment, incredulous, before slowly tilting and falling flat on the grass at his side.

One of the guests, Charles Gainer, sprang to his feet and dashed to King's aid. As he stooped to help the older man, something struck him in the knee, showering the other members of the party in chips of bone and spots of blood. Charles Barber spun around and saw the cause of it – lying in the grass on the other side of the creek was a man with a rifle, aimed straight at him. It was Batson. Charles had only just processed this shocking information when a puff of smoke was seen to blow from the weapon's firing mechanism. William McGrath, seated on a blanket with a sandwich in his hand, screamed in pain, hit in the shoulder. David Sheppard, who had barely been raised to his feet by the bewildering drama unfolding around him, appeared to snap his head backwards, sharply, unnaturally, before falling to the ground.

As the men and women screamed and scattered for cover behind boulders and trees, bullets chopped the grass and earth at their feet. For minutes, which must have seemed eons to those crouching for cover, Batson fired repeatedly from the other side of the creek, evidently taking aim at Mrs Barber. Charles, who had been in the line of fire the entire time, had not been hit, standing like the one remaining skittle as all around had fallen.

Unarmed and with no means of escape, the party began to fear Batson would make his way across the water. After telling the women to stay down and move for nothing, Barber procured a horse and made a dash for Jingellic, where he would raise the alarm with the police. McGrath, despite his wound, stood and bolted for his house, shouting out that he would return with a rifle. Apparently hearing this, Batson was seen to stand and run into the nearby scrub.

It was dusk on Sunday evening when two young local girls by the name of Bryant, who had spent the afternoon in town playing tennis, were driving a sulky along a bush track that led to their farmhouse near Lankeys Creek, not far from Jingellic. On the road ahead they saw a figure emerge from the ferns and step into their way, brandishing a rifle. Terror quickly turned to bemusement as the girls recognised the man as Claude Batson, the local idiot, with whom they had been in a neighbourly way since childhood. Unaware of the afternoon's events in Jingellic, the girls stopped and spoke with Batson, who asked if they might be so kind as to allow him to stay at their farmhouse for the evening, as he was on his way to some place out of town. The girls readily agreed, and the three rode together to the Bryant home.

It was only after their arrival that Batson revealed to the girls and their mother his deeds for the day, apologising to them for the inconvenience. He implored that they not try to alert the authorities, though he insisted he had no intention of hurting them. The Bryants accepted Batson's guarantee and, in return, gave him their own. A fitful night's sleep was had by all.

At daybreak, the Bryant girls and their mother awoke to find Batson loitering in the kitchen, his rifle tucked under his arm. While Mrs Bryant fixed him steak and eggs for his breakfast, Batson, assuming his position by the mantelpiece, proceeded to finger and fondle the ornaments there – as was his wont – while he boasted of his exploits the previous day, and of those he intended to perpetrate in future. He was on a bushranging expedition, he said, which had always been his destiny. He was armed to the gills, with thousands of rounds of ammunition and provisions buried in the nearby hills. From his hiding place, he declared, he could keep an army of police at bay, and wage war on the township of Jingellic, where there were many who had wished to do him harm, though their names he would not say.

The would-be bushranger's swank was suddenly interrupted by the barking of the Bryant family dog. Peering out of the window, Batson spied two troopers approaching on horseback, one of whom – though Batson had no way of knowing it – was Trooper Tom Morris, the first Australian to be recommended for a Victoria Cross after serving in the Boer War in South Africa. Without a word, and leaving his bag of ammunition and provisions behind on the kitchen table, Batson bolted through the back door of the farmhouse and into the orchard, the two troopers in swift pursuit. Morris called out to the fugitive to stop, but Batson paid him no mind, increasing his speed as he weaved through the fruit trees, dashing for the safety of the hills. Morris fired but missed, whereupon Batson was seen to spin and return fire. Morris felt Batson's bullet cut the air as it sped by his ear. Morris raised his rifle to fire again, taking careful aim to bring his man down. He pulled the trigger, but his rifle jammed. By the time he looked up, Batson had reloaded and was taking aim. Both troopers took cover as Batson's shot cut through the leaves that hung by their heads. When they looked up, Claude Batson was gone, escaped through the trees and into the New South Wales hills.

The next day, the newspapers screamed with news of Claude Valentine Batson, the madman of Jingellic, who was on the loose in the Upper Murray district. David Sheppard had died of his wounds, and King was not expected to live. McGrath and Gainer remained critical. Claude Batson was now a murderer, the feared bushranger he had always dreamed of becoming. Newspapers spoke of his rat cunning, his expert marksmanship, his thorough knowledge of the terrain, and the known fact that Claude Valentine Batson was mad – crazy enough to wage a one-man war against the society whom he felt had wronged him. Reports of his boasts to the Bryant girls confirmed that Jingellic was now under siege.

Terrified civilians armed themselves and nailed their windows shut. A posse of more than thirty police and as many as sixty armed civilians combed the surrounding bushland. Roads were blocked, and checkpoints were set up on all bridges that spanned the Murray River.

It was Wednesday afternoon, at about three o'clock, when a boy who was milking a cow on Charles Barber's farm looked up to see a naked man approaching from the direction of the Murray River. As the man came closer, the boy recognised him as Batson, unarmed and dripping wet, with not a stitch of clothing nor a weapon to be seen. He told the boy he had swum the Murray River to elude police who were guarding the bridges. He asked the boy if anyone was home at the Barber residence, to which the boy replied honestly that there was not, as they were all being attended to at a hospital in Albury. Batson bade farewell, making his way to the Barber house, where he was seen to enter, emerging later in just a coat and a pair of Barber's trousers, running across the fields barefoot in the direction of the hills on the Victorian side of the Murray.

The next day the newspapers trumpeted that Claude Batson was now in Victoria, having boldly breached the Murray, nude, much to the embarrassment of the New South Wales police. The Victorian authorities sprang into action, convinced as they were that crafty Batson must be maintaining a second headquarters on their side of the border, in the inhospitable ranges that were honeycombed with crevices in which it was said the sun had never shone. A crude note found in the Barber home, allegedly written in Batson's hand, announced that the fugitive was off to commit suicide by cyanide, but it was dismissed as a ruse – most probably, the newspapers speculated, Batson had planned his war in advance, with supplies and ammunition buried in the Victorian hills. A special squad of mounted police were freighted from Melbourne, and local Victorians were warned to arm themselves and stay inside at nights.

Sightings of Batson began occurring everywhere, on either side of the state line. Farmers took long shots at anyone who looked suspicious, or half-naked, and newspaper reports had Batson leaping about the countryside like a flea on a map. On Thursday, a senior policeman was reported as speculating that the war between Claude Batson and the people of Victoria might go on for many months, the cost in lives impossible to predict. The reports also told of how close Trooper Morris had come to nailing his man during the shootout in the Bryant's orchard, the discovery of the clothing Batson had discarded on the New South Wales bank of the Murray revealing a bloodless bullet hole in the sleeve of his jacket.

But the papers of Thursday revealed something else, too. Reporters hungry for details of the life of Claude Valentine Batson were encountering not the hostility they might have expected, but a strange sense of commiseration for the man who'd been mocked for the whole of his life, by the very people who were now at his mercy. Residents who'd known Batson all of his life alluded to the 'privations' he'd endured, both as a young lad and as the known local simpleton. The passing of David Sheppard – a popular man – seemed all but lost in the reflections of a people labouring not under fear, but guilt.

On Friday morning, just after eleven o'clock, two young farm hands were milking cows in a shed on a property not far from Barber's home, when Claude Batson appeared at the window. Though he looked in a dreadful state, both boys recognised him, as they knew him well. One of them greeted him cheerily, and Batson responded with a weary smile, before asking if they'd mind if he came inside and had a drink of milk. The boys consented, and were alarmed when Batson entered the shed: he was dreadfully thin, dressed in nothing more than a woollen cap, a coat and some ragged trousers, with no shirt or shoes, his hair matted, his face unshaven, his feet red and swollen and covered in lesions. He trembled as he bent down to swig a cup of milk from a bucket, and the boys realised this might be their chance to pounce on the fugitive who'd eluded police for nearly a week. They seized his arms and forced him to the floor, impressing upon him the wisdom of him giving himself up before he was shot. Batson, too weak to resist, was held to the ground by one of the boys while the other went to raise the alarm.

Police swarmed the farmhouse, whereupon Batson was arrested and driven to the Jingellic Hotel, troopers propping him up on the verandah like a prize animal captured on a hunt. Word spread quickly and people from miles around descended on the scene until there was quite a crowd. In a low, feeble voice, trembling terribly as he stared at the ground beneath him, Batson told of how he had barely slept since Sunday, and had eaten so little his insides ached. He had lain in the scrub for days and nights, shivering, with nothing more than a pistol, which he had buried in the hills many months before, for reasons he could not say. Sometimes, in the darkness, he'd watched the police lanterns as they'd moved slowly up and down the hillsides, and there were moments, he said, when searchers were so close he might have reached out and touched them. When asked why he hadn't shot at anyone, Batson replied that he'd known many of his pursuers by name, and that he had no reason to dislike them.

As Batson spoke, his tired eyes peeping out occasionally from under his cap, many of the local men who had hunted him for days were moved to tears.

It was never to be known why Claude Batson fired at the picnic party that day, why he had grievances with some and not others, what those grievances might have been, or whether they were real or phantoms of his mind. But a curious episode took place during a hearing conducted by the bedside of the recuperating Thomas King. Interrupting his own testimony to ask if he could have a private word with the defendant, King whispered something in Batson's ear, and Claude's whispered response sent King into such an excited state as to force the hearing to be adjourned. What was said that day we may never know.

On Monday, 14 April, in the year of 1924, newspapers reported that Claude Valentine Batson had been officially declared insane by authorities. He was confined to a mental asylum for the remainder of his days.

UNDER A
MALEVOLENT STAR

Stand a distance from the Melbourne Cricket Ground while a contest takes place inside of it, and one would swear some meal for giant gods is being brewed inside – a steady simmer rises, falls, goes silent, rises, falls again then, suddenly, some angry heat boils all to roaring point, the depth and girth of the swirling noise enough to tear the whole joint down. It's a sound that carries all the way across the lush, green grounds of Fitzroy Gardens, only fading short of the buildings along Spring and Flinders streets, which enclose their own cosmopolitan racket. Viewed from the sky, the elms that line the paths radiating from the centre of the gardens make the shape of the Union Jack, the flag of King and Commonwealth at whose behest the ANZAC legend was born. But they also make the shape of a spider, eight legs stretching to all corners of the park. Enthusiasts of Greek mythology will recall Arachne as the vain young girl who hanged herself by her own woven threads, the goddess Athena bringing her back to life as a creature who must sit and wait for those unfortunate enough to make her acquaintance. But this is all unnecessary stuff. Our next story begins at the football, where players wear distinctive colours so that everyone knows which team they're on . . .

The Collingwood football club should have won the Anzac Day clash in 1999. They had earlier trailed the Bombers by forty points, a mighty resurgence in the final quarter seeing the Magpies come within eight points, the roar of 70 000 spectators in their sails. But when Anthony Rocca missed a sitter from right in front in the dying moments, flags dropped, shoulders drooped, the clock no longer mattered. Collingwood fans were already leaving when the siren blew.

John Whiteside and Kristian Dieber were on an Anzac Day roll. It had been a good, exciting game – the Anzac tests always were. They had been stirred by the solemn service before the game – *The Last Post*, the minute's silence. Good boys, they were, from decent families, moved by the gravity of the day.

John was twenty-eight, the youngest of five, born and bred in Ferntree Gully to the east of Melbourne, birthplace of Shane Warne, the cricket player. John was just fourteen when his father died, and his mother had passed away just the year before. But he had a good job and a steady life. He had never been in trouble with the law. Kristian was twenty-four, from Ringwood, not far from where his friend lived. He had a university degree in economics and coached little kids in cricket. Nobody had ever known him to be violent.

On this day John and Kristian had been drinking at the MCG prior to the game. They were drinking still while the contest raged. At the conclusion of the game, they joined the swarm that spilled from the grounds and headed for the MCG Hotel on Wellington Parade, where they drank again for several hours and shot the breeze with friends.

It was dark when they stepped back onto the street, their bellies full of beer. Along the edge of Fitzroy Gardens, the lights of oncoming cars making fiendish shapes amongst the trees, they made their way toward the glow of the city where another pub was waiting. At the traffic lights they stopped and waited. There was a whimper in the bushes. They turned to see a woman on her knees, sobbing quietly in the shadows, her shoes gone from her feet.

They stepped closer, asked if she needed help. The woman appeared to panic, throwing her purse toward the boys and begging to be left alone. John picked it up and tried to give it back. She screamed and sobbed some more. He looked inside for evidence of her name – Euvegina Tsionis, aged twenty-three. Kristian was on the street, hailing her a taxi. It was best that she go home, he said, as it wasn't safe for a woman, drunk amongst the gloom. All sorts of creeps wander the night in places such as this. A taxi pulled up to the gutter. Euvegina said no. She wanted the cops.

Someone asked if she'd been assaulted. Yes, she cried. She'd been raped. There'd been two of them.

A man approached, a jogger. He'd been doing the rounds of the park and, on his last circuit, he'd seen the woman arguing with a man who had been holding her by the arm.

John and Kristian knew the rapists could not have gone far – according to Euvegina, it had all occurred just minutes before they had found her. Fueled by beer, post-football rage and a certain ANZAC spirit, the two charged into the shadows of Fitzroy Gardens, determined to find the culprits and administer the justice they deserved.

The Fitzroy Gardens, like most manicured metropolitan forests, had a history of violence and shame all of its own. In December of 1889, the *Melbourne Daily Telegraph* interviewed City Coroner, Dr Richard Youl, about the alarming number of babies being found abandoned in town dumps and washing up in the metropolitan waterways. Dr Youl placed the blame on the 'deplorable immorality in our open gardens and parks', naming Fitzroy Gardens at the top of his list of depots of depravity where 'young ladies sit out in the garden during the hot weather', tempting young men

> *to look askance on their weaker sisters, and being deceived in the goodness and chastity of the one, lose all belief in their general virtue. When that comes about, man's finer feelings sink to the level of the brute beast that roams the field, and he regards woman only as a means whereby animal passions may be gratified.*

In April of 1917 – on Anzac Day, as fate would have it – a young man named Clarence Sefton was committed for trial after a dead baby, wrapped in a brown paper bag, was spotted floating down the Yarra River under the Punt Road bridge in Richmond. The baby turned out to be the unplanned child of a young, unmarried woman named Millicent Berger, who claimed Clarence Sefton to be the father. When Clarence insisted the newborn boy be placed in the care of strangers until such time as he and Millicent were wed – which he promised would be soon – the mother had reluctantly parted with her child, spiriting the baby from the hospital late one night and handing him to Clarence on Victoria Parade in the city. Clarence vigorously denied it was he who had later thrown the baby into the Yarra, or dashed its brains out on the riverbank before doing so. All the way to the gallows he swore he had handed his little boy to another man, whose name he couldn't recall, and whose face had been hidden by the dark shadows cast by the elm trees in Fitzroy Gardens.

And it was from those same shadows that Nancy Condon cried out for help in 1942, police finding her bloodied and naked in the bushes, her assailant, a returned soldier named Robert Joseph Lacey, caught by police who gave chase through the gardens.

It is unlikely John Whiteside and Kristian Dieber were familiar with such local history as they charged through the gardens on Anzac Day, 1999. They knew even less about the men for whom they searched, having launched themselves upon their mission before extracting a description of the offenders from Euvegina. All they knew was that there were two of them, and that they were to be punished.

They came upon a family strolling in the park. They should get out of here, the boys said. There were rapists afoot. The family thanked them for the warning and made their way out of the park. John and Kristian continued into the gardens.

In the darkness, they saw two strangers ambling slowly toward them from the city side of the park. Could these be the rapists? There were two of them. They were walking slowly, cautiously, as if having something to hide.

A woman had been raped, they shouted, waiting for a response. The two strangers stopped. They looked startled, indignant, afraid. That's terrible, they said, two actors on a stage. The police should be called. John and Kristian assured the two men that the police were on their way. They watched for some response from the two strangers, some expression of guilt betrayed on their faces or in their shifting demeanour. The strangers were nervous, moving about, trembling, looking for an exit.

Suddenly, one of the strangers shouted at the other to run, both of them bolting toward the edge of the park and the city beyond, where they would surely vanish into the crowds and buildings, never to be found. John and Kristian gave chase. These were not the powerful men they had been when they'd forced themselves on the helpless young girl. They were cowards. They must be stopped.

One of the rapists tripped and fell. John and Kristian began laying in with fists and feet. If they could hammer him hard enough, break him, they could safely pursue the other. The rapist curled up and screamed as he was punched and kicked in the head and legs.

The other rapist was coming back, shouting at them to stop. John broke away and charged at him. The rapist turned and ran back toward the lights of the road. He was limping. Perhaps he had been hurt during the rape, when Euvegina had fought back. John caught up to him on Lansdowne Street, the stranger staggering into a car parked by the side of the road. He slammed him into the vehicle, swinging punches to his head and chest. He felt the smack and crush. A friend of his, a woman, had once been raped by a stranger such as this, and John felt the hate burn in his gut. This bastard would pay.

But the rapist turned and fought back, throwing punches wildly in the air. John hit him hard in the jaw – once, twice . . . four times. But the rapist kept coming, with the power of a guilty man pressed. They wrestled into the gutter. For the first time, John felt afraid. The rapist had a hold of him, by the head. He couldn't see. He was going down. He called out for Kristian. He needed help.

Kristian left the other rapist on the grass and ran to the aid of his friend. He saw the rapist struggling, trying to get free. Perhaps he had a knife, or a gun. There was no time to discover. They had to put him down. Kristian took hold of his arms and held tight. John hit him hard, and again. The rapist was shouting, cursing at them, like a witch on fire. Then he slumped against the car, his blood smearing on the bonnet as he slipped to the road and was still.

The other rapist had escaped, across the road, to the entrance of a hospital on the other side of the street. They could not let him get away. They dashed across to search for him. Some people had gathered – they had not seen the rapist flee. Then John saw him standing in the distance on the footpath, behind a man and woman who were shielding him. They ran toward him, but the man and woman stopped them, trying to calm them down. That man was a rapist, John and Kristian said, and he had to be brought to justice.

But he couldn't be a rapist, the woman cried. He was gay.

David Campbell met Keith Hibbins in the early '80s at the Market Hotel in South Yarra. David was thirty then, a farm boy from Wandin who was raised by his grandparents. Keith was twenty-eight, an architect, tall, lanky, confident. They fell in love the night they met, and bought a house together in Collingwood in 1992. They had never been apart.

On Anzac Day in 1999, Keith and David, now in their mid-forties, had spent the day in Marysville in north-eastern Victoria, visiting the falls, stopping in at a winery before heading home. It was about six o'clock when the couple went out to buy some dinner, parking their Volkswagen outside a hospital on Lansdowne Street, beside Fitzroy Gardens, where they knew there to be an after-hours cash machine. On the way back to their car David suggested they take a stroll through Fitzroy Gardens, to take in the night air. Keith moved with a limp, a fall from a roof in 1992 leaving him with metal pins in his arms and in his legs. They walked slowly.

To them, the men who charged at them from the shadows seemed frantic, breathless, reeked of too much beer. They were angry, leaning in too close, babbling something about rape. Keith and David were not rapists. But they were homosexuals, a breed often hunted by drunken, angry men. When Keith cried out to run, David knew exactly why.

In the dreadful days after that night, David Campbell could do nothing but pace and pray for the love of his life to keep living, to wake up and get well and return the world to normal. Doctors and policemen tried to console him, telling him Keith was strong and would pull through. But as the days went by, Keith lying, voiceless, battered and dark with bruises, it looked less likely. He'd sustained terrible trauma to the head. There was a chance he might be permanently damaged. Someone told David that Keith might survive to be a creature with thoughts no more complex than those of an insect. David had to be sedated to get through the nights, waking each morning to a few precious moments when he thought it had all been something dreadful he'd dreamed through the night.

On 6 May, the phone rang, and a voice told David to hurry to the hospital. Keith was dying. David made it just in time to have Keith breathe his last breath of air while cradled in his partner's arms.

John Whiteside and Kristian Dieber were charged with the murder of Keith Hibbins. On the advice of their lawyers they pleaded guilty to manslaughter. All they'd intended to do was arrest the guilty, the rapists who'd violated a woman out in the open. They swore they thought they'd had the right men. Why else did they run? Why else had they both fought back? It was a full day after the fateful evening before they'd heard there had been one rapist, not two, Euvegina's description of the man who had grabbed her and forced her into the rear of his utility, ripping at her clothes, not at all similar to either Campbell or Hibbins.

In court, witnesses told of the brutality of the killing, a beating so merciless it burst eyes, tore arteries and flooded Keith Hibbins's brain with blood. The defence argued that these were not violent people, just two boys trapped in a squall they couldn't control, an event that was driven by a swirling fate in which all players were pitifully caught. They had meant to do good, not harm. It was a slim defence. A man was dead, viciously beaten by the accused. The law guards innocent lives jealously, and views vigilante killers as no different to murderers.

But Justice Philip Cummins saw things differently. In a summation remarkable for its melodrama, Cummins repeatedly referred to an 'unfolding tragedy', a 'cruel confluence of events' that guided two fine young men on their brutal quest. It was society, not the boys themselves, that was to blame for the tragic misunderstanding. That Keith Hibbins ran, said the judge, was not an indictment on the savagery of John Whiteside and Kristian Dieber, 'both young men of good character', but rather a fact that

> *brings shame on us all: shame that our society has been so inept for so long in eliminating violence or the risk of violence against homosexuals, and shame that by our failure homosexuals have become inured to violence or the risk of violence against them.*

He pointed out the 'long history of the power of citizen's arrest: generally, from Norman times and particularly, from the time of Henry II and the Assize of Clarendon'. He quoted Shakespeare, from *A Midsummer Night's Dream*, and from *Julius Caesar*: 'Men at some time are masters of their fates; The fault, dear Brutus, is not in our stars, But in ourselves . . .

'But you,' he said, 'and the victims were under a malevolent star that Anzac night.'

And then he set them free.

A later appeal by the prosecution found that Justice Cummins had erred, and thus John Whiteside and Kristian Dieber were sentenced each to six years in prison.

So ended the tragedy of Anzac Day, 1999, a day that claimed more victims to add to the slaughtered of battle and the wounded of war. Keith Hibbins was dead, his lover of fifteen years destroyed by a loss he would never replace. John Whiteside and Kristian Dieber were in prison, their families and friends crushed by the fate of two boys who had never been in trouble in their lives.

And then there was Euvegina Tsionis, the original victim in this sad enterprise, who, like so many Australians, began Anzac Day celebrating the freedom for which so many had fought and died in bygone days.

She had intended to go to the seaside with her boyfriend that fateful day, but went to the pub instead. She smoked a bong at breakfast time, then drank with her boyfriend from morning till dusk. She was drunk, and they argued as they drove through the city that night. She wanted to keep drinking, he thought she should come home. The fight became heated, noisy. When the car stopped at the lights in Wellington Parade, just beside the darkness of Fitzroy Gardens, Euvegina opened the passenger door and ran out into the night. Her boyfriend called out after her, gave chase, grabbed her by the arm, but she fought her way free. She was too far gone. He got back in the car and drove away.

It was cold and dark in Fitzroy Gardens as Euvegina staggered around in the shadows, her shoes falling off, her singlet top falling down her shoulder. She fell beneath some bushes and began to sob. She was drunk and so sad.

Some men approached, asking if she was all right. Someone asked if she'd been raped. To Euvegina, it really felt like she had.

WHAT'S EATING MRS MOUSLEY?

The French poet Henri Michaux observed that 'more than the all too excellent skills of the metaphysician, it is the dementias, the backwardnesses, the deliriums, the ecstasies and agonies, the breakdowns in mental skills which are really suited to "reveal" us to ourselves'. One might assume that this was even more the case in the days before we had television and drugs to keep us warm, therapists armed with new names for moods to distract us from simple truths, and aged care homes to relieve us all of the guilt of not wanting to deal with the old and lonely. This is the story of a woman whose heart was camouflaged by the chaos that comes at the end, but whose love, forgotten even in her time, still touches lives who'll never know. The action begins in the Melbourne suburb of Windsor, in a house next to the green gates of the Presentation Convent, which remains there today, though the house and all who dwelled within does not . . .

Maria Sarah Clare Mousley was approaching her sixtieth year when her husband, Francis, much younger than she, deserted her for another woman. That was in 1904, and until then life had been charming. They were wealthy – Maria's inheritance had seen to that – and together they had enjoyed the frills and gaieties the high society of Melbourne had to offer. Now she was alone, in her mansion on a one-acre property on Dandenong Road, her fortune unable to rescue her from the poverty of a broken heart. Childless, her only family being a sister back home in London, she was as destitute of love as the nuns who drifted in the grounds of the convent next door.

There were friends, of course, who rallied and cared, but none who stayed through the cold winter nights, or nuzzled her neck when she craved affection. They had their own husbands, families and lives, the very things Maria had not. Which is not to say that Mrs Mousley was without her means – highly educated, well read and finely cultured, she could lose herself for days in one of the many books from her library, or close her eyes to the gramophone's song and recall the things that had happened to her once, when she was young and pretty, her life an abundance of delights yet to be. In the evenings, people passing in the street would stop and listen as Mrs Mousley played the classics on her piano. But a house can be as bleak as a forest to the miserable, its little organisations – lamplight on pictures, painted walls and tapestry chairs turned this way or that – all the more lonesome for being devoid of shadows but one's own, each elegant touch unseen by those who might commend the host on keeping such an enchanting home. Such was life for Mrs Mousley after Frank went away.

She was not entirely alone. There were animals – the many dogs she reared, the cows in the yard, poultry and the occasional vermin that dared to venture out from beneath the boards. These creatures would come to form the community in which Mrs Mousley spent her private hours and with whom she increasingly shared her life, her thoughts, her meals and memories. Friends warned her to control them, to get some cats to chase the rats. But these creatures were friends to Mrs Mousley. She didn't want to scare any of them away.

The first sign of trouble came in 1910 when Henry Rider, an inspector for the Prahran Council, was called to the house on Dandenong Road by neighbours who had become concerned by the barking, squawking, chattering and the smell. Mr Rider saw the dogs had multiplied – he counted thirty-two in all, many of which slept in Mrs Mousley's bed, or in beds in other rooms of the house. The floor was littered with feathers that fell from the birds that flapped from mantel to chair, or that roamed from room to room, no longer caring to fly. The rats seemed content to go about their affairs in plain view of the other animals that paid them no mind. Mr Rider warned Mrs Mousley to control this burgeoning menagerie – the rats, he said, would bring disease, which might spread to other homes and to the city sewers. She promised she would.

But the next few years saw things get worse. Mrs Mousley began to drink – with friends at first, who warned her not to fall into the grip of alcohol and the fearful melancholy it might bring. She heeded their warning for a time, taking the Pledge of Temperance, which was popular in its day. But as the animals multiplied, Mrs Mousley's friends began to pull away, their visits becoming less frequent, her loneliness all the more crushing for being constant, uninterrupted, unnoticed, a sunken fact of daily life. Then in early 1916, she learned that her sister had passed away in England. Now she was truly deserted on earth.

So she turned to the bottle again, alone, drinking in the mornings just to colour the day, to give voice to the animals, and to bring closer those memories that she cherished so. In time, the scenes that played in the rooms of her mind became more real than the happenings in the here and now. Her life lost its depth, all the sounds and visions from her past – memories which, when positioned in sequence, had shaped a continuous chain of people and events who came to represent her life, her 'experience' – were now concertinaed into one act alone, in which neither past nor present could be discerned from the other. For Mrs Mousley the only distraction from this milieu were the animals, who needed her so desperately. She devoted herself to their meals and their pains, ignoring those of her own.

It was around this same time, too, that Mrs Mousley began to think of the children – not her own, of course, for she had none, but the children she was sure Frank Mousley would have sired with the woman who had taken him away. She professed to friends her wish that such children be beneficiaries of her wealth and estate, the many thousands of pounds in her bank account, the properties on Bourke Street, and elsewhere in the city. Her friends thought her insane – these children of whom she spoke, if they existed at all, were the gremlins of the very affair that had sentenced her to that dungeon of the heart in which she currently dwelled. But Mrs Mousley was certain. It was the dusk of her life, her joys and agonies passed through, her battles won and lost, and there was nothing she could do to change her fortunes. Those children, however – the closest to her that lived in the world, or would ever exist through the years to come – deserved whatever love she could give. The unborn child is innocent of the wreckage that lovers bring to the world. Had things been different, they might have been hers.

It was past midnight, just before Christmas in 1916, when Joseph Christensen, a veterinary surgeon, was awoken by a strange panting and scuttling that rolled down the street outside his home. The sound became louder until Mr Christensen peered out of his window to see Mrs Mousley standing amongst a swirling herd of dogs at her feet. There were dozens of them – pugs and mongrels, cattle dogs and pointers of every size and colour – scampering, scratching, gnawing at bones. Having known Mrs Mousley for many years, Mr Christensen was alarmed at her appearance – she was unkempt, frayed, and it appeared she hadn't washed for weeks. Her legs were bare of stockings and she wore but a petticoat that stopped at the knee, an old shawl slung around her neck and a garish blonde wig crowned with a peculiar kind of hat. She appeared somewhat confused and vague, the sweet smell of alcohol and stale cigarette smoke hanging from her like an invisible fog.

Mrs Mousley apologised for the hour but insisted one of her dogs was sick and required urgent attention. She couldn't point out which one, exactly, and Mr Christensen could see nothing wrong with the creatures that dashed about at their mistress's feet. But he promised he come to her house in the morning to have a closer look, and at that Mrs Mousley and her loyal pack departed.

The following day Mr Christensen was disgusted at the state of Mrs Mousley's abode. The once stately dwelling was robbed of its grace, the furniture tattered, the floors scuffed and caked in animal refuse and assorted litter. Empty bottles lined the skirting boards, and Mrs Mousley, once again, seemed puzzled in drink, oblivious to the chaos into which she had descended and altogether unperturbed by the stench of the dogs and birds and rats now greater in number. One whole room in the house was reserved for the cows, which slept on carpets darkened and damp with their droppings. In the corner, a fireplace crackled for their comfort alone. Mrs Mousley asked Mr Christensen if he knew of a way to convince the cows that the fire would do them no harm, as they would leave the room frightened whenever she lit it, which was a shame, she said, as she'd had it specially made for them. Mr Christensen urged Mrs Mousley to take the cows to the butchery as they were both very old and lame. Before he left, Mr Christensen noted the cows were being fed on a diet of cauliflower and cabbage.

Over the next few months Mrs Mousley's deterioration became obvious to those who knew her. The local butcher, from whom she bought meat for the dogs, saw she was constantly dirty and drunk, wore the same tattered clothes and no boots, and never seemed to purchase any meat for herself. The local tobacconist thought her insane. Neighbours noticed her mixing with harlots and vagabonds, smoking and drinking with them on the street, in plain view of good people who might see.

In November of 1917, Henry Rider from the Prahran Council was once again called to Mrs Mousley's residence, a petition from neighbours objecting to the disintegration of her property and the malodorous stench. Mr Rider found Mrs Mousley drunk and asleep on the floor in her living room amid barking dogs and rats in their hundreds, who scurried madly as he entered the premises. In a nearby room Mr Rider found a female pug dog dead from starvation, her eight little pups piled close to her belly, where they had starved, too. A cow lay in a bedroom moaning in pain for lack of milking. Rotting meat lay everywhere, the entire house so covered with faeces that no part of the floorboards or carpet could be seen. When Mr Rider woke Mrs Mousley from her slumber she refused to allow him to bury the dogs. Nor would she agree to poison the rats. The animals were her pets, she said – the only friends she had in the world – and she would not live if any of them went away. Mr Rider issued her with a summons. The neighbours, he told her, could take no more.

In court Mrs Mousley paid a fine and promised to tidy up her home. Instead she paid contractors to build a fence taller than a man could see, completely surrounding her property, against the prying eyes of neighbours who might complain. For the next year of her life, Mrs Mousley was rarely seen by any living creature other than her animals. A friend who entered the home in December of 1918 found the house had virtually disappeared beneath a jungle that chattered and howled in feral tribute to the wild and lonely woman who was its queen.

On 5 February, 1919, police were called the mansion on Dandenong Road. The smell and the noise had become worse than ever, the past few days and nights having been impossible for the neighbours to bear. Nobody had seen Mrs Mousley since 1 February, when a friend had waved to her as he passed by. She was drunk, no doubt, somewhere inside.

After knocking for some time, policemen forced the door, a putrid rush of air pressing the officers back for a moment to gather their wits and cover their faces with their handkerchiefs. As they cautiously moved down the hall, the sound of their footsteps gave rise to a ferocious trembling of the floorboards and walls as thousands of rats darted for subterranean safety. Then from the murky living room into which they entered, a dreadful growl rose up from the darkness, a malevolent choir of hell's own hounds. As the officers' eyes adjusted to the gloom they saw that the dogs were gathered around a mound in the middle of the floor, protecting it from the advancing intruders. It was Mrs Mousley, naked and dead, as she had been for days, her animals forced to fend for themselves. Her face was gone, as were her hands and feet, the flesh and muscle eaten down to the bone.

Mrs Mousley's house no longer stands on Dandenong Road in Windsor. But there is another house in which her spirit lingers, on a leafy corner in Sydney's Lane Cove, just off Epping Road. It was built in 1921 by a Francis Mousley, who'd come into some money the year before. Today people still stop and stare as they pass, so charming is the old two-storey abode – the gentle slopes of its roof, the fairytale windows, and the lush gardens in which it dwells. It's the kind of home in which one imagines a child would enjoy a magical youth.

Francis Mousley's children grew up in this house – two brothers and two sisters, now all gone. One went on to become a photographer, who flew over Hiroshima after the Bomb went down. He died years ago and, today, his surviving son worries, like all sons do, that he never got to tell his father how much he loved him. But there is nothing he could have said that wasn't already expressed so clearly by a woman who lived many years ago, who none of them ever knew and who knew them not, but who felt so deeply that it took her mind, and gave everything she had to the ones she loved.

THE STAR WHO NEVER WAS

Every boy in history has dreamed of something. In times gone by, those dreams were of adventures in strange worlds, mastery of the sea and air, or victory in battle. But in the second half of the twentieth century, in the dawning of our age of clowns, every next boy's dream was of being a rock star, little more than a singer of songs and a creator of puddles on the seats of young girls. For most this dream was fleeting, a momentary delusion chased from the psyche by maturity, marriage, a family and other such vital pursuits. But for some the longing for rock and roll greatness is a sad corpse to be rediscovered every time the mind goes in search of what might have been. Why the psychiatric profession has yet to invent a name for the peculiar brand of depression one suffers after failing to sell jingles to children is a mystery, as is the ultimate fate of the young man at the centre of our next story.

Dim the lights, switch off all hi-fi systems and pull up a chair next to the bed of your most impressionable child, for like some pop culture Aesop fable, the saga of Marcus Montana is a cautionary tale about the elusive nature of rock and roll stardom, and a sweet lesson in how respect is often earned in ways one least expects . . .

It was the winter of 1989, the year of Tone Loc's *Funky Cold Medina* and Madonna's *Like A Prayer*. About to see their last number one hit were an American duo called Milli Vanilli, who would soon be exposed as mere sock puppets for the voices of others. A new decade loomed large.

So too, it seemed, did Marcus. Advertising told us that Marcus was 'coming', but didn't say when or exactly why. A doe-eyed boy sulked out at us from posters that hollered his name, but there was no hint as to why his pending arrival was of the slightest importance. He may have been an evangelist or the face of a new men's fragrance. That was none of our business. All we were meant to know was that he was on his way.

Teaser advertisements, as they were known in the industry, were popular in the 1980s. Designed to create a buzz in a vacuum, the teaser sucked in the masses while starving them of information. The theory was that the common people would develop a hunger for anything if you could convince them they've been deprived of it. But most were hip to teasers by the end of music's most useless decade – they knew that the best way to sell faeces was to hide its true identity until it was deep in the hapless consumer's belly. And thus 'Marcus is Coming' might have slipped by as just another forgettable page in the book of failed entertainment industry confidence tricks. But there was a difference.

The 'Marcus is Coming' campaign was so massive that few who were alive in Sydney at the time have forgotten about it. It wasn't just posters but billboards, the sides of buses, the backs of taxi cabs. Marcus was everywhere, and inner-city Sydney began to wonder – not as the fish beguiled by the dangling prawn, but as the cynical audience that it was.

Late one evening, a respected Sydney sound engineer took a call from a colleague employed by EMI recording studios in the city, who'd been working on demo tapes recorded by some local musician. He'd been at it for hours, he moaned, to the point where his ears appeared to be playing tricks on him. He wondered if his friend might be so kind as to relieve him and have a try at mixing the tapes himself.

Arriving at the studio and hearing the demos, the engineer immediately understood why his friend had become so exhausted. The sound was a grim one – a guitar commandeered by an amateur thrasher, a lonesome voice in search of a tune. The engineer did the best he could, but you can't make a symphony from a busted windmill. Before returning to the peace and quiet of his bed, he left behind what he felt was a document of lousy songs most exquisitely mixed.

A few days later, he received another call. The person who'd made the music on the demos was impressed with his work and wanted advice.

It was Marcus. Marcus Montana, no less.

The engineer was star struck. Like everyone else in Sydney, he'd been tormented for weeks by the sight of Marcus's face, name and vague promise of arrival, and he'd had no idea that the boilers over which he'd slaved at EMI were the work of the boy himself. He listened without prejudice as Marcus explained the time had come for him to perform his songs to the world, and he needed to put together a band, fast. He wondered if the engineer knew of any musicians who might be up to the challenge, assuring that they would be handsomely paid for their services. Intrigued by the possibilities, the engineer, a musician himself, agreed to ask around and get back to Marcus at his first opportunity.

The Sydney inner-city music scene of the '80s was not famous for its wealthy troubadours, and the engineer had no trouble rounding up a company of musicians interested in paid work. All of them had dreams of their own, and some would even go on to earn fame, but that was years away yet (their names do not matter here, any more than the real identity of the boy in whose service they were to labour). They were told they would be paid $100 each for a rehearsal and $120 per performance – excellent money for the time – and that they were to study the songs on the demo tapes and master them before the first rehearsal. They were to leave all other details to 'The Family', from whom they would receive orders for the next few months of their lives.

The notion that rock and roll fame might be purchased was not particularly novel in the year 1989. Frank Sinatra, it was commonly known, had cruised to fame in the 1930s thanks to a cosy relationship with New Jersey racketeer Willie Moretti, who took a shine to Frank and ensured he was the preferred entertainment in every dive east of the Hudson River. (It was said that when Sinatra found himself inconveniently bound to an agreement with Tommy Dorsey, to whose band the young Sinatra had contractually hitched his wagon for life, a few of Moretti's enforcers helped Dorsey overcome his reluctance to release Frank from his obligations by sliding the barrel of a revolver down his throat.) The career of Alan Freed, the American disc jockey who coined the very phrase 'rock and roll', ended in shame in 1962 when it was revealed he'd been accepting bribes in return for playing certain discs, and the airwaves of the '70s and '80s in America were fed and denied by 'The Network', a coast-to-coast cartel of creeps who bullied radio stations at the behest of the record companies.

But this was Sydney, where a hit local record earned only enough to buy a holiday abroad and not much more, the city's restaurant kitchens and supermarket checkouts manned by hit parade heart-throbs only months out of favour. Surely the rackets worth engaging in were on the waterfront, or trackside, or in the cannabis fields to the north. Why bother trying to muscle a bullseye in such a loose-change gamble as urban pub rock?

But city gossip travels fast, spreading like some exotic disease from taxi driver to drinker and back, and by the following evening the members of the band had each been greased with the good oil regarding the strange enterprise into which they ventured. One had heard that The Family were wealthy fruit wholesalers from suburban markets, the son squandering his family endowment on the rock star dreams he was sure he'd fulfil. Another tale told of an exalted fatherly pact, which promised to grant each son whatsoever he wished upon his twenty-first birthday. The elder of the brothers, it was said, had been a fan of American gridiron and thus had been sent to a big university in Hawaii to learn how to play the game. Marcus himself had a penchant for gridiron, which was why he had chosen the stage name Montana, after Joe Montana of the San Francisco 49ers, who many claimed was the greatest quarterback of all time. But Marcus's greatest dream was of being a rock star. And so, it seemed, he would have it.

It was within the unique gloom of a typical Sydney rock rehearsal room – the grey carpeted walls, orphaned strips of black tape, the sweat and the cigarettes in ammonia disguise, the unstoppable, directionless electronic buzz in the air and the thud-thud-thud of the band at the bottom of the ocean in the room next door – that the boys first, and at last, saw Marcus.

He entered with a shiny new guitar case under his arm that further dwarfed his diminutive stature. He was young, handsome, a Mediterranean matinee idol with a rock and roll swagger thrown into the jeans – Al Pacino, Bruce Springsteen and Arthur Fonzerelli compressed into one. Behind him was a small entourage of sorts, a few cousins who acted in the service of security, and an enthusiastic younger brother, his wide-lapel suit, super-sized shades and snappy, rat-pack hipster jaunt immediately identifying him as Marcus's own Las Vegas-style manager.

It was a start.

Marcus moved around the room introducing himself to the men in his band, each responding in kind to the courteous nod, the nervous handshake, the shy smile and the plea in the eye, each of them feeling he was just a nice kid for whom they would like to succeed. But success in this business was never so easy as simply making a decision.

Out of the shiny guitar case Marcus hauled the most beautiful guitar the band had ever seen. He strapped it on, strummed it, oblivious to the fact it was way out of key. Before a voice could suggest his guitar needed tuning, someone counted a beat and the rehearsal lumbered into life.

What came next took the whole room by surprise. As the first song kicked into gear, Marcus, flailing at his untuned instrument, launched into a series of choreographed moves, a strange cocktail of stadium rock standards and Frankie Avalon beach blanket limbo. Hands clapped over head and the heavens were punched. There were duck walks and moonwalks, star jumps and windmills, fingers pointed at honeys not there. A grand slide on the knees was rudely halted by the unexpected friction of denim on carpet. The band watched aghast as Marcus, all windmill arms and pelvic thrust, seemed to be performing for multitudes far beyond the four enclosed walls of the rehearsal room.

The exhibition went on for the remainder of the rehearsal, during which, unbeknown to the poor boy himself, every member of Marcus's band had decided that he would never make it.

On 2 October, 1954, a young Elvis Presley made his debut performance at the Grand Ole Opry in Nashville, Tennessee, the seat of country music and spiritual home of such country gentlemen as Hank Williams, Tex Ritter and Uncle Dave Macon. The audience applauded politely, but Elvis's suspicions that he hadn't gone down too well were aroused when Opry manager Jim Denny wished him well with his truck-driving career back in Memphis. Elvis swore never to return to Nashville, a promise he kept to the end.

Perhaps this was why Marcus Montana chose to record his first single in Nashville, Tennessee, as something of a homecoming for rock and roll, he and Elvis as kindred spirits in a world of critics who ruthlessly take aim at dreams. Or perhaps he simply realised a single recorded in Hit City, USA, would already be halfway to greatness in the eyes of the easily impressed people of Sydney. Whatever the case, sometime early in 1989, Marcus, at great expense to The Family, had flown to Music Mill Studios in Nashville to record 'Tell Him I'm Your Man', his first would-be smash hit single.

After the first rehearsal, when it became clear to Marcus (if nobody else) that this band was to be a going concern, the singles, which had been independently pressed by the thousands, were released from their cardboard boxes and distributed to stores all over the city. The cover of the single featured the same photograph of Marcus that had graced the posters, just to ensure everybody made the connection, and the news that the songs were recorded in Nashville was displayed prominently on the back cover.

The music press slaughtered it. Radio mocked it, one prominent Sydney DJ playing it every morning before rudely tearing off the needle and ensuring his listeners heard as yet another of the brittle discs shattered against the studio wall. Columnists from the daily newspapers used Marcus to up the laugh count whenever gags were thin on the ground and, in the street press, the very name Marcus became shorthand for fool.

The music press of the '80s, however, was an animal easily tamed, and had Marcus been hip to its simple machinations things might have been manifestly different. The key to receiving good press – or, at least, no bad press – was to be found in the advertising departments of the various magazines and newspapers that struggled for survival, embroiled as they were in a competition so fierce that even the most credible organ could not resist an opportunity to be fertilised with funds that might otherwise nourish its neighbour. There was no such thing as an advertising department that was closed to negotiation, and it was rare that an artist gracing the front cover of a music magazine would not also be represented inside somewhere by a full page, fully-paid advertisement. The booking of a series of adverts over several issues was all one needed to grease the wheels for glowing reviews, in-depth interviews and enthusiastic mentions in gossip sections.

Too late did the Marcus Montana machine realise its folly in plastering an entire city with posters that merely whispered a name. Buildings, buses and taxi cabs were not renowned for providing healthy editorial in return for one's dollar. In fact, far from being a cool name to drop, the tawdry mystery of the 'Marcus is Coming' campaign had made the boy a figure of ridicule, his name a groovy new buzzword for any spectral thing dubiously promised and doubtfully on its way whether one liked it or not: Santa Claus; the friend late for tea; the cheque in the mail; venereal disease; the Russians; the end of the world.

Unfortunately, The Family's way of rectifying the problem was entirely ignorant of the nuances that disguised and legitimised the music business payola of the day, preferring instead a more ham-fisted approach consecrated by Hollywood wiseguy stereotypes.

Late one afternoon, the editor of rock and roll gospel, *Rolling Stone*, looked up from the desk of his Sydney office to find his doorway darkened by a certain Las Vegas-style hipster, his wide-lapelled suit, large sunglasses and furtive demeanour – like that of a spy being followed – suggesting he meant deep business. The man introduced himself as the manager of Marcus Montana, a fine new talent who belonged on the cover of *Rolling Stone*. The editor was less than convinced and told the man so in no uncertain terms. Upon hearing this, Marcus's manager stood and walked to the window, whistling a tune that spoke of no business behind him that he wished to see. On the chair he had left a briefcase open, and inside were bundles of $50 bills.

Politely, the editor asked him to take his money and leave.

One morning, Sydneysiders awoke to find that the city had changed – the 'Marcus is Coming' posters were now nowhere to be seen, replaced with 'Marcus is Here!' The city braced itself for the arrival they'd been promised for months, which materialised on a crisp Sunday afternoon in the outdoor arena at Darling Harbour. The Family had spared no expense, booking out the open-air stage usually reserved for TV personalities and family entertainment.

This time the media had paid attention, advising the populations of this grand occasion, not wishing to deprive Sydney of its chance to see, at last, the man who had littered its walls for so long.

Backstage, the air was one of strange anticipation. For Marcus this was the moment for which he had longed, the performance that had doubtless played out as both triumph and tragedy in so many nightly dreams, and the knot in his gut manifested in an expression of terror on the poor boy's face. The others, too, were nervous, though for entirely different reasons. Some 1000 souls had gathered on the grass, a great many of them music industry luminaries and musicians from local groups with cool reputations. If Marcus wondered why his band all looked so strange with their wigs and sunglasses and caps pulled down tight, he didn't give voice to it. He was so nervous he scarcely had any voice at all.

The voice of Marcus's brother introducing the man for whom Sydney had been waiting spelled time for the boy whose dream had come to visit him, and an uneasy Marcus climbed the stairs to the stage, his band behind him whispering encouragement, as a flutter of cautious applause filled the air. And then the show began.

For those not so predisposed, the experience of performing for the very first time, in front of a large number of people, is one that can scarcely be conveyed by written or spoken word, in part because the mind races so violently that few men or women can precisely remember the whole of the experience. Epinephrin, adrenalin's neurological running mate, is both an eraser and blender of memory.

The shy and inexperienced Marcus must have been hit with an overdose of the stuff as he launched into the first number of his career. He didn't so much as make mistakes as fail to do anything remotely right, strumming when he was supposed to pluck and singing when he was meant to be quiet. And when the moves came out – the Frankie Avalon jaunt – there was none of the triumphant authority of before, but anxious hand claps, worried windmills and heavens most bashfully punched.

Behind Marcus, the band, struggling to provide a musical smokescreen for the frontman's obvious shortcomings, dared not concentrate on anything but their instruments. Once or twice, however, they couldn't help but glance outward to see how the audience was holding up. What they saw was a crowd who were quickly realising that the figure on stage in front of them – the Marcus of the posters and the teasers and the colossal ad campaign – was little more than a pretender with money. A general hilarity began to ripple through the assembled. What had begun as a growl of amused disappointment snowballed to full-blown hysterical laughter.

The performance reached its nadir with a tune the band had come to know only as 'The Ballad'. Slow and melodramatic, after the fashion of the old blues heartbreakers, 'The Ballad' was clearly designed to reveal the singer's amorous, more quixotic side amid so much pelvic horseplay. There had been trouble with 'The Ballad' during rehearsals, its lingering tempo scarcely conducive to the camouflage Marcus required but, here, amidst the madness of performance adrenalin, it was a disaster. Nervous, Marcus panicked and began singing the lyrics two beats ahead of time. The band tried to stop him, shouting at him to either stop for two beats or go two beats ahead, but Marcus was too far gone and terrified to comprehend what they were trying to tell him. For four minutes, Marcus was an arrhythmic, atonal juggernaut, the band, in a futile attempt to capture the singer, speeding up and then slowing down again, like a record on a turntable spun at the whim of some mischievous child.

Meanwhile, down on the lawn, observant punters had already noticed the blonde American woman who'd been snaking through the audience, whispering in ears. With the attention to discretion that had now become a hallmark of The Family's first foray into the music business, she'd been wandering from young girl to young girl, in plain view of all, offering $20 to anyone bold enough to dash on stage as a delirious fan and plant a passionate kiss on Marcus's cheek. At least one young woman complied, celebrating the completion of her covert mission by skipping from the stage waving her $20 note high above her head.

In the wake of the Darling Harbour fiasco, the rehearsals concentrated on the weak points. 'The Ballad' came in for particular scrutiny. So, too, did the band members themselves, each of them quietly pulled aside to receive a message from The Family: there was to be no more smirking on stage.

The Marcus Montana roadshow then embarked on a week of performances at local suburban shopping centres, attracting the fleeting attention of the passing midday crowds. One such performance ended when the management of the complex itself complained about the noise. On another occasion the band found themselves competing with the muzak that was piped every day through the establishment, and which nobody had bothered to switch off.

But the coup de grâce was to be the performance at Selinas at Coogee Bay, the biggest pub-rock room in Australia, and the end of the beginning for Marcus Montana. The advertising for the event had been massive, every wall and pole from the city to the outer suburbs plastered with news of the event. To guarantee a last minute victory snatched from the jaws of humiliation, Montana

Inc. had ensured a full house by orchestrating a series of support acts that would appeal to the baser instincts of both sexes: the Australian Manpower strip show for the ladies, then the Penthouse Pets for the gentlemen. The plan worked, some 300 people filing through the doors to witness the spectacle.

But a certain fire had gone from Marcus's eye since that first performance at Darling Harbour, and those who cared for the boy could see it. It had taken less than seven days to demolish the dreams of a lifetime, and he trudged through the performance that night like a man on his last day at a job for which he no longer cared. He didn't even seem to notice the audience members mocking him wholesale, the girls leaping up to dance behind him and the drunken louts appearing by his side, playing guitars that were never there.

Backstage, Marcus said his goodbyes, thanking everyone for the toil they had invested in his endeavour, then bade them all a humble and heartfelt farewell. The dream, it seemed, was over.

Weeks passed before Marcus received a call from one of his former band members, asking if he'd be interested in performing one more show. Marcus was unsure – his brief experience on the rock and roll stage had not been encouraging, and the single was selling so poorly that most stores were now refusing to stock it, even when offered copies for free, lest it take up the space of some other, more profitable record. He was doubtful as to his ability to find another venue that would be interested.

But Marcus was assured it was all taken care of. The band had pulled a few strings of its own, procuring a one-time-only spot on the coming Saturday night at a reputable joint on Sydney's Broadway. They would play for no fee – they had not worked so hard on his songs only to stand by and watch the boy quit so easily. What did he have to lose? Reluctantly, but gratefully, Marcus agreed.

What he couldn't have known was that he was being betrayed by his own band, the members of which had belatedly realised the comedy value of Marcus Montana. Broadway's Lansdowne Hotel was a venue that showcased music from the grungy underground, the crowd promising to be made up entirely of the band's friends, cosmopolitan urchins who were hip to the joke. Unbeknown to Marcus, he was returning to the spotlight not as a rock star at all, but as a clown.

It was the night before New Year's Eve when Marcus took the stage for what would be his last show of all time. From the moment he was introduced, the crowd, like extras in B-grade film, rushed the stage in the most ridiculous display of mock Beatlemania Sydney had ever seen. Women were screaming, tearing at Marcus's clothes and guitar, begging for sex, while grown men pulled at their hair and cried out his name in admiration and despair. Marcus's cousins, acting as security, linked arms to hold back the seething mob. Marcus was reduced to a rabbit in the headlights, bewildered, and for a moment he may have wondered whether his dreams had all come true at last.

But it was midway through 'The Ballad' that the reality seemed to dawn on the boy as the crowd screamed and laughed and slam-danced and shouted abuse from the front of the stage. One could see the very moment when the penny dropped. Marcus looked to the floor at his feet, swallowed hard and seemed to say something the audience couldn't hear. Then he lifted his head and returned to the microphone, eyes closed, singing his way to the end of the song, the crowd no longer there in his world.

This is how he continued until the whole nine songs were done, soldiering through the chords he could never master and the corny moves that never looked right. The bogus performance from the crowd continued, but the frenzy cooled as many became astonished at what they were witnessing. Marcus Montana, or whoever he was, seemed to be saying goodbye to the boyhood fantasy he now knew was only moments from death, and he would do so whether the people in front of him screamed or laughed or wished it away.

On the last chord of the very last song, Marcus nodded, thanked the audience with a cursory smile – polite, embarrassed and disdainful at once – slung his guitar and marched through the crowd to the door and the waiting Mercedes outside that spirited him away into the night.

Marcus Montana was never seen again, though Sydney rock and roll folklore has never forgotten him. The single is now a collector's item, the posters coveted as ancient scrolls, and those lucky enough to have witnessed his coming boast of their good fortune, like apostles of some cargo cult who swear they caught a glimpse as the Lord passed by. There are those who say that, on that last night, Marcus made it after all; that to hang on and ride the rhapsodies of youth, eyes closed to the world, is what it's all about. Others speak of a comeback tour, where Marcus's dreams might be relived by all. As if he who died a hero's death might wish to be awoken.

THE SHOW

In the criminal underworld that once ran amok in the working class New South Wales city of Newcastle, a man who was known to have been liquidated was said to have 'gone to the islands', an oblique reference to the old BHP blast furnaces on Kooragang Island in Newcastle Harbour, which one would imagine disposed of cumbersome bodies and nuisance DNA very effectively indeed. 'He's gone to the islands,' they'd say, 'where the climate suits him.' About a half-hour drive inland from Newcastle is the town of Maitland, considered the tougher country cousin of the more glamorous seaside ruffian. The Lord tried to drown Maitland in '55, floodwaters taking twenty-five lives and thousands of homes, and providing the locals with a grotesque spectacle when a man was winched by helicopter into the air from the roof of his home, dangling like a circus acrobat from the harness on the end of a long cable. A sudden gust of wind blew hats from heads and raised mist from the raging waters, the helicopter lurching sideways, the dangling man trailing below toward a row of swinging high-tension power lines. There was a blinding light, like a flash from a photographer's bulb, and when everyone looked up again the helicopter and the dangling man were gone. The whole of the town was watching that day.

But nobody saw what happened in the shadows of night three decades later, when the Show came to town, and a pretty young girl walked into the laughter and lights to disappear forever . . .

Trevor Kirk is seventy years old and lives in an old sawmill shack on a lonely country road near Stroud in New South Wales. He sleeps on a mattress accessible by an indoor track that meanders through bricks and metal and piles of papers whose purpose is not readily clear. It's a bunker for one who survived the apocalypse that rained on him and spared the world.

Amongst piles of documents, press clippings and the stray little ornaments that cling to Trevor's life are photographs – 7000 of them, he says – that record the world in which he lived before, of days in the sunshine and open air. There's Trevor, in black and white, a much younger man. He is smiling, which is something he doesn't do much these days, and with him is his wife, a striking brunette, whose eyes appear to be focussed on something beyond the photographer's lens, which nobody will ever see. They used to win best-dressed couple every time. Trevor had a special thing for her, but you don't often get two people who love each other to quite the same degree. She left, for the last time, in '83. Trevor was still pining for her when the Show came to town.

Here are his daughters, Larissa and Melissa, the younger two of the three, bounding in the yard of a nice brick home. And there is Stacey Lee, tall, pretty and sixteen, her hair after the fashion of Doris Day. She has the body of a supermodel, calling all boys with its secrets. Her eyes are excited, her lips slightly parted, a word on the tongue that is yet to escape into the world when the shutter snaps. It might have been 'Dad', or 'do', or 'don't'. Whatever it was, Trevor says, it is precious, and forever lost. We will never know.

It was dawn on Friday, 17 February, 1984, that Trevor Kirk first learned that something was wrong. The previous evening, Stacey Lee had ventured with a friend, Annette Tyson, to the Show in

Maitland, the annual gathering of rides and amusements that attracted the people from miles around. She and Annette had loitered in Sideshow Alley, amongst the shooting galleries, the haunted houses, the barking of the spruikers and the stench of animals, the friends parting at half past nine, agreeing to meet later at the main gate. Stacey Lee, her friend would later recall, had seemed distracted by the attentions of someone from within the fairground – Annette could never remember who. It hadn't mattered at the time. Stacey Lee was a big girl, adventurous and sharp. She had nothing to fear from a place of fun, with so many people around.

But the meeting time had come and gone. Annette had tired and gone home. Now it was morning, and there was still no sign of Stacey Lee.

By mid-morning, Trevor was fighting a rising panic, convincing himself all would be well. It was not unlike Stacey Lee to wander off – when the family had lived at Warkworth, near Singleton, the young teenager had been prone to sneaking out of the house at nights for a midnight swim in the river. She did such things. But when the next day passed with neither word nor sign, Trevor knew that something was wrong. He drove the streets of Maitland in search of her, returning home at dusk when there was no luck. As the clock ticked through the night, the realisation loomed that something wicked may have taken place. All Trevor could do was hope Stacey Lee had survived it, and would stride through the door with little more than a half-hearted apology and a strange story to tell.

Early on Saturday morning, a cleaner at the showground noticed something bulging from beneath a tarpaulin behind the shooting gallery. Underneath was the body of Stacey Lee Kirk, her eyes shut tight, her jeans pulled down, her t-shirt raised on her smooth, dirtied belly. Her mouth was wide open, her own panties stuffed inside, a pair of men's underpants taut around her neck, twisted and blue. Someone had used her before she had died, to the sounds of the laughter and clanging bells.

When Trevor heard, his first thought was that Stacey Lee was having a joke on them all. In the weeks leading up to that night, she'd been playing 'Auld Lang Syne' on the family organ, over and over, until Trevor had complained. It was a dreadful song, he said – they had sung it when the *Titanic* went down. It was a melody of death.

Stacey Lee didn't care. For some reason, she said, she liked it. She'd been roaming the house for days, whistling its tune, as if she was going away for a long time, and was singing goodbye to those she loved.

In the days that followed the discovery of Stacey Lee's body, police interviewed hundreds of stall holders, locals and fairground itinerants, but nobody appeared to have seen or heard a thing. Detectives found the show workers secretive, clannish, like the circus carnies of dark folklore. No sooner had the investigation begun were the tents collapsing in clouds of dust, the scene of the crime packing up and clearing out as the Show rolled along to the next town.

Trevor could not accept that his little girl was no longer of this earth. He had raised her, watched her grow, witnessed all the joys and sorrows in a life that had seemed so long, now no more lush with time than the snap of a twig. Every room or doorway in which she'd once stood seemed suspicious in its emptiness, lifeless objects threatening to betray her hiding place with whispers that she was here or there. Sometimes he was sure he could hear her in the house; the creak of an elbow, or the sound her hair made when she brushed it from her eye – the gentle sounds of a soul in the world, only noticed when they're gone. She came to him in dreams, haunted waking moments, tortured him with memories of smiles now warped by the many riddles of her death. Did she suffer? Did she know it was the end? Did she cry out for him? What trifling thing was he doing at the very moment of her last breath?

But more tormenting than any of these things was the thought of the one who killed her, still alive, still breathing air, somewhere, the memory of Stacey Lee cruelly accompanied by his lurking absence, everywhere. There was no clue as to who he might be. Perhaps he was a worker from the Show, one of the scum who manned the rides or galleries, with the fag on the lip and the rag in the jeans pocket. Or perhaps he was a local man, one whom Trevor might pass in the street. He may have known him all his life.

Trevor began to see the face of his daughter's killer everywhere he looked, in the men who muttered together in the pub, or in whom handed back his change at the corner store. Might that be him who just passed by, within a touch? Those brake lights in the distant dark – might they be operated by the man who killed his Stacey Lee?

An inquest left an open finding. The investigation ran stone cold. The months went by. The world became content, it seemed, that Stacey Lee was murdered, that her killer was living free and there was nothing that could be done.

And then the day arrived when the Show came back, rumbling into town without a care for the girl it had crushed one year before, the sound of the games and wheels and barking spruikers mocking the anniversary of Trevor's daughter's death. He forced himself to go, to walk through the lights, the laughter and the dark, just to see. Perhaps he'd spy a guilty face, or overhear a whispered conspiracy.

In Sideshow Alley, amongst the ghouls and shooting galleries, police had erected a mannequin dressed as his daughter, designed to unlock stubborn memories. All Trevor could think was that she wasn't anywhere near as pretty as Stacey Lee.

In 1991, police appeared to be on the edge of breaking through. They charged sideshow food operator Ricky Stephens with the murder after three show workers signed statements claiming that 27-year-old Stephens had confessed to the crime. Three of Stephen's friends were also implicated, confirming police suspicions that more than one person had participated in the rape and murder of Stacey Lee Kirk. Ricky's father, Dick Stephens, was a patriarch, the Brisbane family having built their millions from food stalls that journeyed the length of the country with the Show. Trevor Kirk felt that justice was close at last. But at a committal hearing the witnesses retracted their evidence on the stand. The case fell apart, and the magistrate allowed Ricky Stephens to go free. There was talk of tampering, though an independent investigation found no evidence of it. Ricky Stephens, it seemed, was innocent.

The decade went by with hopes raised and dashed, Trevor Kirk sinking into frustration and madness as he drove alone in coal trucks for sixteen-hour days, rolling from one side of the state to the other with nothing on his mind but Stacey Lee's killer. He became vengeful and bitter, harassing the police with phone calls and letters, his life disintegrating around him as he clipped articles from the papers and wrote formal requests for court documents, poring over the millions of words contained in transcripts and investigative reports in a vain quest for something that might stand out as a clue. He worked with every one of the thirty-five policeman who worked on his daughter's case, and watched helplessly as many of them gave up in despair. He begged the police to allow him to infiltrate the Show, to work on the very stalls in Sideshow Alley where his girl had disappeared, so that he might learn something new. He came to blows with one of the detectives. He never gave up.

Then, in February of 2002, Trevor took a call from police telling him they were reopening the case. There had been advancements in DNA technology, and now they could test the semen that had been found in Stacey Lee's body to match it conclusively against that of her killer. They had covertly obtained DNA samples from various sideshow itinerants and carnival workers on whom early suspicions had fallen. It would only be a matter of time. Trevor felt a wave of hope as he hung up the phone.

At that very moment, Trevor Kirk and his daughter's killer were hours apart, though they had been closer in the past. His name was Ian Raymond Sargent, now a truck driver for a coal company in the New South Wales town of Picton. On the night when Stacey Lee Kirk was murdered, Sargent had been just twenty years old, married with a child, another on the way, and living on the outskirts of Maitland. He'd been working at the the Show that night, on the shooting gallery in Sideshow Alley. He had been questioned by police in the days after the murder, and had admitted to flirting with Stacey Lee, but his wife had provided him with an alibi. Nobody was yet to know, but DNA tests would ultimately prove it was Sargent who had summoned Stacey Lee into the darkness, and into oblivion forever. It was Sargent for whom Trevor had been searching for all of these years and, now, at last, he was within reach. But the gods had one more torment left in store for Trevor Kirk.

On 21 February, 2002, just days after police reopened the case into the rape and murder of Stacey Lee Kirk, Sargent was driving his truck on the Pacific Highway at Grafton when he lost control and crashed into a tree. A blood sample from his autopsy would prove Ian Raymond Sargent was the killer.

Trevor Kirk doesn't believe his daughter's killer died on the eve of being brought to justice. It's one bitter truth he refuses to accept. There are others, he says – a conspiracy. They're still out there. So he continues to sift through the transcripts and documents, piled high in his sawmill shack on the side of a lonely country road. It's a maddening task, he says, but he has to keep going. The police have closed the case on Stacey Lee Kirk. He can't let his daughter down.

When not working on the case, Trevor passes the time by inventing things, contraptions and machines to make life easier for the people of the world – like the perpetual motion engine, which he claims is the answer to the world's energy crisis, and which he'd take to market, if only the oil companies would allow it.

He's been inventing these things, he says, ever since Stacey Lee went away.

A SORRY END INDEED

Before leaving England to take his post as the first Governor of New South Wales, Arthur Phillip declared his opinion that the death penalty was too good for perpetrators of two particular misdeeds: murder and sodomy. 'For either of these crimes,' he fumed, 'I would wish to confine the criminal until an opportunity offered of delivering him to the natives of New Zealand, and let them eat him. The dread of this will operate much stronger than the fear of death.' Needless to say there was no Mardi Gras in the early colony – no rainbow flag, no pride, no rest for them whose love was deemed wicked under threat of arrest and imprisonment (an invasion of privacy that remained enshrined in the law of Tasmania until 1 May, 1997). Consider, then, the plight of the two gentlemen in our next tale, who guarded their friendship jealously against the scorn of all around, and who dreamed – perhaps – of a day when they might walk hand in hand through a world that would not exist for another hundred years . . .

Edward Feeney was a reserved man, so little is known about his life. It is said that he was born in Ireland in 1834, and came to Australia some time before 1853, as a private in the Queen's army. He left no papers, no manifesto, but for a few letters and the odd declaration written in the final days of his life. Charles Marks was more elusive still. All that is known of him is that he was twenty-eight years old in 1872 – eight years Edward Feeney's junior – and that he loved his friend to death. 'Ned', as he called Feeney, was a man without whose company Marks could not survive – so he told others when the nights were late, the wine having loosened the doors of his heart.

Whether Marks and Feeney cared for one another after the fashion of man and wife was not known for sure – nobody ever caught them in the act, or burst in on its aftermath – but the circumstantial evidence seemed to whisper that it was indeed so. They were rarely seen apart and appeared to enjoy an intimate bond that others thought peculiar. They shared a single room in the Great Britain Hotel in Flinders Street and worked together as wardsmen at nearby Melbourne Hospital. At night they were regulars at A. B. Clay's Wine Bar in Bourke Street, at the Treasury Gardens end, where the late hours would see the alcohol melt away their armour, each falling in the arms of the other, declaring such affection as to alarm the bar's more Victorian patrons.

Sometimes, the slender walls of their lodgings in Flinders Street betrayed the sound of midnight lover's quarrels – cries, curses and pleas for forgiveness, all overheard by one Henry James, a young man who dwelled in the room next door. Marks had explained these storms to James as squabbles over women, that he and Feeney were forever becoming enamoured with the same girl. But evidence of such women was scarce in the world that Marks and

Feeney shared, never one without the other at his side, no room for girls or other creatures that might invade their mutual fondness.

It could be said that, together, Marks and Feeney had a propensity for melodrama. On one occasion, after Feeney had left for work one evening, a distraught Marks had knocked upon Henry James's door, a letter in his hand which he insisted be delivered to Feeney upon his return, by which time Marks would be somewhere in the country, dead, he declared, by his own hand. When Henry James expressed no interest in such folly, Marks snatched the letter back and stormed into his room. Another time, after a particularly ferocious spat, Feeney had taken poison, though evidently not enough to kill himself, and Marks had responded by slashing his throat with a razor, the attempt so feeble as to draw not a single drop of blood.

In the sober daylight hours, however, Marks and Feeney were as gentlemen – quiet, discreet, careful as to whom they spoke, polite and respectable in every way. If they were lovers they never told a soul, and Feeney was known to become heated if anyone dared peep into his private affairs. To he and Marks, whom they loved, or how, was not the business of others, but theirs alone. The judicial leer of society was not welcome behind their door, any more than it was at the foot of a matrimonial bed. That the lords of the land – those charged with the task of administrating the colony, quelling violence and keeping bedlam from the shores – might be concerned with the tender sympathies passed between two individuals must have seemed the most burlesque of notions to these two men of private ways. At other times, it was too tragic a truth to be borne.

Such anguished thoughts appeared to pray upon Marks and Feeney as the month of March dawned in the year of 1872, a despair in their tempers noted by Mrs Clay, who owned the bar in which they drank. Perhaps they'd grown tired of the world from which they were forced to hide, disgusted with the society that branded their love a crime, that forced them to duck and weave and deceive just to save their hearts from an undeserved shame. Whatever the case, it was in the early days of that month that the sky turned dark for Marks and Feeney and a pact was made, one that would end their lives with the high romance and melodrama that had always attended their relationship on earth.

On the afternoon of Tuesday, 5 March, they purchased pistols from the local armoury and made an appointment at a photographer's studio in the city. There they posed for a portrait, the pair of them standing, facing each other, their pistols raised at the other's heart. The photographer did not ask why – he thought them just two theatrical types. His flash bulb burst and, satisfied they had left their image in the world, Marks and Feeney departed for the wine bar, arriving at about three o'clock, taking the same table they had always shared on their nights of drinking and affectionate talk. There they drank as they quietly wrote letters to family and friends back home, occasionally stopping to whisper to each other, mischievously, like two young girls playing a hush-hush game. As the day grew old and the bottles emptied, their behaviour became more of the demonstrative kind, each fondling the other warmly, and at one point Marks lay his head in Feeney's lap, declaring again his love for 'Ned', and that he could not live without him.

It was dusk when Marks and Feeney stood to depart, leaving the letters on the table where they had written them. As they paid their bill, Marks declared to Mrs Clay that he and his friend were 'going home', and they brandished their pistols as proof of it. Mrs Clay expressed her astonishment, though she scarcely believed it. But she was used to the couple's histrionic behaviour and she knew better than to pry into Feeney's mind.

The two men left the wine bar and made their way into the Treasury Gardens. Once there they bade each other farewell, an embrace that lasted for all of time. Their friendship was not for this world, with its rules for love and laws of hate. They would leave it behind, taking with them the secret of their ardour. Nobody would ever know. They packed their pistols and faced the other, each barrel aimed at a cherished heart. On the count of three they would both fire.

What went wrong we will never know – whether Marks lost count, or just his nerve – but it was Feeney's gun alone that fired. Packed with too much shot, it exploded in Feeney's grasp, blasting his lover's heart from his chest and crippling the hand that pulled the trigger. When police arrived, alarmed by the report, they found Feeney at his dead friend's side, smoking a cigar, whispering words of love into the ear of the one who'd been spared a life without his Ned.

Edward Feeney was charged with the murder of his friend, tried, found guilty and sentenced to death. He might have saved himself had he confessed to the special nature of their love, but that he would not do. The letters he and Marks had written revealed little, save that they had decided to end their lives together. The judge pried and the papers wondered, but Feeney was private to the last, sitting quietly in his cell, determined to take his personal business to the grave. He even gave a statement to the hangman on the eve of his last day on earth, renouncing the rumours that were spread. Charles Marks would not be betrayed at the final hour by his Ned.

On Tuesday, 14 May, 1872, Edward Feeney was taken into the yard at Melbourne Gaol and pinioned to the gallows. To the newspaper men and the others who gathered there, he appeared to show no fear as the mask was drawn down upon his face and the noose pulled tight around his neck. But the hangman, who was nearer, saw the trembling in the doomed man's hands, and heard the whispered prayers that he uttered to the end.

When the bolt was pulled, Feeney fell awkwardly, his rump striking the side of the scaffold, breaking his fall. And thus he twitched at the end of the rope, a dangling man in hell. For two whole minutes did he suffer, until at last he was still.

His body was removed for post mortem to nearby Melbourne Hospital, in the very halls where he and Marks had shared so many glances. There Edward Feeney was stripped of his clothes and laid face down upon a table, naked under the prying eyes of doctors who had once known him, though had not known him at all. Into the room was ushered a phalanx of eager medical students from Melbourne Hospital who gathered at the feet of this most private man.

Keen to learn the truth, the doctors opened Feeney's legs and pried apart his buttocks. The surgeons peered, the students glared. Yes, they all declared: the rumours of Charles Marks and Edward Feeney were all true.

THE LAST TROOPS

The memorials to the dead of war mark the nation in their thousands, the names and dates of those who were loved and lost. They died 'in action', the tributes say, and we are left to ponder the loud and terrifying last moments of those remembered, whose bones are often to be found far from the places that consecrate them. But there is a memorial near Rockingham in West Australia that is different to the others. The boys who died are here, in their own land, underneath the slabs of stone that speak of them. They died as a result of the Great War, though the dates of their deaths tell of a time of peace, after the armistice of 11 November, 1918. The wounds from which they perished were not given them in anger, but were the result of the sheer, dreadful luck that befell them, as the last troops to sail from Australia for service in the Great War when the century was young . . .

On the morning of 30 October, 1918, the HMAT *Boonah* departed the West Australian port of Fremantle loaded with 164 crew and 931 Australian soldiers bound for service on the battlefields of Europe. Few on board knew where they were headed, their ultimate destination a wartime secret, understanding only that they were sailing to the aid of their brothers in the fight that had already claimed so many. The soldiers aboard, from Melbourne, Adelaide and West Australia, were anxious and frightened, but determined to do their duty. For three years the papers had been filled with the names of the brave, and those who remained when the war was over would be either the lucky or the cowardly. Whatsoever lay ahead was preferable to the shame of having stayed behind. As the ship crept through the headlands unheralded by fanfare in the early morning light nobody was to know that it would be the last troopship to set sail from Australia for the Great War.

The *Boonah* was originally a German freighter, captured in Sydney Harbour at the outbreak of war and converted to a troopship by the Commonwealth, taking her place in the Second Convoy carrying diggers to Egypt before the Gallipoli landings. She was a seaworthy vessel, but not built for comfort, and the hardships of war came quickly to some, seasickness laying many of the young men down within hours of departure, the stench in the confined quarters making the air unpleasant to breathe. After days of steaming through the Indian Ocean, the sea became a giant of rolling waves and stormy skies, the soldiers confined below sometimes for days on end as the rain and the waves smashed over the ship. One night a part of the railing was ripped from the bolts that held it to the deck and sucked into the sea forever.

The men passed the days as best they could, with boxing bouts and other games, and gambling by candlelight after the lamps were extinguished at ten o'clock. It was a camaraderie built on anxiety, necessity and nothing else to do. After two weeks of endless ocean, of stormy weather spotted by sunny days, the hills and trees of land at last loomed over the horizon on the morning of 16 November, the *Boonah* sailing into the South African Bay of Natal. Lingering off the port of Durban, the troops aboard were anxious for the chance to step onto dry land for the first time in weeks. They could see the clock tower in the centre of town, and smell the rich aromas of a new and exotic land. Almost immediately, however, the ship was ordered to drop anchor and wait until boarded by port officials, who came with astounding news: while the *Boonah* had been at sea, an armistice had been signed between the Allies and the Central Powers. The war was over.

The news that should have been greeted with delight by the young men on board was instead received with a peculiar quiet – an unexpected, disillusioned joy. That their lives were to be spared seemed a blessing hidden behind some imaginary curtain that veiled the dead who'd gone before, and the valour that would never be known by those who were now free to return to their homes. Like boxers laced and limbered for the fight that never came, the soldiers of the *Boonah* felt cheated by a victory that was, for them, cheaply purchased.

But there was more news that would prove to be unpopular with all: the *Boonah* had been quarantined, and none could leave the ship, which was to turn back to Australia after several days at anchor, once stocks had been replenished and coal supplied for the return trip. At first, the soldiers were furious – to deny them leave was inhumane; the bustling city sounds beckoned them from across the bay. But then they heard the meaning of it: the dreaded Spanish Flu had taken grip in Durban, and if the *Boonah* were to take it on board the results would be catastrophic.

The Spanish Flu, a pandemic that swept the world between 1918 and 1920, would ultimately claim in two years more lives than the Great War had in four. At the time the *Boonah* was anchored off Durban, it had already killed millions in Europe and America, travelling on crowded troop transports and festering in the trenches, returning home again in the bodies of the wounded and the dead. Nobody knew where it had been born (its name was derived from the devastation it wreaked upon Spain in 1918, where it reportedly took eight million souls) but the first cases of it had been reported in the military camps in the United States, where troops had mingled in close quarters with those returning from the front. Rumours abounded that the virus was a weapon devised by the German army, spread through the Allied ranks by agents posing as nuns or the surrendering wounded. The deadly affliction took its victims swiftly – within hours of the initial feverish symptoms, the sufferer would become too weak to stand, their face turning blue, their bowels opening, blood seeping from their mouth, their nose, their eyes, their lungs filling fatally with blood then drowning the host. A madness would take hold before the end, and permanent damage to the mind was likely in those fortunate enough to survive it.

The panic that came with news of the virus saw city streets all over the world filling with masked ghouls who dared not breathe the air. Windows were sealed shut. Domestic pets were slaughtered lest they roam the streets and bring the illness home. Businesses closed down when workers were seen to catch the commonest colds. The British press was reporting it as the most devastating pandemic since the Black Death, the fourteenth century plague that decimated half of Europe's population. Others called it the wrath of God, who was raining pestilence on men who dared to wage such diabolical war against their brothers.

The Australian people had not met with the Spanish Flu in 1918, though they had heard of it. In the month before the *Boonah* sailed, news from America told of how 851 New Yorkers had died of the virus in a single day, while Chicago's crime rate had dropped by half, the city's hardened criminals being quietly slain in their beds, or simply too frightened to venture out. It would take until the year of 1919 for the panic to take hold in Australia, the creeping virus crossing oceans with soldiers returning home to their loved ones. Theatres, churches and schools would close, and police would man the borders of the states. Anzac Day services were cancelled. Fraternisation with soldiers would be discouraged. But this was all in the future as the *Boonah* lay anchored in the Bay of Natal, its decks crowded with young men who'd sailed the sea to die heroic deaths in battle. For none would death come so gloriously.

For days the troops remained on board, the heat forcing most of them onto the decks to sleep, the lights of Durban winking at them in the night, the sounds of music and laughter and the clink of glasses – a city celebrating the end of war – drifting across the bay. To some, the sounds they heard did not tell of a city crippled by pestilence. One night, risking infection rather than remaining as hostage to their ship, a dozen cut a raft away and rowed off into the darkness, toward the lights and the gaiety. They were arrested within moments of stepping onto shore, the strict quarantining of the *Boonah* preventing them from rejoining their ship. They sailed on a later steamer to Australia, unaware as they were of their good fortune until they arrived.

For though strictly quarantined, the *Boonah* still had to be restocked with supplies, thus native labourers were allowed onboard to replenish the reserves of food and coal for the journey home. It was late one afternoon when soldiers on the *Boonah* were greeted with an ominous sight: local stevedores lying exhausted on the deck, sprawled out, sick, too weak to stand.

The *Boonah* pulled away from Durban on Sunday, 24 November, chugging out past the headlands on the Bay of Natal and continuing out to sea on its way back to Fremantle. It had been decided that, on the voyage home, the ship would make a sweep into the Indian Ocean to visit the island of St Paul, a small and remote volcanic land mass known as a haven for shipwrecked sailors. In 1871 the HMS *Megaera*, a British transport ship, was wrecked off the island, the 400 survivors lasting for three months on the barren, rocky isle before being discovered. In 1889 Charles Lightoller, who would later survive the sinking of the *Titanic*, had been castaway on St Paul for eight days until a rescue party came. The loot of long dead pirates, it was said, was hidden in the many caves that burrowed through the basalt on the rocky isle.

But romantic thoughts of shipwrecked sailors, treasure chests or shore leave were dashed when the stony spire of St Paul rose upon the horizon. As the *Boonah* drew into the circular bay through a narrow channel eroded in the rocky walls of the volcanic crater there were no signs of life – just a hollow pyramid of rock and desolation, a seafarer's purgatory, little jets of steam rising like dragons from a land that seemed lost to another time. There was silence on the deck as the *Boonah* sounded its horn, the call echoing back from the vast, forbidding walls of rock. The *Boonah* turned, crept out of the crater and continued on its journey, the spire of St Paul gradually sinking out of sight until it was no more.

The ship was five days out of Durban when the first signs of illness appeared. Men called into sick parade with headaches, fever, bloody noses. The *Boonah* was still days from Fremantle – enough time for the virus to kill them all. The ten beds in the hospital were quickly filled, and recreation areas were commandeered for the growing numbers of the sick. Within a day, ninety cases were reported, and the following day the number doubled. Men retreated to their bunks, too afraid to roam the decks or to come in contact with the others. The ship's crew were not immune, and when stokers began to wither the ship slowed to a crawl – it would take them twice as long to get home, the agony prolonged.

Water was rationed to one cup a day and men were ordered, in groups of twenty, to crowd naked in a fumigation chamber where they were made to breathe zinc sulfate fumes for fifteen minutes at a stretch. The medical staff knew not whether this would do any real good at all, but there was no known cure or inoculation for the Spanish Flu, and it was all they could think to do. At least it kept spirits up, convincing the men on board that something was being done.

The first fatality occurred on 9 December, though nobody saw it happen: Staff Sergeant A. C. Thwaites of the Australian Medical Corps had worked tirelessly with the sick and had brought the disease upon himself. He was last seen late at night, pacing the deck with a blanket draped around his shoulders, thinking of something, it seemed, a polite but morose nod to a sailor who bid the man goodnight. In the morning light the blanket was found hanging on the ship's rail, and Thwaites was gone.

In the early morning hours of 11 December, 1918, the war having been over for a month, the *Boonah* limped into the waters off the coast of Fremantle Harbour, the lights of the city comforting those strong enough to stand on deck. The ship now carried 298 cases of the illness, and none on the *Boonah* knew of the debate that had been raging on land as the ship had slowly steamed toward home. Readers of the *West Australian* had been informed on 1 December that a ship carrying 1000 soldiers and the dreaded Spanish Flu was approaching port, the plague to be unloaded into the city when it came. Like all Australians, the people of Fremantle had read the news of the outbreaks overseas. The dilemma was dreadful: their soldiers were returning home, alive, but to innocently unleash death on the nation finally at peace after so many years of conflict. Authorities were terrified of an outbreak on the mainland, and the ship was ordered to quarantine in the waters of Gage Roads, a few miles out to sea, between Rottnest Island and the shore.

By the time medical officers from Fremantle inspected the ship in the mid-morning, there were 337 sufferers in varying degrees of anguish. These men, it was decreed, would be ferried by boat to the quarantine station at Woodman Point, where outbreaks of diseases in cattle had been effectively managed in the previous century. The remainder of the men on board were considered 'contacts' – those who had been too close to the disease to safely be regarded as unaffected. None would be allowed to set foot on Australian soil until all signs of the disease had disappeared, or everyone on board had suffered and died.

And there the *Boonah* remained, the men on board in sight of their homes, but closer still to the death that travelled on the very air they breathed, the vessel that held them nothing more than a dungeon of disease. They'd been spared the horrors of the trenches and the violent deaths that came to so many, only to be left adrift at sea, unwanted by the nation for whom they'd volunteered their lives.

The scene at Woodman Point was pitiful; men were housed in tents and under blankets wet with perspiration, the awful silence punctuated by the chokes and coughs of the dying, the moans of pain and the screams of delirium. Nurses who'd volunteered from a nearby hospital ship shuffled from bed to bed, unable to do anything more than offer water and words of comfort. For Staff Sisters Rosa O'Kane, Ada Thompson and Doris Ridgway their decision to volunteer would be a death sentence, as all three, along with many of the medical staff, would succumb to the disease and live their last hours amongst the sick and dying.

Meanwhile, aboard the *Boonah*, soldiers lingered up on deck, tormented by the lights of Fremantle that flickered in the night. Below the air was thick with the fetid stench of rotting food and the slow creep of disease. New cases of the Spanish Flu hatched every day and the approach of the little boat that ferried the afflicted to Woodman Point was like a harbinger of death that bobbed toward them and away, their numbers dwindling with every visit that it paid.

In editorials and letters to the newspapers, fiery public meetings and civil protests, the people of West Australia raged at the authorities to allow their sons to return home. But the government of the day held fast, determined to prevent infected soldiers from bringing the Spanish Flu onto the mainland. On the ninth day at anchor off the coast of Fremantle, while the politicians fought by letter and word, not a one of which translated into action, the sufferers aboard the *Boonah* were saved by a most appropriate champion indeed. The West Australian branch of the Returned Servicemen's Association, the forerunner of today's Returned and Services League of Australia, stepped in and threatened that its members would storm the ship and rescue the men themselves if the powers that be would not.

The authorities panicked. Suddenly, after nine days of procrastination, the government allowed the West Australian men of the *Boonah* to be taken ashore at Woodman Point, where they would remain in isolation for seven days, their ship granted permission immediately to continue her voyage to the eastern states, sailing out from Gage Roads on 20 December, 1918. For some aboard the tragedy was far from over – six more cases of the disease developed between Fremantle and Albany, and a further seventeen between Albany and Port Adelaide. The Spanish Flu would then take hold in Melbourne, taking with it more than 12 000 souls.

Meanwhile, at Woodman Point, the *Boonah* patients continued to die. At first the casualties had been buried at East Rockingham cemetery but as the death toll continued to rise, it was decided to consecrate a new burial ground in the quarantine station grounds. The death toll at Woodman Point eventually reached thirty – a small number, compared to what might have been. But the heartbreak of the men who sailed on the last troopship to leave Australia for the Great War would stay with them for all their lives. As one soldier wrote:

'We, who have been spared, have returned, not covered with honour and glory and not seeking same, know in our hearts that at least we did our best.'

THE SPY WHO LOVED HER

The sunsets that are witnessed from the sole of the boot that is the Mornington Peninsula, from Portsea at the toe to Cape Schanck upon the heel, cannot be seen from elsewhere on the Victorian coast. The sun sinks well enough when viewed from Phillip Island or Venus Bay, where the land is angled to the sea at about the same degree, but never does the sky seem painted by the same hand, or to quite the same glorious scheme – the flame in the clouds, the blue-green sea and those rays of sunlight that frighten unbelievers.

It was into this picture that Harold Holt paddled on 17 December, 1967, transforming himself from one of the more dreary prime ministers in Australian history to a mystery immortal. That is what happens when you vanish from such a pretty picture – you become interesting. And it was not far from here, just a short walk to Sorrento, where dolphins caper daily in the blue of the bay, that our next story blossoms with all the charm of love anew, morphing into something as intriguing as the shadow of a man who was never there . . .

It was the day after Valentine's Day, 2003, the sort of summer Saturday morning when the young at heart might expect something good to happen – azure sky, a kiss of breeze, everything blessed with that hopeful hue that lives on in home movies from the 1960s, before Kennedy was shot, when the Cold War was still running hot. This was the day when Karen Roberts met Wayne Charters at a motorcycle meet near her home on the Mornington Peninsula.

At forty-one, Karen had almost given up. Her last marriage had done the splits, as so many seem to do, leaving her to care alone for her teenage daughter, Rebecca. They say that life begins at forty, and for Karen Roberts it had been an unheralded birth. She hoped that one day something, or someone, would make all the lousy memories go away, and fill her life with excitement again. Wayne seemed the kind of guy who could make it happen.

She'd just turned and found him standing there, smiling, as if it were the very place he'd meant to be all along, the very spot toward which his whole life had propelled him. He wasn't exactly handsome – he looked a bit like Tommy Cooper, without the fez – but he was brash, warm and curious, with a mystery of his own. There was something going on and Karen couldn't place it. Was this some kind of love at first sight? Had she forgotten what it felt like? Had all these years – the jaded love, the budding into nothing – convinced her that it never happened, and robbed her of the ability to know?

He introduced himself as 'Padre', said he was a carpet layer, and that he used to be a priest. Karen liked that, the way he wasn't ashamed of his past. Life is a journey and, when meeting someone new, it helps to see a passport, of sorts, the stamps and watermarks betraying places their lives have taken them. Some people were loath to show such things, but not Wayne. He did not seem surprised when Karen told him she was a spiritual person, too.

As they spoke, they realised Karen's daughter and Wayne's stepson were friends at school. It was a small world, as they say. Or maybe this was meant to be. When Wayne asked for Karen's phone number, she didn't hesitate.

He called her the next day. They talked for hours about all sorts of things. Karen was amazed at how similar they were, how they'd read the same books and enjoyed the same films, both shared a love of art, how they both hated violence and manipulative people, both shared a belief in a higher power, and in creating one's own reality. Wayne had no time for people obsessed with money or other earthly things. Most humans, he said, disappointed him. If only humanity was more spiritually aware, like dolphins, the world would be a better place.

Karen could scarcely believe her ears. Dolphins were her favourite animals, too, their intelligence and compassion far beyond the minds and hearts of humans. She'd often watch them in the bay, marvelling at them, and knew that there was so very much to learn from them. From the moment Karen heard Wayne mention his love for them – an enthusiasm she always looked for in others – she felt something awaken in her, an energy like she'd never felt. When Wayne asked if she'd like to come over to his place the following day, she didn't fear. She felt it was her destiny to go.

What she saw inside Wayne's home only confirmed the feelings that had been growing inside her. That his apartment was spartan and cheaply furnished didn't matter – material things never did. His walls were festooned with pictures of dolphins, painted in an airbrushed style that Karen particularly admired, the dreamy starbursts and soft pastel colours conveying their other-worldliness, the unique relationship these sea creatures shared with the supernatural realm. When Wayne told Karen that he'd painted some of them himself, she laughed – surely he was only joking. Then he showed her a room in which there were easels and brushes and paint. Just like Karen, Wayne loved art. He'd been too modest to tell her that he was, in fact, an artist.

Wayne showed her photos of himself dressed as a priest, and the religious robes in his wardrobe, which he kept for sentimental reasons, even though, just like Karen, he'd rejected the western concept of God after studying the eastern religions. She was amazed to see his psychology degree – no wonder he'd been so interested in the fact she herself was a qualified counsellor – and she was quietly impressed when she spied a trophy that celebrated Wayne as a tae kwon do champion. He was almost ashamed when she pointed to it. He hated violence so much. But it was important, he said, to be in control of one's energy.

Karen left Wayne's house that day convinced that she had at long last found her soul mate.

They had been together but a month when Wayne proposed to her, with a crystal ring that meant more to him spiritually than any materialistic diamond ever could. Crystals were conduits of divine energy and, with this ring, they would be joined forever on life's path. There had been too many coincidences, said Wayne, and he could ignore his destiny no longer.

Karen said yes immediately. She had fallen in love with Wayne long ago – perhaps, she thought, long before she had met him. It was as if they'd been joined in some other life, an existence she had been made to forget, if only to be rewarded with this sublime moment, her coming together with this beautiful and familiar stranger.

But when Karen told Rebecca, the young girl reacted badly. She did not trust Wayne, nor did she trust his stepson. She'd heard stories. There were those who said Wayne Charters was no good, that he'd done time in prison, might even be violent. A killer. Karen laughed – it was impossible. Wayne abhorred violence. Yes, he was a martial arts champion, but he would sooner hurt himself than another living soul. She insisted to her daughter that she knew this man like she knew her own heart.

But all thoughts planted tend to grow, and Rebecca's words began to take root in Karen's mind until she found the courage to ask Wayne about them. Yes, he said, he had been to prison, but it was not as Karen had heard, or might think. There was an explanation she would scarcely believe, a truth he had hoped he might keep from her, a part of his life he wished he could make go away. It was well, he said, that she had raised it, for she had a right to know.

It was many years ago, Wayne said, that he had been seconded into ASIO, the secret organisation charged with defending Australia's liberty through subterfuge and covert intrigue. It had begun as little more than a youthful interest in the thrilling world of espionage, but Wayne's natural gifts as a spy – his keen mind and physical prowess – had ensured that, before he could do much about it, he had risen through the ranks until he was third-in-charge of the entire organisation. Wayne's work with ASIO had necessitated him being quite the chameleon, drifting to and from various guises and walks of life. Sometimes he'd had to masquerade as a bum, a criminal, a gambler, a drunk – his very occupation as a carpet layer was a ruse. This was, no doubt, the seat of all the rumours Karen's daughter had unearthed. At least, Wayne consoled himself aloud, his performances had been believable.

But there was something else, too, something terrible that had been troubling him, and was bound to trouble Karen. The war in Iraq had just begun, to which Australia had committed itself militarily and morally, and Wayne feared he'd be called upon to serve – not simply as a soldier, but as an agent, a spy, on the very edge of death and in the thick of all the killing. Not only did this grate against his spiritual self but, now that he'd met Karen, everything had changed. Where once he'd been a reckless soul, a man who'd always slapped his thigh and laughed at death, he now had something worth living for. Love, it seemed, made death no laughing matter. He had tried to resign, shortly after that day they'd met, but ASIO would have none of it, and had refused his resignation. There was nothing he could do.

Karen didn't know what to think. Wayne's story sounded crazy, like something from a novel. But then she'd heard of ASIO, and knew that spies existed. Who was she to say that Wayne was not involved in such a world? After all, he was a tae kwon do expert. Why not a secret agent, too? In any case, Wayne Charters was the most honest, spiritual soul she'd ever met and only a sick, perverted madman would spin a yarn like this.

Karen told Wayne not to worry. She loved him, trusted him and, if he trusted her, they would think of something. Their love would find a way.

In 2003 Dr Andreas Bartels and Professor Semir Zeki, neurologists from the University College, London, began looking closely at the parts of the brain that were activated during the swoon of love. Using magnetic resonance imaging, they recorded activity in the brains of mothers and lovers exposed to the objects of their desires, the chief interest of the scientists being the neurological differences between maternal love and the purely romantic variety. The results showed significant overlap – romantic love triggered activity in the same parts of the brain that are active when a parent loves a child, lovers being as neurologically inclined toward the protective instincts of the parents of schoolchildren. More revealing, however, was the locations in the brain that appeared to be deactivated when love flared. Parts of the pre-frontal cortex which are engaged during judgement, critical analysis and evaluations of trustworthiness were less active when feelings of affection were amplified, love's drain on neurological resources effectively dimming the lights in the mind's bureau of intelligence. Love, it seems, is not only blind but temporarily brain damaged, too.

While not being in touch with the world of neurological inquiry, Karen Roberts was at this moment in time a most excellent exhibit for its latest findings, and whatever doubts she had regarding Wayne's story – doubts already expelled by her white-hot love for the man – were banished further into the dark corners of her mind when she was introduced to Craig Hall, whom Wayne presented to Karen as verification of his story. Craig worked for ASIO, too – he was one of Wayne's subordinates – and he confirmed that everything Wayne had told Karen was true. Like Wayne, Craig was worried about the war. Coincidentally he had recently met the love of his own life, and was convinced he'd soon be sent to Iraq, too, where he would surely meet with death. The regime in Baghdad was one of the cruellest the world had ever known, harbouring biological weapons the nature of which ASIO was keen to learn. If Wayne and he were to be sent to Iraq, Craig assured Karen, it would almost certainly be in the name of uncovering the truth about such weapons. Failure would mean a grizzly demise.

The alternative, it seemed, was no better for any of them: Wayne showed Karen the letter he had received from his superiors, rejecting his request for leave to resign from the organisation. It was serious, the words lashing out from stark typewriter print on an ASIO letterhead. Wayne and Craig both insisted that refusal to comply with orders handed down from their ASIO handlers would result in their certain elimination.

Karen suggested they go into hiding – Wayne could come and live with her, change his name, and nobody would ever know. But Wayne insisted it would never work. His money was all tied up in bank accounts to which ASIO had access, and they would know every time he ate a meal, made a phone call or paid for petrol. Indeed, they probably already knew of Karen, and were keeping watch on her, too.

At this Karen became frightened. She was caught up in something too colossal for her to comprehend, much less combat. It wasn't fair. All she had done was fall in love. Perhaps Rebecca had been right without knowing it: falling in love with Wayne Charters had been a mistake.

And yet she felt it was no mistake. Love's alchemy conquers all of earth's minerals, bookish equations and mathematical monsters, restraints and things that crush. All Karen Roberts knew was that fighting her love for Wayne Charters would be harder than fighting all the devious designs of all the intelligence communities of the civilised world. Perhaps, then, their love would also be strong enough to defeat such things.

It was late one night, after many drinks and fraught conversation, that a plan began to take shape. What if all of them were to sneak out of the country under the guise of taking a simple holiday? They could go to some country in Asia, where the sheer volume of international traffic would make it possible to escape to anywhere in the world undetected. Wayne would need to abandon all his own savings and possessions, lest the authorities suspected he was up to no good. But if Wayne and Karen were husband and wife, as they would be in just a few weeks, they could open a joint account about which ASIO would never know. Together they could move to Canada, where they could both begin new careers as spiritual counsellors. They would have to lie low for a while, just until the scandal of Wayne's disappearance blew over, but they would survive. Karen's house alone was worth at least a quarter of a million dollars – perhaps a little less, if she had to sell it fast.

Naturally the idea concerned Karen deeply. She had always been careful with money, the very reason she had savings worth $60 000. But she feared losing Wayne more than losing the lot. It was something that simply had to be done.

Wayne Charters and Karen Roberts were wed in May, in a little restaurant in Sorrento, not far from where the couple had met just a few months before. Craig Hall and his girlfriend, Carol Logan, were wed, too, the only guests being Rebecca and Carol's own daughter, Kim. Wayne and Craig had thought it best to keep things quiet, lest a wild celebration pose a security risk.

Wayne and Karen both cried in each other's arms that night, with the moon beaming down on the dolphins in the bay. For just one moment it didn't matter that their lives were in danger. They were in love, and whatever might be ahead in life's journey was waiting for them both. It was the happiest night of Karen's life.

In the days that followed Karen did as Wayne instructed, for he was the one who knew how to manage this deception without alerting suspicion. She put her house on the market and sold it to the highest early bid, transferring all of her money into their joint account. She then booked several rooms at the Raffles Hotel, Singapore, in her own name, and return air tickets for Wayne and herself, Craig and Carol, Rebecca and Kim – two happy families enjoying a holiday together. Nobody would ever know the truth.

They slipped out of the country without rousing suspicion and, for a few days, the honeymoon was bliss. But it was while island hopping in Malaysia that the newlyweds had their first fight. Late one night, Karen complained that Wayne was avoiding her – not publicly, of course, where he appeared to worship the ground she walked upon, but in private, where he seemed withdrawn and uneasy. She wondered aloud exactly when and where Wayne might decide it was time to consummate the marriage.

Wayne raged at her. How could she be so selfish, he fumed, to be bothered with such a trifle as her own physical fulfilment? They were escaping the clutches of ASIO, one of the most powerful intelligence organisations in the world, and the stress he was under would crush a lesser man. Now was not the time to be anxiously fondling like teenagers at the movies. There would be plenty of time for that later when his spiritual energies weren't so under siege.

Embarrassed by her own childish wants, Karen apologised and let it go. He was right – there would be time for love. She had waited her whole life for this. A few more weeks would mean nothing.

On the ides of June, Karen and Rebecca returned to Australia, as had been agreed. She was to perform a few transactions back home just in case the authorities had grown suspicious by their absence, her appearance again in Australia buying Wayne and Craig precious time to organise safe passage to Canada. Karen was to wait for instructions from Wayne, who had said the most tearful goodbye at the airport, promising they would see each other soon as they walked the long path to their destiny together.

A few days later a text message arrived from Wayne, telling her to wait and stay calm, that he would be in touch once he had a 'secure line'. Days passed, and Karen began to panic, imagining the tragedies that might have befallen him. What if ASIO had found Wayne and liquidated him quietly? Neither she nor the world would ever know.

She checked their bank account and was relieved to see there had been some transactions – at least Wayne was still alive. Then she saw the balance: there was only $6.

She went cold. She wasn't sure what had happened, but she knew something wasn't right. She refused to believe that Wayne had conned her – that the whole of the last few months had been a scam was simply impossible. For that to be true Wayne would be evil, and Wayne was anything at all but evil. But she could no longer stay silent and alone. Something had gone terribly wrong. There had to be someone whom she could turn to.

She picked up the phone and dialled the number for the police, even though it was the very thing Wayne had told her to never, ever do. Surely, she thought, not everybody worked for ASIO, or was out to get the man who loved her.

Detective Sergeant John Coburn was. And, when he heard the very name Wayne Charters, he had some dreadful tidings to deliver to Karen Roberts.

Mr Charters had first come to the notice of police in 1978, when he was charged with fraudulently obtaining unemployment benefits while working. It was the beginning of a career of deception and fraud that spanned three decades and saw Wayne Charters regularly leaving courtroom doors swinging in his wake: charged with being an unlicensed private investigator in '79; with theft by deception in '81; with obtaining property by deception after getting a $22 900 loan for the establishment of the Congregational Church of Australia in Boronia in '89. In 1991, he was charged by federal police with setting up a false church, the Lutheran Order of St Paul Australia, and with operating numerous bank accounts under false names and using forged certificates telling of fraudulent degrees in theology and medicine. Incredibly, however, the court gave Wayne Charters a suspended sentence when he presented forged certification claiming that he was intellectually disabled.

In 1992 he was charged with passing thousands of dollars in bogus cheques, and again in 1997, for which he received three years in jail. In June of 2002, he'd set fire to his own real estate office and two carpet businesses, attempting to frame a seventeen-year-old apprentice who was nearly imprisoned until Wayne skipped town, his sudden disappearance confessing his guilt. He'd been on parole when he met Karen Roberts, on the day after Valentine's Day, 2003.

In the months that followed Wayne's vanishing, Karen drifted though each day battling breakers of shock, thoughts of love returning momentarily to be dashed once again by sheer disbelief. Even then, after all that she'd learned, some hopeful part of her dreamed that there'd been some mistake, that Wayne might some day march through her door with an explanation that would make everything beautiful again.

It took until 2006 for those feelings to even begin being laid to rest at last. In a Victorian County Court, Karen listened to the evidence against Craig Hall, arrested while trying to sneak back into the country, now charged with four counts of obtaining property by deception, and with stealing the suit that he wore at his wedding. He'd been sharing a jail cell with Charters late in 2002 when Wayne convinced him to take part in a scam sure to work. It involved a lonely divorcee, a house and many thousands of dollars in savings. Wayne's stepson had been drilling the woman's clueless daughter, with whom he went to school, for information about the things her mother loved, the enthusiasms she looked for in others – dolphins and such – so that Wayne could become the man of her dreams. All Craig Hall had to do was go along with the plan, to 'marry' his de-facto girlfriend, to play the spy coming in from the cold, and a grand holiday plus a cut of the winnings would be his.

Even then, Karen's heart surged a little when Hall revealed that he and Charters had been on an island off Thailand at the time of the Boxing Day tsunami in 2004, and that Charters had most probably been washed away to sea. She needn't have worried.

In August of 2008 Wayne Charters was arrested at Melbourne Airport as he tried to quietly enter Australia. He'd been living in China, south-east of Beijing, with a pregnant wife and luxury home. For four years he'd been posing as a doctor, a clinical psychologist, a US Vietnam veteran with a Medal of Honor and a personal adviser to the President of the USA. He was wanted by police when he'd left Australia in 2003, and should have been detained. But immigration weren't looking for a man with a wife and a child and friends who loved him.

At Charters' committal hearing in April of 2009, Karen Roberts would learn it was not, in fact, the dolphin that best symbolised her union with the man who never was, who had robbed her of everything she owned.

According to Carol Logan's police statement, Karen had only just flown out of Malaysia when Charters had turned to his friends and announced it was time to party. 'For the fat cow is gone,' he had declared, 'and she's not coming back.'

A DAY AT THE RACES

The outback Queensland town of Augathella, 90 kilometres north-east of Charleville, is home to meat ants said to be capable of carrying weights a hundred times their own, a legend that greatly benefits the local rugby league team, the Mighty Meat Ants. Once known as the Burenda Township, Augathella takes its name from the Aboriginal word meaning 'waterhole', a reference to the nearby Warrego River, which rises and falls with the floods and droughts that play tag upon the stoic local population. The racetrack is still there, hosting meetings at Easter and Christmas, and so is the Ellangowan Hotel, where one can get a cold beer or, if one so desires it, a cool glass of water. Sometimes, even a warm one will do ...

The summer 1875 had been a scorching one in central Queensland, and the festive season saw drovers and men of the land released from their duties to spend time with their families. Those without loved ones converged on the public houses that rose from the outback plains like temples for lost souls, the rooms at the back reserved as morgues for the dead drunk. And it was to the Ellangowan Hotel, near the isolated cattle station at Burenda, that five friends met as the year drew to a close: James Larkins, Albert Green, James Wilson, William Nolan and Louis Schmidt – all good drinking men who intended to stay in the township so as to usher in the new year.

There was reason to be here apart from drinking. A race meet had been arranged for Tuesday, 28 December, horsemen from all over the state coming together to pit their mounts against those of other riders, the local publican offering generous cash prizes for the victors. It's fair to say that the racing was secondary to the purpose of Larkins and his friends. Having arrived not with horse, but each with a dog (Larkins had two – a cattle dog and her puppy), they were here for the drinking, and the rowdy companionship that such a gathering might bring. Albert Green, in particular, had a reputation not as a rider but as a man who was rarely seen sober.

The day began in the public house, men from near and far flexing for the coming contests as rum was swallowed and beer was guzzled. So intense was the carousing in the Ellangowan Hotel that the race meet was all but forgotten, and it was not until three o'clock in the afternoon that the publican finally convinced the loud and wobbly mob to remember the gala for which they had come.

By all accounts, the scenes that followed were hardly a mirror of the elegant derbies at Ascot or Kentucky, drunken jockeys astride their mounts, galloping to the hollers of the boisterous crowd of men who staggered and gambled in the afternoon sun. Fights broke out continuously, the nearest policeman miles away in Charleville, the rabble left to its own lawless instincts, and any man who stepped up to quell the strife was beaten for his trouble. During one race, a rider, finding himself behind by a head in the final straight, took out his whip and lashed the face of the jockey who threatened to best him. A newspaper man there to report upon the sport described the day's events taking place 'amid scenes of drunkenness and bestiality sickening in their details – a living disgrace to any civilised community of white men'.

Whether Larkins and his friends were a party to such outrages in not recorded but we at least know that they drank heavily, and continued drinking at the Ellangowan Hotel for the next three days, long after the hoi polloi had gone, salving the oncoming crush of their hangovers by beginning each day in the bar again, the hot sun rising and setting on entire days spent by the trickle of the barman's tap. They saw out the year there, heralding the first moments of 1876 with brandy and beer, and toasts to a happy and prosperous year ahead.

On the Saturday morning of New Year's Day, 1876, James Larkins awoke with an angry head, but was determined to make a move this day. Encountering some resistance from his friends, who seemed happy to remain at the Ellangowan Hotel for the rest of their lives, Larkins proposed they purchase some bottles of whisky to drink upon their way, thus a leisurely journey would be had by all. If they started now they would make the Nive Downs station by nightfall, where they might take meals, procure horses and bid each other farewell as they made their way to their respective homes.

After a few glasses of beer to right themselves, the band set off at eight o'clock in the morning, their dogs at their heels, along what was known as 'The Postman's Track', which ran through the low scrub from Burenda to Nive Downs. They had with them two bottles of Hennessy whisky and two billycans of water.

After some time the sun rose in the sky, its rays baking the land and everything upon it. The temperature soared into the high forties as the men marched on, the alcohol curdling their blood. They stopped and camped for a while under a tree that offered no more shade than a lamp post, so thirsty they drank all the water they had, convinced that Nive Downs could not be far. They each took a swig of whisky, to soothe the looming agony of their hangovers, and then they walked some more. But the sun began to make noise in their heads, the heat and the alcohol soaking all the moisture from their bodies. They grew weak with discomfort.

They camped again, beneath a tree whose shade was a touch more nourishing than the last, and gulped the remaining drops of the whisky, the only liquid they had, whose anaesthetic would serve as the most temporary of medicines. Exhausted from the heat, and lulled into lethargy by the whisky, Nolan, Schmidt and Wilson declared they could not go on, but would rather stay, taking turns in the puny shade of the tree until Green and Larkins might return from Nive Downs with water and more whisky to fire them on their way. Larkins told them not to stray from their post as he and Green, pursued by their dogs, made off in the direction they believed Nive Downs would be.

They walked for an hour – maybe more – until their heads began to throb with pain under the searing sun, their bodies as sponges parched in an oven, their dried brains rattling in their skulls. Their tongues swelled. Their throats stuck closed. Their quickening heartbeats pulsed in their temples and their bodies shook with the delirium tremens, their bloodshot eyes like billiard balls in their sockets. And above all torments, the maddening thirst, the thought of tiny drops of water as diamonds in their minds.

The pounding in Larkins' brain became so excruciating he wrapped his head in a handkerchief, tied tight as to distract from the endless thud inside. He could go no further, and told Green so as he lay down in hopeless agony. Green said nothing but merely stared at him for a moment, before marching off determinedly, his mutt giving chase, leaving Larkins behind in the company of his own forlorn dog and her puppy.

There James Larkins lay, under the snarl of the afternoon sun, drifting in and out of consciousness, awaking now and then to brush the ants from his body. Just when he thought he could take no more, the sun began to retreat beyond the horizon, taking with it the blinding, scorching heat. But his thirst remained – such a a terrible thirst that it made him cry each time it peeped through the madness, his body so dry of moisture that he had not even tears to drink. With what strength he had, he dug at the soil in the hope of finding water deep in the earth, but she was dry and thirsty, too. He would do anything, he thought, for the slightest drop at all.

He looked at his dog. She had moisture. There was blood inside her – a pint of it, maybe two. That it was the juice of a living thing – indeed, the man's 'best friend' – didn't matter, as such trifles don't when one is insane with thirst. He took a knife from his bag. As if realising what her master had in mind the dog bolted into the scrub, howling as she went. She was never seen again.

But the puppy did not have the wisdom of her mother, and lay still at Larkins' feet. He reached over and took her in his hand. She was young and small, and would surely quench but a fraction of his thirst. But he needed moisture so terribly. He held the puppy against the ground, took his knife and pressed it into the throat of the animal, who screeched and howled for a moment, then was still. Larkins raised her to his mouth and sucked until the puppy was empty.

The air was still hot but the blood from the puppy had given him just enough strength to stand. His clothes were heavy upon his back so he stripped them off and pushed ahead, naked in the night, the moon lighting the track ahead of him. For hours he staggered on, calling out to his friends until his parched throat could call no more. There was never an answer but for the scuttle of lizards and snakes and other creatures that lurked in the scrub at his feet. The sky was turning pink ahead – the angry sun coming back to murder him – when at last he saw the silhouette of a windmill on the horizon. It was Nive Downs.

He crawled on hand and knee toward it, a journey that took him hours, until at last he saw a man emerge from a house and walk toward him. Larkins began to speak, but the words hardly came, and then he felt sick. He was taken inside the house, fed water, and rested upon a bed whereupon he fell into a dreadful delirium, a pit so deep he could not rouse himself in the moments when he realised he was within it.

James Larkins awoke in the afternoon to the sound of men in the house, murmuring to each other, a gravity in their voices. He rose, believing the men to be his friends, only to find they were strangers from a neighbouring station. He began to tell them his story, about his companions, who were lost along the Postman's Track in desperate need of water and salvation. They might still be alive – the men must hurry. It was then revealed to Larkins a shocking truth: the date was Tuesday, 4 January, 1876. He had been asleep for two whole days and more. His friends had been found.

William Nolan and Louis Schmidt had staggered naked into a Burenda cattle station the previous night. They had left James Wilson at the tree where he lay, for he had been too weak to move, and though they had encountered Green along the way, he, too, was too muddled of mind to stay with them. Both Nolan and Schmidt had survived the days by digging themselves into the sand to escape the sun, their faces parked in the shade of the low scrub, the pair of them continuing on in the cool of the night. A flight of cockatoos had led them to the Warrego River on Monday morning, from which they drank and swam until strong, following the river until arriving at the Burenda station later that night.

Parties of men had gone in search of Green and Wilson at first light. It was midday when one of the party spied an anthill in the distance. As he approached, to his horror, the little mountain of ants appeared to whisper to him. It was James Wilson. He had survived in fifty-degree heat for three days, lying exactly where the others had left him, unable to move, dreaming of water as the meat ants had swarmed on his naked flesh. At the moment a bag of cool water was held to lips, he murmured something, and then passed away. Not far away, a smaller anthill marked the spot where his dog had succumbed before him. Albert Green was found later, his body black from rigor mortis, and burning under the open sun. He had died not long after the others had left him.

So ended the festive season for five good drinking men who, just days before, had toasted the new year with whisky and beer, warm handshakes and grand declarations of great things to come. For the rest of his days James Larkins would be haunted by the knowledge that his mates had died while he slept, a memory as harsh as a sun without shade, maddening as a thirst without a drink, and as lonely as a man without man's best friend.

THE HEIST

Captain Cook named Byron Bay after John Byron, circumnavigator of the world, who would later become the grandfather of English poet Lord Byron, a man as famous for his recklessness as his verse. It is fitting then, that today, the seaside municipality that bears the name is a magnet for both dreamers and the well-to-do, a strange coexistence of newfound wealth and those who'll have none of it, their escape from the commercial vulgarity of decent society having landed them here, where so many of the joys of life on earth are abundant and free to be picked or indulged. An excellent summation of the town's soul can be found when one looks east from a window of the Great Northern Hotel in Jonson Street, from which one will spy a fish and chip shop, an art gallery, a Just Jeans outlet, a fitness headquarters and a Tree of Life store – suburbia, elitism, modern commercialism, vanity and spiritual anarchy in one blow. It's no wonder Byron Bay attracts so many part-time cultural dropouts, who can screw the system and still get a burger in the dead of night when nobody's watching.

But one should never make the mistake of thinking such urchins don't envy those who prosper in the world which they eschew – Byron Bay boasts one of the state's most alarming burglary rates, and the rich aren't responsible for the piracy. What follows is an account of two such vagabonds . . .

Meet Anthony Prince and Luke Carroll, two fine young fellows whose lives came together in the waves of Byron Bay on the New South Wales north coast. They shared a love of surfing, cheating the breakers of fate. They had grown up and gone to school just miles apart – Prince had graduated in 2003 from Trinity Catholic College in Lismore, while Carroll had been a student at Marist St John's College, Woodlawn, just a short drive inland. They were good Catholic boys from middle-class families, in which trouble had always been kept at the door by decent meals and television, and occasional fantasies of lives lived large.

Prince was a prankster, the class clown, his capers never amounting to anything more serious than some ruse designed to cause a laugh when discovered. His record was as white as snow and so was his future, with no grand plans or colourful goals that might stand out against the void. His father would accuse him of living in a fantasy land and that appeared to be his greatest crime. So it was with Carroll, for whom life was a lark. Nobody ever thought he'd amount to much, but most people don't, vicariously living good lives and bad through the deeds of the heroes and devils from the movies. He had never picked a pocket, lifted goods from a store, raised his hand against a woman or man not his size. For Prince and Carroll, life was little more than an endless pursuit of good seas and nights not spent alone.

Some time in 2004 the pair decided they'd seen everything there was to excite a couple of young men in Byron Bay. They'd surfed all the waves and been drunk in all the dives. It was time to move elsewhere, to some place overseas, where a working holiday would earn them experience and good times to file in the memory forever. They took out a map and a finger pointed to Vail, Colorado, where the ski fields were famous and the night life hectic. If they worked hard, they thought, and saved every dollar, they'd be there by the end of the year.

They both took dumb jobs that meant nothing to anyone, save the customers they served and the bosses who made their fortunes by hiring kids whom they paid less than they were worth. Then they took second jobs of even less influence than the first. For the whole year they toiled, saving as much as they could, until saying goodbye to their friends and their families as they flew out to America for unknown adventure.

They arrived in Vail, Colorado in the winter of 2004. The snow season was crowded, the living was good. It did not take them long to guzzle their savings. They both obtained jobs in a local store called Pepi's, selling sporting goods and ski gear to tourists, the rich and the passing trade. On their days off they hit the snow fields with their boards, sliding down the slopes and then taking the chair lift to do it all over again until spent. At nights they'd drink in the bars until dawn, hoping some meeting would make the future change. One day, they knew, they'd have to return to their old lives, when the money ran out and the fun became scarce. Until then they'd keep working the slopes and playing at their jobs.

One night, drunk and a little wild of heart, the boys shot at the windows of a neighbouring house with pellets from BB guns they'd purchased at a local store, just for fun. The police were called and the boys were cautioned. The cop who attended to the misdemeanour made a note of the boy's names and faces. What they'd done wasn't serious – just boys being boys – but hooligans weren't welcome in Vail, Colorado. It was important to stay on top of the troublemakers.

Soon Prince and Carroll's bank balances were looking spare and the boys began wondering if they'd be going home sooner than they had planned. The signs of wealth around them began to itch in their minds – the big cars that glided through town like chariots, the jewellery and the nice clothes, the wallets full of cash, the flash credit cards people flaunted at the store, the meals on the menus they couldn't afford. They began to wonder what had gone so wrong, why those people, who looked no different to themselves, had so much money where they had none. The working hours at Pepi's became longer, like trawling through mud. There had to be an easier way.

One day Prince entered the local branch of the WestStar Bank, at the foot of the ski slope just out of town. He stood in line to withdraw from the meagre savings he had. He noticed the security was slack, the early mornings lazy and quiet in this vault of riches. He conducted his business with a teller who knew him by name, and never suspected his mind was at work on anything other than his courteous way.

One night he chewed it over with Carroll – just talking at first, over beer and the rash dialogue that it brings. Two people, he said, could easily rob the Vail branch of the WestStar Bank. All they'd need was the nerve, and an escape route that worked – something original. Something James Bond would do. Nobody had ever made an escape on snowboards. They laughed and drank to the thought.

They began to wonder, out loud and together, whether they might not be able to do it themselves. After all, nobody would ever suspect it was them, two fun-loving travellers from Australia who were known by the locals as friendly and good. They discussed it the next night, and the next night again, and before they knew it they were hatching a plan, a conspiracy that would take them from the centre of their dismal world to the very edge of another, where the daring succeed and the weak stay toiling. They imagined the relief of no longer having to worry about money, working jobs that paid them next to nothing. They could leave Vail with the loot and go somewhere else, to Mexico or Cuba, or home to Byron Bay, where they would live like a lord's bastards, safe from their deed by the inscrutable curve of the earth.

By the time the two good boys fell to sleep in the morning hours of Monday, 21 March, 2005, they were caught in a fate of their own design, an idea that had become a juggernaut, a destiny from which they would not escape. Just one night of dreams would estrange them from their old lives and usher them into the history books, where the names of Prince and Carroll would live next to those of the world's most romantic villains – Butch and Sundance, Bonnie and Clyde – but with a footnote they'd wish forever they could hide.

In the morning Anthony Prince and Luke Carroll awoke to find the weather good and the feeling just right. It would be today, they agreed. They would do it now, or wonder till death what might have been.

Prince put in a call to his boss at Pepi's. He was sick, he said, and needed the day off. Together he and Carroll dressed in clothes for the slopes, so they would blend in with the crowd as they made their getaway. They worried that some might recognise them – they were known about town, and were friendly with the tellers in the bank, who might suspect it was them through the camouflage of their masks. Anthony came up with a sterling idea. They would don the name tags that they wore at Pepi's, only bearing names of people who didn't exist – Trevor and Wayne, or names of that ilk. That would throw people off the scent, they thought, sending cops dashing all over in search of two phantoms while the real bandits made their escape.

They filled their backpacks with the tools for the heist: zip ties from a local hardware store, with which they would strap any bank staff who dared make a scene; a pillowcase, in which they would carry the loot; walkie-talkies, so they could communicate if they were separated in the mayhem; and weapons, the same calibre of firearm used by Clark Griswold when he held up Walley World in '83. They strapped on their packs, pulled down their balaclavas and made their way to the bank at the foot of the slopes.

They arrived just after nine o'clock, whereupon Prince realised he'd left his ski pass at home. The pass was essential – without it they wouldn't be able to escape via the snow. Carroll waited anxiously while Prince went back to fetch a new pass from the store that furnished them. It was nearly ten o'clock when he returned. The bank was about to open.

While the two boys from Australia watched, a teller arrived – a woman they both knew – and opened the door to the bank, her hands full, carrying a cake for somebody's birthday. It worried the boys for a moment that they might be about to ruin someone's special day. But there was no time any more for such sensitive thoughts. They must harden their hearts. There was crime to be done. The woman fumbled the cake in her arms as she placed her key in the lock and opened the door. To the boys' amazement, she left it ajar. This was their chance. They sprang into action.

The masked bandits burst through the door of the bank, forcing the terrified woman to the ground at gunpoint, shouting their demands: nobody would get hurt if they did what they were told, the pellets rattling in guns held by hands that had only ever fired in jest. As Prince kept the staff covered, Carroll forced a teller into the backroom vault, shoving her roughly toward the safe, apologising when he saw she'd hurt her arm. Regaining his criminal composure, he took the pillowcase from his backpack and coarsely demanded she fill it fast. The woman was shaking as she stuffed piles of notes in the bag, desperate not to give this masked fiend any reason to shoot her. She had heard of bank robbers who would kill just for kicks, for whom the money was secondary to the power they wield. She hoped these two would not be so cruel.

A customer entered the bank – Prince had forgotten to lock the front door. Through his mask – with a gun in his hand and customers at his feet, their hands behind their heads – Prince politely explained to the ashen-faced gentleman that the bank was experiencing technical difficulties, and to come back later when the problems would surely have been solved.

Carroll emerged from the backroom vault with the pillowcase bulging, ordering the teller to lie face-down on the floor with the others. He then warned the staff not to raise the alarm for at least half an hour or else they'd come back and it would be curtains for all. And with that the boys fled with the loot.

Their nerves were electric as they walked briskly through town to a nearby McDonald's store. They went together to the toilets, to shift the money from the pillowcase into their backpacks. It was only then they discovered the extent of the heist – they had robbed the WestStar Bank in Vail Village of over $120 000. They would never need to work again, at least for a year. They recorded the moment, this dramatic turn in their lives, with a few photographs; posing with the notes fanned out in their hands, smiling like boys who had pulled off a prank.

As they stuffed the cash into their backpacks they realised there was too much to fit. Frantically they took piles of the lowest denominations – the one dollar bills, of which there were stacks

– and buried them in a refuse bin, along with their weapons and the tools of their dastardly newfound trade.

They hustled across to a restaurant at the foot of the slopes where their snowboards were waiting to whisk them away from the scene of the crime. Their plan was to ride to the top of the largest mountain and snowboard to freedom. There was a line at the lift. The adrenalin thumping through their veins would not allow them to stand and wait. They hurried over to another lift, where the line was shorter. It seemed like forever before they were on a chair, being hoisted to the top of the mountain, away from the pandemonium they had left behind.

At the top of the alps they strapped on their boards and rode like valkyries, weaving through trees and leaping over hillocks with their ill-gotten gains strapped to their backs, the music of life at big volume, top speed. They had done the deed so few dared to do. They were rich – not yet famous, but wealthy would do.

At last they arrived at the bottom – not far, in fact, from where they had started. They hailed a bus to Denver, two hours away, smiling at the conductor as they paid their fares. The bus passed through Vail, where they saw no sign of disorder or turmoil, people going about their business as if it were but an ordinary day. It didn't seem to occur to the boys that their wild escape on their snowboards had done little more than deliver them back to the very place from which they had come, where the people and buildings were just the same, but themselves changed, forever.

They arrived in Denver later that day, grabbed a bite at Burger King to consider their options. Perhaps it was time to go home, back to Byron Bay, to the warmth of their homes, their family and friends. Prince wanted Mexico, where he'd heard that crooks can give American law the slip. Did the world yet know it was them who had committed the crime? They couldn't know. Better to be in Mexico than Byron Bay, should the law come looking for them. They took a cab to the airport, where they inquired about one-way trips to the land of sombreros and nachos. They were told there were no more that day, and that they only sold return tickets anyhow. The boys decided to take a hotel room, to stay out of sight till the following day.

On their way, they stopped off at a jewellery store where they fancied a pair of $20 000 Rolex watches. But when they tried to pay with stacks of five-dollar bills, the assistant warned them that was no way to carry money. People might think they'd been up to no good. She suggested they go to a bank for a cheque, or for larger denominations.

At a similar store down the street, however, Carroll purchased a $9500 diamond, and Prince a splendid $2000 ring. Their money had seemed as good as any to the sales assistant there.

Once at their room in a five-star hotel, the boys watched the television for news of the damage they'd done. There was none. They appeared to have made it scot-free. They barely slept that night, only beer calming their nerves.

Meanwhile, back in Vail, police had been gathering as much information as they could from witnesses and employees of the bank. The police had been initially alerted by a customer who'd told police that a man in a balaclava, with a gun and hostages, had told him to come back later. He'd doubted the man was a bank employee.

The shaken staff were saying the boys had seemed familiar, their accents Australian, the mannerisms peculiar to Anthony Prince and Luke Carroll, two boys from Australia, who came into the bank regularly. Others noticed their tags were from the ski shop called Pepi's, with the names erased and replaced with others. The police went to Pepis where they learned that Prince had taken the day off sick, and had then been seen by another employee purchasing a new ski ticket for a day on the slopes. As far as his boss was concerned he was already in strife.

Police were then informed of the toy guns and walkie-talkies that had been found abandoned in a garbage bin at McDonald's. One policeman recognised the weapons straight away – they were the same ones that had been used weeks before by Prince and Carroll, when they'd been shooting out neighbours' windows for a lark. They checked with the ski fields and found the boys' passes had been scanned on the slopes that morning, within an hour of the heist having taken place.

Then a call came in from a jeweller in Denver, who said two suspicious young men had tried to purchase expensive watches with five-dollar bills. Another store called to say boys buying diamonds had paid with bank notes that appeared to be stolen.

Their descriptions and photos were sent out to authorities, to police on the beat, to bus terminals and airports. Prince and Carroll were on the lam. They could not have gone far.

The next morning Prince and Carroll awoke, hungover, a little nervous, the reality of their deed having crept into them as they slept. They had to sneak out of town, discreetly, without a sound. So they hired a limousine to take them to the airport – the type of vehicle that makes people stare, in the hope of catching a glimpse of a star. They tipped the driver with a big wad of cash.

It was only when they were outside the airport that the boys wondered whether they might look suspicious. What if security went through their baggage and found over $100 000 in tightly-packed bills? They stuffed the money from their bags into pockets, in pants and under shirts, crammed into money belts. They dumped a backpack with $26 000 in a garbage can in the airport car park. Some vagrant, they thought, would hit the jackpot.

Inside, Prince and Carroll purchased their tickets to Mexico, grumbling about having to pay for return flights they would not use. They passed through the metal detectors, their bags sliding through the checks. They were home free. They could scarcely believe two boys from Byron Bay had devised and engineered such a spree. They could already taste the tequila as they marched toward their flight. Then they felt the hands on their shoulders. The authorities would like a word.

Hustled into an interrogation room, Prince and Carroll were told they had been identified as two criminals wanted by police. They denied it. They were good Catholic boys from Australia. They were surfers, loafers, dreamers – not crooks. Then the evidence began piling up: the wads of cash, the backpack from outside, the diamond rings for which they couldn't account. When police asked them to explain the photos found on their digital camera – smiling young thieves celebrating with great fans of notes – the two confessed.

The tears flowed freely in court in September of 2005 as the two boys and their families pleaded for clemency. The parents of Anthony Prince had already released a hair-shirted apology to the people of Vail: 'We are the parents of Anthony Prince, one of the two boys who robbed the WestStar Bank last Monday,' it read.

We are so sorry for the damage inflicted on your community by this event. We offer our sincere and unconditional apologies to the people of Vail and especially to the two female employees of the WestStar Bank. We also apologise to the local family and to the staff at Pepi Sport who sponsored Anthony and provided the opportunity for employment. We fail to comprehend how our son, who was raised in a family with strong ethical values and all the love and support in the world, could contemplate such an act. We will never understand the reason why. We know this act was so out of character for Anthony and we know that his remorse is absolute. Our thoughts are with you all.

Lawyers for Prince and Carroll argued that the crime wasn't serious, that the guns had been toys and robbers just boys. The press saw the lighter side, too: 'Dumb and Dumber' they called them, the stupidity of their exploit broadcast around the world. But the judge didn't see it that way – he saw two young men wielding firearms, no different to Dillinger and Pretty Boy Floyd. He sentenced Anthony Prince to five years and Luke Carroll to six, for injuring the woman whom he'd pushed into the vault.

The boys sobbed as they were led away to Allenwood Federal Correctional Center in White Deer, Pennsylvania, where the evils were real and the nights long and cold, where hardened criminals paced in their cells, having been without women for years on end, where the days were spent sweeping leaves and serving food in the kitchen for $7 an hour. These were the spoils of an adventure cooked up in the minds of two ordinary boys from Byron Bay, who had looked at their lives – the nights out on the tiles, the days of work with ordinary pay – and dreamed of an existence that waited beyond, but for something daring done.

A HOWL IN THE NIGHT

The entrance to the old Beaumaris Zoo is still there in Hobart, the bars and wire good enough to keep in the ghosts of beasts that are no more. The crater that the fence surrounds is contaminated ground – the military used it as a fuel dump in the '40s and, today, no living thing must dwell within it. On the gate, little steel silhouettes of the animals – an elephant, a lion, a monkey, a toucan, a polar bear, and the mythical thylacine – seem to plead on behalf of the beasts that inspired them, their eyes wide in shock over what happened here.

There is a duck pond, empty of water, but littered with jetsam and a drink can faded by years of sun – a zoological exhibit for its time – and the only survivor of the bygone days is a concrete toilet block that stands like a bunker from the years of war. What happened here robbed from us all, and we mourn the loss like death-bed lovers who never met the girls or boys of our dreams. But there was one woman who felt the loss more than most ...

When Mary Grant Roberts passed away in 1921 just two years after her husband, she bequeathed her entire menagerie of animals – critters of all stripe and humour, from Tasmania, the mainland and some from abroad – to the Trustees of the Tasmanian Museum. What had begun as a passing interest in fauna had exploded into a suburban fanatic's assembly of creatures great and small, the Roberts' home, named 'Beaumaris', coming to be known as Beaumaris Zoo, the doors swinging open to the public in 1895. But now Mary was gone and the many hundreds of animals she'd nurtured were now at the mercy of the Tasmanian bureaucracy. The museum had no place to put them, so the ark of lions, birds and weasels was passed to the Hobart City Council, the gentlemen of the Reserves Committee viewing the acquisition as a storage problem above all else. It is to their credit that they decided to honour Mary's memory by relocating the zoo to an old quarry in Queens Domain in Hobart, not far from the Botanical Gardens, where convicts used to toil at breaking rocks and dream of freedom. Beaumaris Zoo, as it was to be respectfully named, was officially opened in 1923.

The curatorship of the zoo fell upon one Arthur Robert Reid, a Scotsman who'd emigrated to Australia in the 1890s. A founding member of the Tasmanian Field Naturalist's Club and a well-known advocate for the protection of native animals, Arthur had been a natural choice, and he was paid a handsome public servant's wage to manage the zoo and care for the animals. He and his family took up residence in a cottage just outside the zoo grounds where they were serenaded to sleep each night by the yawn of the lions and the chatter of monkeys.

Most delighted of all was young Alison Reid, born in 1905 with a feeling for animals in her bones. It was a complicated love – she had been trained in the art of taxidermy by her father and, as a youngster, made a hobby out of mounting animals shot by hunters, so their killings could scream from walls and prance petrified in parlours. But Alison's love for the creatures showed in her work. Sometimes, the grieving masters and mistresses of departed pets would approach her in the hope she could bring the dead back to still life, and to such tasks Alison applied herself with all the tenderness of a mother dressing her child. To Alison, there was nothing more noble than a living beast, and nothing sadder than one who was living no more. To make them alive again, if only frozen in a moment, was to bestow upon the creatures a kind of honour. In this way, they would not be forgotten.

Alison was not yet seventeen years old when her skills came to the attention of the Tasmanian Museum, who offered her employment as a taxidermist in May of 1922. In her spare time Alison helped her father at the zoo, her natural touch with the animals seeing her trusted with the rearing of quails and pheasants and other baby animals. She became particularly fond of the lion cubs, and admired the strength and nobility of the leopard and the great black panther, its gentle roar a comfort in the night. She began spending so much time in the zoo she found herself doing other jobs here and there, cleaning cages and operating the entry turnstiles on weekends, selling tickets to visitors. Both the animals and other workers came to view Alison as a permanent member of the zoo's exotic fraternity.

By 1927 Alison had begun to tire of her job at the museum, obviously finding living, breathing animals more agreeable than the dead and motionless ones even she couldn't bring back to life. It seemed only right to her father that a job at the zoo would allow Alison plenty of time to tend to the animals as she had always done, while at last rewarding the girl for her greatly valued presence. Thus a full-time position was created especially for her at the zoo, the job involving ticket vending, some secretarial work and general care of the exhibits – menial tasks that needed to be done, but were applied to the job description primarily so that the Reserves Committee, which would be paying her wages, would see they were getting something for their money. As with all public service positions, Alison's job was required to be advertised but, being that Alison had thus far been working for sheer joy, the success of her application seemed a foregone conclusion.

But the Superintendant for Reserves, a Mr L. J. Lipscombe, the younger brother of the man who had hired Alison's father, had other ideas. A strong advocate for the Returned Soldiers League, Mr Lipscombe had planned and built the Avenue of Honour in Hobart's Domain, his overseeing of its construction bringing him in contact with many an unfortunate fellow. One was a Mr R. Manson, a soldier who had returned from the Great War having lost an arm. Manson was down on his luck and Lipscombe no doubt felt a duty to use his offices to assist the poor man where he could, applying for the 'vacant' position at the zoo on Manson's behalf, long after the closing date for applications had passed. Despite the man's complete lack of zoological experience or enthusiasm, and the obvious troubles that might arise were Manson called to assist in the gentle handling of new-born cubs, flighty birds and carnivorous animals, Manson got the job, thanks entirely to Lipscombe applying his own weight upon the Reserves Committee, with whom the final decision rested.

Understandably disappointed, and aware that Manson's seven-day-a-week employment would doubtless scuttle the only paid work she'd been receiving from the zoo on the weekends, Alison decided to travel to Europe for a holiday. But when she applied to the museum for unpaid leave they refused, demanding she return to work immediately. Alison thus resigned completely and packed her things for an extended stay in England, leaving Hobart late in 1927 with little money but carrying letters of introduction to the British Museum and the Zoological Society of London. While in London, Alison visited the Regents Park Zoo, marvelling at the cats and the elephants and the lion's cubs, which made her recall the ones she loved at home. She also laid eyes on another creature that made her homesick for Tasmania, and one that would live in her dreams for the rest of her days: the thylacine.

Returning from her European travels to Australia in 1928, Alison Reid was employed once again by the Tasmanian Museum, which had missed her touch, and she was happy to resume her unofficial duty as assistant to her father in caring for the young animals at the zoo, where some of the cubs she had nursed from birth had matured in years but knew her still. The one-armed man had tired of his job but, finding the idea of unemployment even less tolerable, remained at his post, refusing to work on weekends like the animal that won't come out of its den until all the people have gone. Thus Alison received paid work once again, hired to work the gates on Saturdays and Sundays, and tend to the animals in her spare time.

The Great Depression hit in 1930, the panic closing doors and forcing businesses to shed their men and women like leaves from autumn trees, tossing people with families to feed to the streets with no money. The museum could no longer keep Alison, and the zoo was fleeced of most its staff, the turnstiles closed at weekends, the population pared down to the animals, Arthur and a chosen few. The Reserves Committee knew that Alison's work was a labour of love – and in times like these, it's love that is always counted upon to tidy up the mess of greed.

The year of 1930 was nearly over when, one night, Arthur and Alison heard the animals making noise. Something wasn't right, and Arthur went to investigate. As he searched through the grounds for the cause of the commotion, he came across an aviary whose cage had been disturbed. He knew instantly what had happened – the birds were exotic, expensive and easy to transport, and they would fetch a tidy sum for anyone brave enough to take them. Suddenly Arthur saw a man standing in the shadows. A struggle ensued, the man beating Arthur savagely before escaping into the night. His attacker was eventually arrested – a local man named Fischer – but the harm done to Arthur would be permanent, his left eye having to be removed, a cancer growing in its place. For three years Arthur soldiered on as best he could but as the cancer took its toll, it was Alison who did his work, keeping accounts and records clean, feeding the animals and making sure they were locked inside their dens before the gates were closed at the end of the day.

Sometimes she'd hear the animals cry to her through the night and, with her father's keys, she'd enter the zoo herself to find them locked outside their sleeping quarters, the staff having gone home without unlocking the little doors that kept them from hiding from paying customers through the day. She came to know the special sound the female thylacine would make – a peculiar bark like a sharp, hoarse cough – when she wanted to go inside and sleep. It was a sound Alison would not forget.

As Arthur's condition worsened and his working days grew shorter, the Superintendant of Reserves, Bruce Lipscombe – L. J. Lipscombe's brother – seized the moment to save money for the Hobart City Council. He proposed that Arthur be paid part-time, instead of a full man's wages. Everyone knew that Alison was doing Arthur's job, and would do it still, because of her love for the animals. Arthur responded by proposing that Alison be employed full-time in his place, whereupon he would assist her as he could, much as she had him. Mr Lipscombe, the third member of the Lipscombe family to serve on the Reserves Committee, rejected the offer, on the grounds that the council didn't want to be seen as party to nepotism.

The issue was unresolved when Arthur succumbed to his cancer in 1935, Alison burying the father who had taught her so well of the nobility of living creatures, and of the respect one must have for them above all things. Bruce Lipscombe took over as caretaker curator of the zoo, the council noting disingenuously that there was 'no one in the council's employ with any knowledge of the care of animals needing attention'. However, they would allow Alison and her mother to stay in the cottage next door to the zoo rent-free, provided Alison volunteer her services to Mr Lipscombe at no charge.

Alison and her mother were down to the threads they wore and the borrowed roof above their heads. They pleaded to the council for money – surely Arthur's years of service, and the fact he'd died from wounds incurred while on duty, mattered for something when it came to the care of his loved ones, who were clearly needed by the animals in the zoo, if not the men who presumed to manage them. Reluctantly, the council agreed to a modest stipend for Alison and her mother, enough to allow them to live a Spartan existence in the cottage, as slaves to circumstance.

Mr Lipscombe's first act as caretaker curator of Beaumaris Zoo was to staff the establishment with 'sustenance workers', victims of the Depression who worked not for any love for animals, but for food, just to keep themselves alive. His second was to insist that Alison hand him her father's keys to the zoo, despite him having no need for them, save as symbols of authority. At nights

Alison could barely sleep as she listened to the cries of the animals locked outside their dens, the workers consistently failing to open the doors to their sleeping quarters before leaving for home.

She appealed to Lipscombe for the keys – he had no use for them after hours – but the man refused. Alison went over the man's head and appealed directly to the Town Clerk, Mr William Brain, explaining to him that the animals were being deprived of the care to which they had been accustomed. Mr Brain responded to her heartfelt request by suggesting it was her father's incompetence that had made such nightly visits to the zoo necessary in the first place – if he'd instructed workers properly, he told her, visits to the zoo to remedy neglect would not have become the habit. It was one she would have to break.

The zoo became an infirmary for the pitiful unemployed, who wandered the grounds like spooks until the time came each day for them to go home to their own suffering broods. Each morning Alison would wait at the gate for Lipscombe to arrive, the turn of his key allowing her to enter a world of increasing squalor – food left rotting in the animals' filthy cages, the doors to their dens rarely ever opened for them, the coats of the mammals matted and damp from nights spent in the miserable cold. One morning she entered to find that the mighty black panther had perished in the night. When the deaths became more frequent, Alison knew she had to try once more.

Alison went personally to Mr Brain and begged him once again for the keys. There were seventy-five cages in the zoo, she explained, and she couldn't inspect them all in the afternoons before Mr Lipscombe closed the gate and locked her outside. The sustenance workers did not care for the animals – they couldn't be expected to. They had troubles of their own. But somebody had to save the creatures before they perished one and all. The thylacine was the last in captivity. Should they lose her, there was no telling where another might be found. Once again, Mr Brain refused Alison her own set of keys. However, he promised to take the matter up with Lipscombe at his first convenience.

And he did, writing Lipscombe a letter expressing his concern, as had been conveyed to him by certain other parties, as to the running of the zoo. Lipscombe responded with a letter of his own, addressed to Alison Reid. Though a new caretaker had yet to be found, one would surely be employed some time in the near future, and it was only fair and proper that the caretaker of the zoo be housed in the cottage in which she and her mother now dwelled for free. 'I am informing you of the position,' he wrote, 'so that you will have plenty of time to make arrangements for another cottage.' He closed by adding that, in light of these new developments, and the fact that their arrangement was thus cancelled, rent would have to be paid on the cottage during the remainder of their stay.

Alison and her mother had no money, no way to pay the rent. Their only home and purpose for fifteen years had been the zoo. They knew they'd have to go. In those last weeks, Alison lay awake at nights to the sad cries of the animals, the groans of the lions as they exchanged their woes, and the barking cough of the thylacine, who seemed to plead to her alone. The Bengal tiger died in the days before she left. One day in June of 1936 they departed the cottage, to stay with relatives far from the Beaumaris Zoo, the sad sounds of the animals replaced by a silence that was almost as difficult to bear.

September was extreme, sub-zero temperatures at night and close to forty degrees in the day. The tree that hung over the thylacine's cage lost all its leaves and gave no shade, leaving the animal in its care to burn in the day and freeze at night. On the night of 7 September, 1936, the last thylacine ever known to humankind closed her eyes and went to sleep forever.

Alison Reid lived a long life, watching and listening, silently, as debate raged over what killed the Tasmanian Tiger, a relic of a time now cherished, but gone, as if never having been at all. In 1996, at the age of ninety-one, she wept as she spoke of the howl in the night, a cry that haunted her through the decades, from a creature whose warmth was in her touch, still trembling in her hands, but vanished from the universe.

The following year, on 10 April, 1997, Alison Reid passed away in the night, thus moving through the gates of a world that none can know but the unfortunate and the brave, the soldiers and the sufferers, the victims and the disappeared, and those so beautiful they were never meant to be upon this earth.

COP

Australia has always enjoyed an uneasy relationship with its police, a distrust many ascribe to the myth of Australia being 'founded by convicts'. It's a half-truth at best – the convicts no more founded Australia than the Jews founded the Holocaust. The uncomfortable truth, so easily forgotten, is that it was those in authority, not the slaves, who truly fashioned a civilised nation from an ungoverned wilderness. Being that every three convicts to disembark the First Fleet were lorded over by a policeman – and that the quickest way to earn one's freedom was to inform the guards of the misdeeds of one's neighbour – it is more accurate to state that Australia was founded by police and their snitches. Dwell upon that as you read this tale of a stakeout gone wrong, a bust turned bad, a good deed poisoned in the mind of a thankless nation.

Michael Kennedy still gets menacing phone calls from those who believe that the terrible events of years ago were the fault of the police. They call anonymously, promise to burn down his house, rape his wife and terrorise his children. He is not welcome in certain neighbourhoods, on the threat of death. But Michael has been a policeman for nearly four decades. He is not intimidated. He will retire soon, when he's had enough. But he will never accept what they say about the bloody events of the past, which began when police decided it was time to move on a common thug and bring him to justice for the things he had done . . .

Sergeant Kennedy had been a policeman for over ten years, joining the force in the 60s and rising to his rank before the end of the next decade. He knew it was risky and thankless, but he liked the work. It paid well, and it was gratifying to know you were hosing scum from the street. His wife would have preferred him to have a safer job – she worried for herself and their five children, should anything happen to him in the line of duty. But what he was doing was right. It was because of men like him that families like theirs felt safe from the murderers, the rapists, the thieves and others who believe the world is theirs to fondle.

The 70s had been a bad time for Australian police, the perpetual misfortunes of officers all over the nation painting a picture of a force that was incompetent, corrupt and, worst of all, unable to keep itself safe, let alone the innocent communities in its charge. The decade was only eight months old when a young constable drowned while assisting residents living nearby the flooded Coliban River in Victoria. The following year, in June, Constable James Deacon was killed in a traffic accident near Oakleigh, his back crushed under the wheels of a vehicle as he lay dying in the middle of a crowded street. A Constable Curtin of Violet Town suffered a fatal head wound in similar circumstances the following May. Constable Patrick Barrett stepped into the path of an oncoming train in Melbourne in '76, and the following year, in September, Constables George Armytage and Michael Costigan were shot dead by Sam Getting at the Royal Hotel in Bourke, the offender committing suicide later.

Just days before Michael headed out on the mission that would dramatically change his life, Dubbo policemen Sergeant Wallings, Senior Constable William Souter and Constable John Walsh made the news when an attempted bust went sour. Wallings was killed instantly by a bullet that ripped his heart clean out of his chest, his assailant escaping into the night, the other two policemen failing to hit him with a single shot.

These were dangerous times. The public hatred of police – now something of a national outlook – was buoyed more by police incompetence than corruption, or the hard enforcing of the law. The people no longer felt safe from the ratbags and hoodlums who burrowed through civilisation like they owned it. A public victory was needed, desperately. So the police decided to go for a known gangster, one much harder, more cunning than the others. Taking him down would send a strong message.

But there was no way they were going to repeat the mistakes of the recent past, blundering in with badges and uniforms, making themselves targets for a man known for his detestation of police. This time, they would go disguised as ordinary bums, so that nobody would know they were cops.

Michael knew that the man they were hunting was no greenhorn, and would probably smell a cop coming around the corner, disguise or not.

The target hailed from a family of crooks, his father an ex-con and police informer, his uncles and brothers well known to the warders of Pentridge and Beechworth correctional facilities before the boy was even in his teens. Members of the family were constantly before magistrates, unable to settle differences between themselves, let alone with their suffering neighbours. They considered education a folly for the rich, yet were vain enough to believe themselves the most set-upon mob who'd ever walked the streets. The police 'had it in' for them. Everyone was framing them. Talk to the family and you'd learn not a one of them had ever committed a single transgression, despite their multitudinous arrests, most of which saw them slipping away from convictions due to technicalities.

The man himself had been in and out of institutions from an early age, mostly for theft. He did his apprenticeship in the prison system, which pumped out kids more brazenly criminal than they had been before they went inside, and by the time he emerged back onto the street he had a reputation with police as racist and violent and frightened of nobody. He had once beaten a man who'd had the temerity to knock on the front door of his family home. Arrested later for gang-related activities, he was released without charge when witnesses refused to give evidence, intimidated by members of the young man's family. The following year, he bashed some marketing dude for no other reason than that he annoyed him, responding to the man's complaint to police by threatening both him and his wife in their home. He'd been three weeks out of a three-month stint in prison when, for the entertainment of drinkers at a local pub, he bashed a policeman who was trying to pinch him for theft, a crime for which he received three years jail, during which he socialised with friends and family who came and went like return vacationers to some dark holiday resort.

Prisoners who spoke with him recalled his boasts of plans to kill cops upon his release.

Free again, he appeared to go straight for a while, before inevitably drifting back into the same old hustles and rackets, and it was only a matter of time before he was apprehended; this time assaulting the arresting officers in a wasted rage in the middle of the main street. A lenient magistrate let him off. But when news came down that he'd assaulted another off-duty officer, the cops got busy, a special task force of officers ordered to shake down their snitches and hit his known hangouts.

Michael had pumped his informants for anything they knew, but few of them coughed up. Then an anonymous letter arrived, telling police they would find their man holed up in some dive overlooking Bridge and Holland, not far out of the centre of town.

Michael gathered his team and they loaded their revolvers. He hoped they wouldn't have to use them. This was to be an arrest, not a firefight, but they weren't to take any chances with this hooligan.

Word got out that the police were looking for blood.

Michael and his officers moved out, acting casual, keeping their eyes peeled for suspicious traffic. Assisted by neighbourhood locals, they made headquarters in a spacious, deserted flat not far from where they'd been told their quarry was hiding out. Then they settled down for the night, keeping lights and voices low. Perhaps they'd see some movement through the night. The man they sought was tall, well built. He couldn't hide forever. He stood out in a crowd. Just one month before, a policeman from Melbourne had arrested a known wanted man when the poor sap, wanting to use the facilities, had knocked on the door of the detective's home. You never know when you might get lucky.

While the others kept watch, Michael passed the time by writing a letter to his wife, his ear staying tuned to the sounds outside, lest he hear a voice, a name, some signal of alarm among the creatures of the night as they went about their business. There were those who feared the man Michael pursued, and they wondered what he would do if cornered. He was dynamite waiting to be lit.

Michael missed his wife and his children. He was just 36 years old, and already he'd created five little lives that would grow and make whole worlds on Earth. His youngest boy was barely two. What would become of them, if something terrible were to happen? It was something he often feared. But this was the very reason he was here, hiding in the dark, in pursuit of a man he didn't know, and didn't even despise. Should Michael succeed, it would not be simply him who was rewarded, or the reputation of the police repaired. It would send a signal down through the years, so that every slasher, beater of the weak and two-bit hustler would hear. The hoodlum would no doubt claim innocence, as he had always done. But that was a matter for the courts, which had been lenient with him before.

The night passed without sign or incident, the sun rising on the deserted scene outside. Michael knew their man would not be snoozing. He'd be up early, on the move, trying to remain one step ahead, creeping on to another town. Michael took a man to reconnoitre the neighbourhood, leaving the other two constables to keep watch on the premises.

Hours later, Michael returned, entering the flat to find the younger of the two constables standing upright, looking alarmed. He announced that their search was over – the thug was here, among them, hiding, keeping him covered. There was nothing to be done but to surrender all weapons.

Michael reached for his revolver. The thug rose from his hiding place and fired. Michael rolled for cover, his training kicking in. Shots fired, shells raining to the floor, splinters exploding from the woodwork. He saw one young constable fall, shot in the chest. There were too many guns – the gangster had come with a crew. He retreated, bolting from the flat, taking cover across the way as the shots continued to whistle past him. He fired back, reloaded, fired again. He couldn't see how many they were. The terrible risk was now an awful reality. This was no longer about merit, or reputation. He was fighting for his very life.

As he turned to sprint for cover something tore at the skin and bone under his arm, burning his body from bottom to top. He staggered forward and fell against something. He was badly hit.

The crook and his friends came upon him, stood over him. They were pumped. They'd just outgunned the police. Michael wanted to live. He had a wife and children. He wanted to see them. He couldn't die like this, so suddenly.

The thug didn't see it that way. As he raised his gun to the wounded man's heart, Michael might have been consoled by the thought that at least the world would remember Ned Kelly as little more than a murdering piece of scum . . .

Sergeant Michael Kennedy shares the name and rank of his great-grandfather, who was murdered near the flat beyond the creeks of Bridge and Holland, at the gully now famous as Stringybark Creek. Some Kelly sympathisers don't like him – they call and abuse him, or slander him in print. If he ever comes to Beechworth, they say, he'll die, just like his great-grandfather did before him. It's a cult just like any other, its apostles no different to kids whose pop star pin-ups can do no wrong.

Years ago, the descendants of Kelly handed back the watch and the letter that their famous ancestor had stolen from the pocket of a dying man, further robbing the family of what little of their father they might have had. Nobody knows which one of the gang cut his ear off. Some say it was an animal. Michael reckons they don't know how right they are.

They say it was a merciful killing, that Ned put him 'out of his misery'. But the man was alive – it was the last shot that killed him. It would have been more merciful to take him back into town, where at least he might have said goodbye to his family. But that wasn't convenient for Ned. To kill for convenience is just blue murder.

Michael doesn't understand the deification of Ned Kelly. He was going to derail a train, full of police and reporters, all with families who loved them, and he would have succeeded had it not been for the brave actions of a man whose name most people in Australia don't know. If he were alive today, Ned Kelly would be all over the tabloids, pilloried as a national creep. Instead, there are museums and statues in his honour.

There are no such tributes to Michael's great-grandfather, a good man, who died taking care of his family.

SOURCES, ACKNOWLEDGEMENTS AND SOME EXPLANATIONS

MOLOCH

One of my earliest memories is of travelling to Luna Park by train in 1970, all the way from Newcastle, only to refuse to be dragged through the entrance, whose wild-eyed, open-mouthed face I found completely horrifying. Sydney artist Martin Sharp finds this memory ominous. In 1979 he had been but one in a long line of artists charged with the task of redesigning the leering visage that lured the children inside, and it's fair to say his part in the carnage bothers him, his shambling mansion in Double Bay a gallery to clippings and relics from the night he sincerely believes was in some way orchestrated by the spirit of Moloch. I'm indebted to Martin for his assistance, and for putting me in touch with Jenny Poidevin. In journalism one meets many people who are supposedly from life at its top – movie stars, rock stars, assorted big nobs who believe they exist in the uppermost extremes of experience. People like Jenny, who have actually been to the very precipice beyond which sane existence ceases, tower over such folk when it comes to life's intensity, and they tend to have a more profound effect on those whom they meet (the reason why, I think, many journalists are so cynical about the petty concerns singers of songs and players of parts, who 'generously' give their time to the media). It was obviously difficult for Jenny, even after the passing of so much time, to recall her story for me, and I'm forever grateful to her for persevering. Various supplementary details regarding the events of 9 June, 1979, and the consequent coronial inquest come from the *Sydney Morning Herald* (Monday 11 June, 1979, page 1, 2 and 3; Saturday 16 June, 1979, page 3; Thursday 16 August, 1979, page 1; Friday 17 August, 1979, page 6; Tuesday 4 September, 1979, page 4), and information on the background of the park comes from *Luna Park – Just for Fun* by Sam Marshall (Luna Park Reserve Trust, 1995) and *Spirits of the Carnival* (Paperbark Films, 1995).

CLOSER

Statistical details on the wartime career of Robert Bungey came from: *RAF Fighter Command Victory Claims* by John Foreman; *A Chronology of Australian Armed Forces at War 1939–45* by Bruce T. Swain; *RAAF Saga* by RAAF Directorate of Public Relations, 1944; *These Eagles* by Australian War Memorial, Canberra, 1942; *Royal Air Force and Fleet Air Arm News and Announcements, October 9th, 1941*; and the service record of R. W. Bungey, Australian War Memorial, Canberra. Further details of the activities of his various squadrons were gleaned from *First Impact* by Dennis Newton, *The Brotherhood of Airmen* by David Wilson and Movietone News ('Australian Fighters with Big Punch', November, 1941). Biographical details were provided by *The Bungey/Bungay family history: the story of the Bungey/Bungay family in Australia* by the Bungay Family History Committee (pages 181–184), which can be found in the State Library of New South Wales. More precious than any of these sources, however, was Richard Bungey, who kindly allowed me into his father's life, and his own. I was well into the research for this story when, going through newspapers in the Mitchell Library, I came across a report that, unlike those before it, told of how Richard had survived, that somebody I'd accepted to have been dead for half a century was still with us. The shiver that washed over me when I heard his voice must surely have made a noise. I should also thank Milton Howard of Adelaide for his insights into the rare experience of having flown the Spitfire in wartime.

THE MOTHER OF ALL LIES

For biographical details on the life of Merle Oberon, I relied heavily on *Princess Merle: The romantic life of Merle Oberon* by Charles Higham and Roy Moseley (Coward-McCann, 1983), an exceptional Hollywood biography for its refusal to salivate about its obviously flawed subject. Additional information came from *David Niven: A bio-bibliography* by Karin J. Fowler (Greenwood Publishing Group, 1995), *Hollywood Greats of the Golden Years: The late stars of the 1920s through the 1950s* by J. G. Ellrod (McFarland, 1989), *Fade To Black: A book of movie obituaries* by Paul Donnelly (Omnibus, 2003), *Merle Oberon: Face of mystery* by Bob Casey (Masterpiece@IXL, 2008), *Olivier – The life of Laurence Olivier* by Thomas Kiernan, (Sidgwick & Jackson, 1981), and *Silver Birch: The spirit speaks* by Tony Ortzen (Psychic Press, 1995), a ludicrous book containing an account of one of Merle's many attempts to communicate with the dead. What originally drew me to this story, however, was Marée Delofski's strange little documentary, *The Trouble With Merle* (Australian Broadcasting Corporation, 2002), in which Marée, determinedly perched behind the wheel of her VW Beetle, motors around Tasmania in search of the Hollywood star's roots, finding instead something of a Merle Oberon cargo cult on an island gripped by denial. It's well worth a look.

A MELBOURNE TRIPTYCH

The tragic tale of Mr Greer's last night at the opera comes from excited reports in *The Argus* (Monday 26 July, 1880, page 1; Tuesday 27 July, 1880, page 1), the *Maitland Mercury* (Tuesday 27 July, 1880, page 8; Saturday 31 July, 1880, pages 4–5; Thursday 5 August, 1880; Saturday 10 December, 1881), the *Brisbane Courier* (Monday 2 August, 1880, page 3; Wednesday 24 August, 1881, page 3; Tuesday 8 November, 1870, page 3; Thursday 10 December, 1885, page 3; Thursday 17 December, 1885, page 6; Tuesday 29 December, 1885, page 5) and the *West Australian* (Tuesday 24 August, 1880, page 2; Friday 24 September, 1880, page 3; Friday 1 October, 1880, page 3). Mrs Sarah Williams' act of extreme parental dereliction was recounted to readers of the *West Australian* (Friday 4 December, 1885, page 3; Saturday 5 December, 1885, page 6; Friday 18 December 1885, page 3). Details on the unhappy romance of Peter McQuade and Jessie Cameron come from reports in the *Melbourne Daily Telegraph* (Saturday 15 March, 1890, page 2) and the *Brisbane Courier* (Friday 21 March, 1890, page 6). All were accessed through the National Library of Australia. They were the days when there was rarely any such thing as a byline in the newspapers, but I like to think these anonymous journalists might have dreamed of their work entertaining someone over one hundred years later.

THE PUGILIST

My interest in this case began when, in the days after the death of David Hookes in 2004, I traded my suit and hat for a tracksuit and sneakers and parked myself all day against the bar of the Beaconsfield Hotel in St Kilda, in the hope that I might lasso something useful as it drifted from whispering staff and muttering patrons. Two things were palpable: a sense of surprise and bewilderment that such a quiet, well-mannered fellow like Zdravko could find himself on the end of a manslaughter charge; and a sense of the inevitable with regard to Hookes who, the staff claimed, was no stranger to trouble at that particular establishment. (Interestingly, just a few weeks prior to the Hookes incident, a barmaid at the old Savoy Hotel on Spencer Street in Melbourne, just a few kilometres from the Beaconsfield, told me there'd been a major fracas in their lobby involving a party of 'well-known former cricketers', to which police had been called, and which had somehow been kept from the media). Which is not to say that justice was done on either 18 January, 2004, or 11 September, 2005, when the verdict was delivered in *DPP v Micevic*, but simply that there are two sides to a tragedy like this. While I'm well acquainted with the court proceedings, this chapter is based entirely upon interviews conducted with Zdravko Micevic, who is understandably reluctant to discuss the event in question, and I thank him for entrusting me with his story. It's fair to say he's deeply concerned about reopening public debate on this incident, and it's significant to me that at no time during the conversations I had with him did Zdravko ever take a wounded posture. 'It's a bit rich,' he once said, 'to refer to myself as the victim.' Thanks also to Louis Korica for his assistance.

JOAN OF ANTWERP

I first read of this incident in a book by an American: *Holy Homicide – An encyclopedia of those who go with their god and kill* by Michael Newton (Loopmaniacs Unlimited, 1998) – a difficult book to track down, but worth any effort for the author's delightful contempt for his subjects. Details of Joan Vollmer's torture and death come from transcripts of *R v Vollmer and Others*, County Court of Victoria, 1994, courtesy of the Office of the Victorian Director of Public Prosecutions. Additional details were taken from 'Death In The Name of God' by Larry Writer (*Who Weekly*, 22 February, 1993). Useful, too, was the excellent essay 'Delivering Demons, Punishing Wives:

False imprisonment, exorcism and other matrimonial duties in a late 20th century manslaughter case' by Adrian Howe and Sarah Ferber, which appeared in *Punishment and Society* (Sage Publications, Volume 7, Number 2, 2005, pages 123–146). As a sober, critical summary of the entire outrage, it can't be topped. 'While it may not be novel to suggest that western societies and their law courts have yet to throw off their pre-modern origins,' Howe and Ferber conclude, 'it remains remarkable that at no point in the proceedings did anyone question the notion that to hold a reasonable belief that someone has a supernatural force in their body is in fact a contradiction in terms: it relies fundamentally upon an act of faith, ordinarily the antithesis of reason.' My thanks to Sarah Ferber for providing me with a copy of her work.

THE AGONY OF ARTHUR DACRE

Details of the troubled life and disastrous end of Arthur Dacre and Amy Roselle come from reports in the *Brisbane Courier* (Monday 7 May, 1894, page 5; Monday 18 November, 1895, page 5; Tuesday 19 November, 1895, page 4; Wednesday 20 November, 1895, page 5), the *West Australian* (Wednesday 12 December, 1894, page 5; Tuesday 19 November, 1895, pages 3-5; Thursday 21 November, 1895, page 6; Tuesday 26 November, 1895, page 6), the *Sydney Morning Herald* (Saturday 15 June, 1895; Monday 18 November, 1895, page 1; Tuesday 19 November, 1895, page 1; Wednesday 20 November, 1895, page 1), all of which were accessed through the National Library of Australia. British and American reports were found in the *Cardiff Western Mail* (Saturday 8 December, 1883, page 3; Thursday 8 December, 1887, page 3; Tuesday 19 November, 1895, page 3; Thursday 21 November, 1895, page 7; Tuesday 24 December, 1895, page 5), *Reynolds's Newspaper* (Sunday 9 December, 1883, page 5; Sunday 16 December, 1883, page 5; Sunday 23 December, 1883, page 4; Sunday 24 November, 1895, page 6), *Lloyd's Weekly Newspaper* (Sunday 9 December, 1883, page 7; Sunday 16 December, 1883, page 3; Sunday 23 December, 1883, page 2; Sunday 24 November, 1895, page 4) the *Pall Mall Gazette* (Friday 14 December, 1883, page 9; Monday 24 December, 1883, page 4), the *Aberdeen Weekly Journal* (Monday 14 May, 1888, page 4), *The Era* (Saturday 24 May, 1890, page 14; Saturday 4 October, 1890, page 7; Saturday 23 January, 1892, page 10; Saturday 29 December, 1883, page 3; Saturday 23 November, 1895, page 9) the *Liverpool Mercury* (Tuesday 24 December, 1895, page 7), *The Stage* (Friday 30 May, 1890, page 13), the *New York Times* (Monday 12 January, 1884, page 3; Tuesday 30 December,

1890, page 1; Tuesday 19 November, 1895, page 1), and the *New York Clipper* (Saturday 15 November, 1890, page 1), all of which were accessed through the State Library of New South Wales. Additional details come from *London's Lost Theatres of the Nineteenth Century* by Erroll Sherson (Ayer Publishing, 1925), the *Cambridge Illustrated History of British Theatre* by Simon Trussler (Cambridge University Press, 2000), *A Playgoer's Memories* by H. G. Hibbert (Riverside Press, 1965), *The Disreputable Profession: the actor in society* by Mendel Kohansky (Greenwood, 1984) and Don Shewey's essay, 'The Actor As Object of Desire' (*American Theater*, October, 1990). I have to confess to having developed quite an affection for Arthur Dacre along the way. In my experience with creatures from the acting profession, I do believe him to have been a man greatly ahead of his time.

THE LODGER

Reports on the sad fate of the family Gray come from the *Courier-Mail* (Monday 26 February, 1934, page 11; Monday 12 March, 1934, page 13; Tuesday 13 March, 1934, page 13; Wednesday 14 March, 1934, page 13), while reports of various drowning accidents come from the *The Argus* (Monday 7 February, 1916, page 9; Tuesday 20 February 1917, page 4; Thursday 25 October, 1923, page 16). All were accessed through the National Library of Australia. Dr James Lowson's account of drowning also appears in *The Perfect Storm* by Sebastian Junger (HarperCollins, 1998) and, to the Lowsons of Brisbane, who verified for me the fact that their great ancestor was indeed from Australia, I say thanks for your time (and I apologise for disturbing your evening glass of wine on the beach). Reporting on the Coronial inquest at Boggabilla in 1934, the *Courier-Mail* recorded an interesting exchange between Sergeant Grimes, officer in charge of the Boggabilla police station, and his somewhat cagey witness, Charles Arthur May. 'In what way,' asked Grimes, 'did Mrs Gray suggest her husband had made her life a misery?' 'I would rather not answer that,' May replied, 'in deference to the woman.' It seems that perhaps poor old Frederick Gray might not have been such a legendary milkman after all.

OF MONKEYS AND MEN

Doctor Henry Leighton Jones has been something of a pet project of mine since the late '90s, when I first heard the urban myth about an evil Nazi scientist who'd performed weird operations on Lake Macquarie simpletons during the post-war years. It took me years to get to the bottom of it and, along the way, I spoke to many people, particularly locals of Dora Creek, whose names I no longer recall. Should you recognise yourself in that sentence, buy yourself a beer and put it on my tab. Otherwise I'm greatly indebted to retired surgeon Herbert Copeman, former Honorary Consultant in General Medicine and Endocrinology at the Royal Perth Hospital and one-time President of the Australian Postgraduate Federation of Medicine in Australia. Something of a one-man Leighton Jones fan club, Copeman interviewed Leighton Jones's wife, Nora, in 1973, as well as members of Leighton Jones's transplant team, and I thank him for the wealth of information he passed on to me and for his time. (While visiting Copeman at his home in Hobart, I noticed a framed black and white photo of a young Herbert standing beside an old Typhoon fighter, and consequently discovered that the man who was enthusiastically speaking to me about another man entirely had been a Flying Officer in the RAAF during the Second World War, flying in support of the D-Day invasion of Normandy, swatting V1 'doodle bugs' over London and strafing German tanks near Schoenberg during the Battle of the Bulge on Christmas Eve, 1944.) Thanks also to Jackie Parker for recalling to me his childhood memories of Doctor Leighton Jones, and to David Quick for his assistance. Additional information comes from *Life: A study of the means of restoring vital energy and prolonging life* by Serge Voronoff (E. P. Dutton & Company, 1920), *The Monkey Gland Affair* by David Hamilton (Chatto & Windus, 1986), *The Lancet* (Volume 338, Issue 8779, Friday 30 November, 1991, page 1367), *The Journal of the E. E. Cummings Society* (October, 2000, page 44-45), and *The Independent* (Saturday 8 October, 2005). Local reports were found in the *Northern Territory Times* (Thursday 27 January, 1916, page 10; Thursday 3 February, 1916, page 9; Thursday 29 June, 1916, page 9; Saturday 1 October 1921, page 9. Tuesday 19 September, 1922, page 2; Saturday 15 October, 1921, page 3; Friday 24 April, 1925, page 6) and the *Canberra Times* (Friday 22 December, 1933, page 1; Wednesday 11 December 1935, page 2; Tuesday 26 October, 1943, page 3), all of which were accessed through the National Library of Australia.

A BOAT WITH NO NAME

In the aftermath of the terrible events of 19 October, 2001, the vessel that had swallowed the lives of 353 people was at last given a name: *SIEV-X*

(Suspected Illegal Entry Vessel - X). For a time the Australian media showed interest in the human tragedy, until it became lost in the inevitable sea of conspiracy theories, advocacy journalism and zealous political activism in the guise of humanitarianism, the Navy corralled into having to explain its failure to rescue passengers from a uncharted fishing boat that had sunk in seconds in inclement weather, clandestine agencies of the military accused of deliberately scuttling the vessel before it launched, and hecklers of the government pouncing upon bureaucratic clumsiness as proof of pure evil intent. Within weeks the plight of the passengers had been all but forgotten in the sloganeering, a truly heartbreaking story from modern times reduced to the most tedious political whodunit of the decade, the sight of the very word *SIEV-X* reason enough for even the most unromantic Australian to turn to the following page. For this reason, I gave the political questions surrounding *SIEV-X* a wide berth, it being much less interesting to me than the straightforward horror of the incident. Amal Basry's story comes from correspondence between herself and Mary Dagmar Davies, and I'm very grateful to Mary for providing me with same. Various other details come from transcripts of a videotape made of survivors in Bogor immediately after the incident, translated by Keysar Trad of the Sydney Lebanese Muslim Association and which are available to read online at Marg Hutton's comprehensive website, sievx.com, and 'Perilous Journeys' by Arnold Zable (*Eureka Street*, April, 2003). For the background to the political story, it's hard to go past *Dark Victory* by David Marr and Marian Wilkinson (Allen & Unwin, 2003).

A GRIM FATHER'S TALE

It had always been a concern of mine that the innocent families of murderers, rapists and others of despised criminal notoriety are victims, too, yet are forgotten at best and, at worst, reviled as being somehow responsible and thus deserving of the misery they suffer. For this chapter I relied upon the 'Psychiatric Report of Martin Bryant' by Paul E. Mullen, Professor of Forensic Psychiatry, Monash University, which was tendered as evidence in *The Queen v. Martin Bryant* (Supreme Court, Hobart, 19 November, 1996), as well as reports from Martin's school teachers and diagnostic assessments as supplied to Julie-Anne Davies for her excellent feature, 'Making of a monster' (*The Bulletin*, Tuesday 4 April, 2006). I also relied on Michael Gawenda's 'In Cold Blood' (*The Age*, Friday 3 May, 1996). It might interest some to know that there is a burgeoning conspiracy theory that lumbers along on the internet today, one that claims Martin Bryant is innocent, but a patsy for the usual suspects.

THE CHOSEN ONES

Details of the strange journey of Scott and Wendy Longley were taken from the journal *Recollections* (The Australian UFO Abduction Study Centre, Volume 3, Issue 3, June, 1996) and that fine journal of record, *Woman's Day* (Monday 29 April, 1996). Additional information came from *The World* (Volume 1, Issue 3, September, 1994), *UFO's: A report on Australian encounters* by Keith Basterfield (Reed Books, 1997) and *The Oz Files: The Australian UFO story* by Bill Chalker (Duffy & Snellgrove, 1996). I spoke to a number of people associated with this case who, for one reason or another, weren't comfortable having their names attached to this story (the fact that Scott is a martial artist may or may not be a factor there), so I thank them quietly. One expressed a good deal of hostility toward the Longleys – it is folk of their stripe, he fumed, who make it difficult for the many 'genuine' cases out there to be taken seriously. I cannot say that I share his outrage or disappointment.

FRIDAY THE THIRTEENTH

Details of the day that changed the lives of the family Robinson come from the recollections, written and oral, of Jack and Mary Robinson, contained in the excellent documentary *Black Friday* (Australian Broadcasting Corporation, Film Victoria and Moira Fahy, 2003). As it turns out there have been more recent tales of bushfire tragedy every bit as striking and sad as the Robinson's ordeal but, somehow, the distance of this particular one – and the fact that Jack and Mary Robinson are now with their children who perished in the fires – makes it stand out for me. I made an effort to speak to Tom Robinson, who is still alive and living within shouting distance of the very spot where, at the age of four, he lay on the ground with his family as the flames roared over their heads in 1939. Rather wisely – and perhaps, necessarily – he declared: 'I don't remember much about that.' While I would normally never recommend that anyone subject themselves to reading a Royal Commission document, Judge Leonard Stretton's *Royal Commission Report into the 1939 Victorian Bushfires*, presented to both Houses of Parliament by His Excellency's Command in Victoria in 1939 is an exception. 'Men who had lived their lives in the bush went their ways in the shadow of dread expectancy,' writes Stretton in the Report's dramatic introduction. 'But though they felt the imminence of danger they could not tell that it was to be far greater than they could imagine. They had not lived long enough. The experience of the past could not guide them to an understanding of what might, and did, happen.'

THE ART THE WORLD FORGOT

The story of the hapless Mertz Collection comes from *The Harold E. Mertz Collection of Australian Art* (Christies Australia, 2000) and *Ladies' Legs and Lemonade* by Kym Bonython (Rigby, 1979). Additional details come from reports in *The Age* (Friday 30 June, 2000, pages 4 and 5; Wednesday 5 July, 2000, page 7; Tuesday 3 October, 2000, page 5; Monday 29 April, 2002, page 3; Saturday 9 March, 2002, page 5), the *Weekend Australian* (Saturday 8 December, 2001, page 35), *The Australian* (Wednesday 16 February, 2000, page 19; Friday 23 November, 2001, page 19), the *Sydney Morning Herald* (Friday 24 March, 2000, page 13; Tuesday 25 April, 2000, page 11; Tuesday 20 June, 2000, page 14; Thursday 29 June, 2000, page 3; Friday 30 June, 2000, page 17; Saturday 19 August, 2000, page 9; Tuesday 5 September, 2000, page 5), the *Washington Post – Times Herald* (Saturday 2 April, 1967, page 7; Friday 30 September, 1966, page 3; Saturday 11 March, 1967, pages 1 and 3; Sunday 19 March, 1967, page 10), the *Christian Science Monitor* (Monday 27 February, 1967, page 4) and the *New York Times* (Sunday 7 March, 1954, page 57), all of which were accessed through the State Library of New South Wales.

CROCODILE TEARS

The newspaper reports that built this chapter are stated and dated within the text, so I won't bother repeating the exercise here. I feel somewhat compelled to point out that I personally never had a problem with Steve Irwin any more than I cared too much about him – my intention is not to make any sort of mockery of his memory, but simply to present the printed, two-faced facts that do seem lost to memory altogether. However, such declarations in my experience do little to stem the inevitable propulsion of conspicuous, self-soothing outrage. I refer all such complaints to 'The Eulogy Song' by The Chaser, which is freely available online.

GOODBYE MR RIVER

The modern celebrity is relatively easy to profile, as he has generally left his thoughts and reminiscences behind in newspapers and magazines, as unreliable as they may sometimes be. I thus picked the bones from various magazine interviews conducted with Michael Hutchence over the years, notably: *Spin* (February, 1988); *Sky* (September, 1990); *Rolling Stone US* (November, 1990); *The Face* (September, 1991) and *FHM UK* (March, 1994). I also found an article by Michael's friend, Andy Gill, in the *London Telegraph* (Wednesday 5 December, 2007) to be useful for the author's personal recollections regarding Michael's state of mind toward the end of his life. For Michael's younger years, I subjected myself to *Just a Man: The Real Michael Hutchence* by Tina Hutchence and Patricia Glassop (Sidgwick & Jackson, 2000), a book whose facts must be taken at face value, and *Totally INXS* by Rhett Hutchence (New Holland, 2007), which I found to be an engaging read for the unusual candour of its author. I also consulted *The Coroner – Investigating Sudden Death* by Derrick Hand and Janet Fife-Yeomans (ABC Books, 2004), for the official line of Michael's death. Various other insights were provided me personally by several of Michael's friends, notably Greg Perano and Andrew Hunter in Sydney, and Nick Conroy in Los Angeles, all of whom may or may not agree with some of my conclusions. Aside from that I did a good deal of sitting in rooms alone, drinking and thinking upon the matter, which I find to be a valid methodology when trying to make sense of something that appears to make very little sense at all.

VOYAGE OF THE SAVAGES

'It is a fact that it is hard to teach the Australian aborigines anything useful,' declared an editorial on page 11 of the *Chicago Daily Tribune* on 13 April, 1893. 'They are naturally lazy and indolent, unsettled, and of a roving disposition. They will not stay long at any place, and if raised from their degraded position into more comfortable conditions necessitating the breaking with their natural mode of living, they will almost invariably return to this at their first opportunity, and the same may be said for the half castes, who otherwise are far superior to their sable parents and their relatives.' It's a wonder R. A. Cunningham bothered trying to conscript such losers into his grand enterprise. This story, while being the natural preserve of the original inhabitants of Palm Island, owes its modern life to one Roslyn Poignant, a Sydney-born anthropologist on whose work this chapter is based. My original purpose with *Australian Tragic* was to unearth stories that had not been widely distributed – from word of mouth, newspapers, official documents and little-known books – and present them in the somewhat sensational style of the old 'penny dreadfuls', but when I came upon Poignant's *Professional Savages: Captive lives and western spectacle* (Yale University Press, 2004), I felt very much like a magician robbed of his trick. *Professional Savages* represents not just exceptional detective work but, in the prose, a standard of imagination and romance one doesn't normally find in the anthropological sphere. If you found this chapter intriguing I strongly recommend you hunt down the illustrated edition of Roslyn Poignant's excellent book. I'm also grateful to Alan Palm Island, a direct descendant of Tambo, for his time and for showing me the final burial place of his ancestor, and to the people of Palm Island – significantly (for me) the only non-metropolitan community in Australia where one can spend a few days without anyone needlessly commenting upon one's hat. Additional information for this chapter came from *Simply Human Beings* by E. G. Docker (Angus & Robertson, 1965), *Weird & Wonderful: The dime museum in America* by Andrea Stulman Dennett (NYU Press, 1997), *P. T. Barnum: The legend and the man* by A. H. Saxon (Columbia University Press, 1989), *There's a Customer Born Every Minute: P. T. Barnum's secrets to business success* by Joe Vitale (Amacom, 1998) and reports in the *Chicago Daily Tribune* (Sunday 6 May, 1883, page 12), the *Los Angeles Times* (Thursday 5 January, 1893, page 5; Sunday 12 November, 1899, page 31), the *New York Times* (Tuesday 26 February, 1884, page 1; Wednesday 9 April, 1894, page 9; Sunday 30 September, 1900, page 14), *The Era* (Saturday 3 May, 1884, page 8; Saturday 14 June, 1884, page 21), *Freeman's Journal and Daily Commercial Advertiser* (Friday 25 December, 1885, page 7), all accessed through the State Library of New South Wales.

A FORK IN THE ROAD

On Wednesday 25 March, 1953, Vincent George Dixon had his death sentence commuted to life in prison – a fact so inconvenient I decided to bury it here in the source notes and acknowledgements. Other details on Dixon's life and crimes come from reports in the *Canberra Times* (Saturday 13 July, 1946, page 6; Monday 15 July, 1946, page 3; Tuesday 26 August, 1947, page

4; Wednesday 24 September, 1947, page 2; Tuesday 2 December, 1952, page 3; Tuesday 16 December, 1952, page 2; Wednesday 17 December, 1952, page 4; Wednesday 31 December, 1952, page 3; Wednesday 28 January, 1953, page 4; Thursday 29 January, 1953, page 4; Tuesday 3 February, 1953, page 2; Saturday 7 February, 1953, page 7; Tuesday 24 February, 1953, page 3; Wednesday 25 February, 1953, page 4; Thursday 26 February, 1953, page 6). I'd like to thank Peter Schinnick for speaking to me about this incident from deep in his past. A unusual sort of fellow, married and still working at close to eighty years of age, Peter seemed more than a little perplexed by my interest in what is, for him, a moment of very personal history that he'd rather leave in the distant dark. It's a dilemma for journalists and writers of non-fiction generally – the bugging of people who have every right to tell you to mind your own business. I just find the idea that a single moment can change an infinite number of lives – erase some, give a chance to others – too irresistibly strange to be left unspoken, and this incident, buried in newspapers half a century old, seemed to say it for me.

LOST CHAMPION

The masculine legends of Australian sport are invariably gentlemen: Les Darcy, whose courteous smile charmed everyone he met; Don Bradman who, despite a somewhat unsociable demeanour, was an upstanding fellow in the true colonial tradition; even Phar Lap is remembered for chivalrous qualities not customarily bestowed upon quadrupeds. But Jim Hall was blessed with no such graces, and it's for this reason, I suspect, that most Australians have never heard of him, and absolutely no literature exists in the local libraries. Almost all of his story I found in newspapers from America, namely: the *Los Angeles Times* (Monday 16 June, 1890, page 1; Sunday 22 June, 1890, page 5; Sunday 8 February, 1891, page 5; Wednesday 25 February, 1891, page 1; Thursday 23 July, 1891, page 1; Tuesday 25 August, 1891, page 5; Tuesday 31 May, 1892, page 1; Saturday 5 November, 1892, page 1; Thursday 9 March, 1893, page 1; Friday 10 March, 1893, page 2; Saturday 18 March, 1893, page 2; Friday 16 November, 1894, page 2; Tuesday 11 August, 1896, page 1; Tuesday 26 September, 1899; page 4; Tuesday 11 March, 1913, page 3); the *Chicago Daily Tribune* (Saturday 24 January, 1891, page 6; Sunday 8 February, 1891, page 3; Monday 9 February, 1891, page 5; Friday 27 February, 1891, page 6; Monday 23 March, 1891, page 2; Saturday 18 April, 1891, page 6; Friday 3 July, 1891, page 6; Sunday 12 July, 1891, page 4; Monday 13 July,

1891, page 6; Thursday 30 July, 1891, page 2; Tuesday 4 August, 1891, page 6; Wednesday 5 August, 1891, page 6; Monday 28 September, 1891, page 2; Sunday 20 December, 1891, page 7; Friday 25 March, 1892, page 7; Monday 2 May, 1892; page 10; Tuesday 31 May, 1892, page 2; Sunday 21 August, 1892, page 4; Thursday 8 December, 1892, page 7; Tuesday 3 January, 1893, page 10; Monday 30 January, 1893, page 12; Sunday 5 February, 1893, page 4; Sunday 12 February, 1893, page 4; Monday 20 February, 1893, page 12; Monday 27 February, 1893, page 1; Tuesday 7 March, 1893, page 7; Wednesday 8 March, 1893, page 7; Thursday 9 March, 1893, page 7; Friday 17 March, 1893, page 7; Tuesday 30 May, 1893, page 6; Monday 19 March, 1894, page 3; Tuesday 21 January, 1896, page 8; Tuesday 26 September, 1899, page 4; Sunday 16 March, 1913, page 1); the *Washington Post* (Sunday 8 February, 1891, page 2; Tuesday 10 February, 1891, page 7; Thursday 19 February, 1891, page 1; Wednesday 25 February, 1891, page 6; Monday 23 March, 1891, page 1; Wednesday 5 August, 1891, page 6; Tuesday 25 August, 1891, page 6; Sunday 21 August, 1892, page 6; Friday 4 November, 1892, page 6; Sunday 13 November, 1892, page 10; Wednesday 25 January, 1893, page 6; Sunday 5 February, 1893, page 6; Monday 27 February, 1893, page 1; Thursday 9 March, 1893, page 1; Friday 10 March, 1893, page 6; Monday 20 March, 1893, page 1; Friday 7 April, 1893, page 1; Thursday 1 June, 1893, page 6; Friday 16 November, 1894, page 1; Thursday 5 December, 1895, page 8; Sunday 20 December, 1908, page 4) and the *New York Times* (Tuesday 1 March, 1892, page 3; Thursday 3 March, 1892, page 2; Wednesday 30 March, 1892, page 2; Wednesday 20 April, 1892, page 2; Friday 19 August, 1892, page 3; Sunday 21 August, 1892, page 15; Saturday 7 January, 1893, page 3; Thursday 9 March, 1893, page 3; Saturday 11 March, 1893, page 3; Tuesday 30 May, 1893, page 3; Sunday 16 December, 1894, page 16; Tuesday 11 March, 1913, page 9; Sunday 10 October, 1915, page 3). All were accessed through the State Library of New South Wales.

WHEN THEY ALL FEARED CLAUDE BATSON

Details of Claude Batson's six days of terror were gleaned from reports in *The Argus* (Wednesday 13 February, 1924, page 19; Thursday 14 February, 1924, page 9; Friday 15 February, 1924, page 10; Saturday 16 February, 1924, page 31; Monday 18 February, 1924, page 10; Tuesday 19 February, 1924, page 11. Wednesday 20 February, 1924, page 14; Saturday 23 February, 1924, page 36; Tuesday 26 February, 1924, page 11; Wednesday 27 February, 1924, page

20; Monday 14 April, 1924, page 10) and the *Northern Territory Times* (Tuesday 12 February, 1924, page 4; Friday 15 February, 1924, page 6; Tuesday 19 February, 1924, page 2; Tuesday 26 February, 1924, page 2), all of which were accessed through the National Library of Australia. Additional details on Trooper Tom Morris come from the *Singleton Argus* (Tuesday 26 June, 1900) and the *Corowa Free Press* (Friday 7 October, 1955). I'd also like to thank Ron Frew, historian of the Tumbarumba region, for his efforts in pursuing the invisible man Claude Valentine Batson turned out to be. Intriguingly, history records that a James Valentine Batson from the Jingellic region served in the Boer War, and again in the First World War with his two sons, Eric, born in 1898, and Reginald, born in 1900 – the same year as Claude Valentine, of whom there is no record. Both the *Tumbarumba Times* and the *Albury Banner*, the two newspapers closest to Jingellic, failed to mention the events of February, 1924 at all. Very odd indeed.

UNDER A MALEVOLENT STAR

The details of this disastrous Anzac Day in Melbourne come direct from *DPP v Whiteside and Dieber* (2000), courtesy of the Victorian Director of Public Prosecutions, as well as reports in *The Age* (Wednesday 24 November, 1999, page 8; Thursday 8 June, 2000, pages 4 and 9; Saturday 24 June, 2000, pages 1 and 3; Wednesday 28 June, 2000, page 8; Wednesday 19 July, 2000, page 3; Thursday 1 August, 2000, page 4; Wednesday 21 March, 2001, page 8) and the *Herald Sun* (Saturday 23 June, 2001, page 14). Details of the 'deplorable morality' of Fitzroy Gardens' past were gleaned from the *Brisbane Courier* (Wednesday 18 December, 1889, page 7), *The Argus* (Wednesday 30 May, 1917, page 12; Thursday 31 May, 1917, page 9) and the *Canberra Times* (Wednesday 20 May, 1942, page 3). I also relied upon *Gay* by Steve Dow (Common Ground, 2001), a collection of essays by the Melbourne journalist, one whole chapter of which is devoted to David Campbell, the only truly innocent victim of this affair, who is still alive today. It's interesting to note that the only person involved in this incident to have been previously known to the magistrates of Melbourne got away virtually scot-free, but for a month or two of correctional supervision after being found guilty of having made a false statement. In court, Euvegina Tsionis admitted that she lied about the rape, but insisted: 'That didn't give them the right to do what they did.' Her health and whereabouts today are unknown.

WHAT'S EATING MRS MOUSLEY?

Details on the life and last days of Maria Mousley come from *The Argus* (Wednesday 5 February, 1919, page 8; Wednesday 26 February, 1919, page 8; Thursday 12 February, 1920, page 8; Friday 13 February, 1920, page 8; Saturday 14 February, 1920, page 21; Tuesday 17 February, 1920, page 5; Wednesday 18 February, 1920, page 13; Thursday 19 February, 1920, page 8; Friday 20 February, 1920, page 9; Wednesday 25 February, 1920, page 15) and were accessed through the National Library of Australia. Thank you, too, to Frank Mousley, descendant of Frank Snr, who knew nothing of the woman who had made his father's childhood so charming.

THE STAR WHO NEVER WAS

There is precious little public information about the folkloric phenomenon that was Marcus Montana. This entire chapter was informed by people who were there to witness it. My thanks in that regard to Toby Creswell, Tim Freedman, Michael Vidale, and the many who posted their recollections of this event when I blogged about it at the *Sydney Morning Herald* a few years ago. I made the odd lame attempt to track down Marcus himself, who still lives, so I'm told, in the Sydney area, but after a strong tip-off that told me he'd rather forget the whole affair I let it slide. That the boy – now a man – might consider his moment in the faded spotlight as too embarrassing to recall is a bit of a shame. In the words of Michael Vidale: 'That last show began with people screaming at him that he was fucked. But he kept going. He always did. I think that impressed them. By the end, they thought he was all right . . . I really do think that Marcus actually succeeded that night. He really achieved something. He made it after all. And to this day, he probably has no idea.'

THE SHOW

My gratitude goes to Trevor Kirk, a very unique gentleman who was generous with his time and his story. As with Jenny Poidevin, Trevor Kirk knows of a life that, thankfully, few of us will experience, and it seems a pity society doesn't reward such people more charitably. Additional details on the death of Stacey Lee Kirk and the subsequent investigation come from reports in the *Sunday Mail* (Sunday 17 August, 2003, page 7), the *Herald Sun* (Thursday

7 August, 2003, page 28), the *Central Coast Herald* (Thursday 12 June, 2003, page 4; Wednesday 6 August, 2003, page 5), the *Newcastle Herald* (Friday 28 February, 2003, page 3; Saturday 1 March, 2003, page 1; Thursday 12 June, 2003, page 5; Tuesday 5 August, 2003, page 3; Wednesday 6 August, 2003, pages 1, 3 and 5) and the *Daily Telegraph* (Wednesday 6 August, 2003, page 11), and 'Inquest into the death of Stacey Lee Kirk', transcript of Coroner J. Abernathy, East Maitland Coroner's Court, 6 August 2003. Eerily, while I was working on this story in February of 2009, 21-year-old Jamie Purdon was beaten to death at the Maitland Show, just a few days beyond the twenty-fifth anniversary of Stacey Lee Kirk's death. His assailant would eventually turn himself in to be charged with manslaughter but, for a few days, the town of Maitland was gripped by a creepy déjà vu as calls went out for witnesses and the carnies closed ranks. The newspapers reported Purdon had been enjoying the amusements at the Show with his girlfriend, Misty-Lea Erikson.

A SORRY END INDEED

Flicking through the newspapers of old, particularly those of the late Victorian era, one notices that suicide was practically a fact of daily life. These were the days before 'responsible journalism', reporters taking pains to detail each victim's methodology of dispatch (*The Argus*, for example, merrily reported that on the morning of Saturday 13 February, 1915, 48-year-old George Stockdale of Kalgoorlie marched into a paddock outside the house in which his wife and children slept, placed a plug of dynamite in his mouth and 'blew his head to pieces'). Their primary intention appears to be to horrify of their readers (on Monday 21 April, 1919, the Melbourne *Argus* reported that Oswald Burmah, who had been missing from his home at Anakie for some days, had been found 'in a concrete dam connected with the Geelong drinking water supply system'). The great bulk of them appear to be suicides brought on by the despairing poverty and general hardships of the day but, occasionally, one jumps out at you as a little more mysterious than that, the reasons for the victim's despondency whispering from between the lines. The story of Marks and Feeney spoke to me in such a way, buried as it was in the pages of the *Brisbane Courier* (Tuesday 19 March, 1872, page 3; Friday 29 March, 1872, page 3) and the *Perth Gazette & WA Times* (Friday 7 June, 1872, page 3), all accessed through the National Library of Australia. Further details come from *The Difficulties of My Position: The diaries of prison governor John Buckley Castieau, 1855–1884* by John Buckley Castieau, edited by Mark Finnane (National Library Australia, 2004) and *Colonialism and Homosexuality* by Robert F. Aldrich (Routledge, 2003).

THE LAST TROOPS

There was no need to go any further for this chapter than Ian Darroch's excellent *The Boonah Tragedy* (Access Press, 2004), a book that involved a lot of research for its author. As with the books of Poignant and Paddle mentioned elsewhere in these acknowledgements, Darroch's book is worth hunting down as the extended story of the *Boonah* is not only sad, but infuriating for the bureaucratic stalemate that prolonged the war for these largely forgotten soldiers, and Darroch does well to cover the political side of the drama without losing touch with the tragedy itself. One of the more heartbreaking finds in his book is a letter written to the *West Australian* by Sister Stella Morris, a volunteer nurse from the *Wyreema*, who told readers of the scene at Woodman Point: '. . . a dreadful silence reigns, broken only by the strangled coughs and choked breathing as the boys are carried in and put into beds that have been prepared by skillful, loving hands. They know they are 'home', but they do not speak . . .'

Sister Stella Morris went on to contract the plague herself though, fortunately, she survived.

THE SPY WHO LOVED HER

Details on the sad love affair of Wayne Charters and Karen Roberts come from reports in the *Herald Sun* (Sunday 27 July, 2003, page 4; Tuesday 21 October, 2003, page 12; Thursday 2 December, 2004, page 24; Thursday 24 August, 2006, page 25; Friday 25 August, 2006, page 15; Sunday 3 September, 2006, page 39; Thursday 16 April, 2009, page 11), the *Sunday Age* (Sunday 4 December, 2005, page 13; Sunday 3 September, 2006, page 8; Sunday 16 November, 2008, page 7), *The Age* (Friday 3 December, 2004, page 10; Thursday 17 November, 2005, page 11; Monday 4 August, 2008, page 2; Wednesday 24 September, 2008, page 3), the *Sun-Herald* (Sunday 4 December, 2005, page 49) and the *Sunday Mail* (Sunday 27 July, 2003, page 9). I advise that this chapter be read while listening to the Bernard Herrmann's original soundtrack recording to *The Ipcress File*.

A DAY AT THE RACES

The story of a most uncompromising hangover indeed comes from detailed reports in the *Brisbane Courier* (Monday 31 January, 1876, page 3; Saturday 12 February, 1876, page 5; Wednesday 23 February, 1876, page 2; Tuesday 16 May, 1876, page 3), accessed through the National Library of Australia. The reasons why this particular tale attracted me should be obvious.

THE HEIST

Details of this farce were clipped from the *Weekend Australian* (Friday 26 March, 2005, page 9), the *Daily Telegraph* (Monday 29 March, 2005, page 9; Wednesday 31 March, 2005, page 24; Wednesday 13 April, 2005, page 17; Friday 17 June, 2005, page 23), the *Sydney Morning Herald* (Monday 13 June, 2005, page 17), the *Sunday Mail* (Sunday 25 September, 2005, page 7; Sunday 29 January, 2006, page 42), the *Sunday Age* (Sunday 25 September, 2005, page 3) and the *Sunday Times* (Sunday 23 October, 2005, page 5). Additional information came from *Westworld Denver News* (Thursday 13 October, 2005). By the time you read this, both Luke Carroll and Anthony Prince should be out of prison, not necessarily poorer nor wiser. Unlike others in these pages, this case has been fairly widely documented, but I had a strong feeling it belonged in a collection entitled *Australian Tragic*.

A HOWL IN THE NIGHT

For this chapter, I relied almost exclusively on *The Last Tasmanian Tiger: The history and extinction of the thylacine* by Robert Paddle (Cambridge University Press, 2003), a terrific little book for which the author interviewed Alison Reid in 1996, just one year prior to her death. In the acknowledgements at the front of the book, Paddle pays respect to the research of Tasmania's leading authority on thylacines, the late Eric Guiler, graciously admitting: 'I have stood unashamedly on Eric Guiler's shoulders'. In what might be beginning to resemble an old episode of *Thrillseekers*, I must now admit that I have climbed upon Paddle's (we should all hope the next bloke to write about the thylacine is a midget). Aside from being engagingly written, Paddle's book exposes one of the enduring mysteries of the Tasmanian tiger, which began in 1968 when respected naturalist, Graham Pizzey, whose newspaper column was syndicated throughout the nation, published an interview with a man named Frank Darby, who claimed to have worked at the Beaumaris Zoo, and whose recollections of 'Benjamin', the last living thylacine in captivity, would go on to form the bedrock of what Australia knew of the animal in the remaining decades of the twentieth century. As Paddle was to discover, evidence of a man named Frank Darby does not exist in the zoo records (Alison Reid had never heard of either Darby or 'Benjamin', and swore the last thylacine was female). Who Darby might have been – or whether he existed at all – is a mystery yet to be solved. Paddle beautifully concludes that the extinction of the Tasmanian tiger is 'the most significant loss we have, as a species, experienced to date. For we are all brothers to dragons and companions to owls, and whenever we lose sight of this in our personal, political and spiritual philosophies, we descend to the depths of self deceit and contempt for others, and we destroy the world as well as ourselves.'

COP

Original source documents for this chapter were *The Jerilderie Letter* by Ned Kelly, 1879 (courtesy of the State Library of Victoria) and *A True Narrative of the Kelly Gang by T. N. McIntyre – Sole Survivor of the Police Party Murderously Attacked by those Bushranger in the Wombat Forest on the 26th October 1878* (courtesy of the Victoria Police Museum). Also useful was *The Last of the Bushrangers: An account of the capture of the Kelly Gang* by Francis Augustus Hare, 1894 (Naval and Military Press, 2006). Where Ned's concerned, there are too many books to mention, but useful for me were *Australian Son* by Max Brown (Georgian House, 1948) and *The Kelly Hunters* by Frank Clune (Angus & Robertson, 1954). Most important of all was Sergeant Michael Kennedy, who gave me his time in early 2009, and to whom I am grateful for sharing his thoughts on his great-grandfather and the folklore that seems to have forgotten him.

THANKS

It is customary for authors to thank their editors, publishers, agents and various others – people who have been paid for their labours. Nevertheless, I feel compelled to blow a particular bugle in salute to Matthew Kelly at Hachette, for this work is very much a product of his guidance, patience, wisdom and gentle diplomacy. Thanks also to the late Matt Richell for being sharp enough to 'get' the idea right at the starting gate, and to Roberta Ivers for her surgical yet painless editing. Finally, credit must be heaped upon my agent, Deborah Callaghan, who originally encouraged me to pursue this idea, and without whom I am a bum.